ALMOST A
REVOLUTION

ALMOST A REVOLUTION

SHEN TONG

with Marianne Yen

Ann Arbor

THE UNIVERSITY OF MICHIGAN PRESS

Library of Congress Cataloging-in-Publication Data

Shen, Tong, 1968–
    Almost a revolution / Shen Tong, with Marianne Yen.
      p. cm.
    Originally published: Boston : Houghton Mifflin, 1990.
    ISBN 0-472-08557-3 (pbk. : alk. paper)
    1. China—History—Tiananmen Square Incident, 1989—Personal
narratives. 2. Students—China—Political activity. 3. Shen, Tong,
1968– . I. Yen, Marianne. II. Title
DS779.32.S47   1998
951.05'8—dc21   98-27356
                                                                CIP

For those compatriots who are still carrying out the struggle for a better tomorrow.

Preface to the Ann Arbor Paperbacks Edition

The 1989 movement has a place in China's modern history equal to the Opium War, the Taiping Rebellion, the 1898 Wuxu Reform, the Boxers, the 1911 Xinhai Revolution, the 1919 May 4th Movement, the Civil War, the 1949 founding of the People's Republic of China, and the Great Proletariat Cultural Revolution. Its significance surpasses that of a mere short-term student movement, not only because of the great number of lives it touched nationwide during the movement, but also because it has long-lasting symbolic and political meaning that will continue to unfold for generations to come.

The mass movement in 1989 raised the fundamental questions that China faced in the 1980s. The questions are:

Can a technologically and economically modernizing China develop, prosper, and strengthen without implementing other Western values?

Can a patriarchal political system cope with the desires and aspirations of its youth and of its future generations living in an increasingly interconnected world and open society?

Can dynastic cycles and the psychology of you-die-I-live in the zero-sum political transitions somehow be replaced by dialogue, negotiation, compromise, and coexistence?

Can order and progress somehow coexist in China?

Is every movement in support of liberal tradition (freedom, democracy, human rights, and the rule of law) doomed to act merely as a prelude to each and every major transformation in China, only to be commandeered later by forces that are conservative and comparatively backward?

These are questions that concern the whole of China: the ruling party, the people, and the emerging political elite. Moreover, they are the same questions that generations of Chinese have faced in their relentless modernization efforts during the last century and a half. The answers to these questions were uncertain then and still remain so today in the post–Deng Xiaoping era.

The 1989 movement dramatically raised those fundamental questions. Furthermore, they connected the old and new all in one theatrical play of love and hate, faith and betrayal, naiveté and realpolitik, hopes and disappointments, dark impulses and a sense of responsibility: factors that are all too human and all too Chinese to be transcended by the noble goals and stated purposes of the spokesmen of the movement. The familiar rhetoric used by both the government and the leaders of the movement; the speed and power exerted without the structure of checks and balances, which can corrupt even the purest souls; the acceleration of tension; the presence of a revolutionary fervor similar to that which inspired the youth of the Cultural Revolution; the broad and lofty claims made by the students; the inability of high government officials to cope with open challenge; the low capacity of the student leaders to genuinely control either the direction of the movement or the pace of its course; the tendency that part of the intelligentsia had to hover between serving as outside critics or as inside participants, as well as go-betweens for the government or as supporters of the mass and students are all symptoms of a nation and its youth caught in a timeless space.

What was exceptional about this movement? It was not a movement of national salvation. The country was not under major external threat or internal turmoil anywhere near to the degree of that existing in previous national movements. However, for the first time, the purpose of a nationwide mass movement was not national survival but the betterment of the overall quality of people's lives.

This was not a top-down, politically elite–engineered movement with a distinctive political agenda. There was no clear bearer of the political consequences prior to the movement. Political forces, both within and outside the establishment, became involved as the course of the events progressed. The reform-minded government faction and the self-styled aspiring liberal political elite outside the government all connected themselves with the all-powerful student-led movement only when it reached a level of national influence. For the first time, a nationwide mass movement was not solely a tool of political games and a product of political design but rather a spontaneous, grass-roots demonstration of the general concerns felt by a large section of the society, albeit primarily urban.

There were several features of this movement that made it remarkable. The fit between student demands and popular sentiment was strong in the area of social justice and general hope for greater freedom and democracy. The general population expressed little criticism of the students' insistence on a dialogue with high ranking government officials and for the generally confrontational ways in which the students conducted their affairs. This was unexpected for a people long accustomed to the paternalistic political mentality and the supremacy of political authority. The reason was not so much because of any clear and present danger that the country faced due to the inability of the government but rather due to the partial yet important success of government engineered reforms and the psychological, intellectual, social, and political by-product—raised expectations—brought about by those reforms. For the first time in China's modern history, the country was enjoying an uninterrupted period of growth with relative social stability. Fast economic growth, like economic depression, often creates psychological uprootedness. Thus, uncertainty and the raised expectations, which were not met, generated deep dissatisfaction in the general population.

The impressive organizational structure of the student leadership was, for the most part, an important and positive factor in the growth of the movement. Anyone outside of the governmental apparatus lacked the necessary experience in mass organization, yet despite their inexperience, the students demonstrated how quickly a spontaneous movement can turn into an orderly operation. This opened up the possibility of a relatively fast mobilization and organizational consolidation of a political alternative to the totalitarian Communist Party and its supporting police state apparatus. While many had hoped for this, more had feared that it was unfeasible. This is not to say that the organizational aspect of the movement is politically mature; on the contrary, the speedy dissolution of leadership following the massacre indicated the immaturity by any sound political standard. It merely indicated a remote possibility of an organizational political alternative in the future based on a spontaneous movement.

However, the movement's importance lies not in what it accomplished, but in what it did not. Nineteen eighty-nine did not see reconciliation between radical public concerns and adaptive public policy. Compared to government crackdowns on previous political dissent, this movement accelerated under a relatively safe environment, and repeated stimuli from the government allowed it to continue. In the early phase of the movement, pressure from school authorities on student leaders, attempts by police to block demonstrations, government manipulation in response to the demands of demonstrators, and temporary setbacks were all practically affordable before the Massacre of June 3 and 4, and in turn, stimulated the movement's growth. From my own recollection, and from the dozens of eyewitness accounts that have come out in the last eight years, it was quite clear that the longer the movement lasted, the less control the leaders of both opposing parties were able to exercise till the bloody showdown in early June. We were also, to a significant degree, led by the course of events, over which the student leadership had little overall control.

In the decade prior to the 1989 movement, almost any public demonstration resulted in a call for fundamental political reforms. The Democracy Wall Movement followed Deng's rise to power in the late 1970s. The reopening of universities and reinstallation of local elections opened up the Election Movement. Japanese revision of official high school textbooks on the Sino-Japanese War triggered the New September 18 Movement and the nationwide student movement of 1986. In this series of events, the 1989 movement cannot be seen as sudden and exceptional. As many fundamental conflicts accumulate, and as long as symbolic anniversaries remain appealing to the public, another mass movement could rise at anytime. Will this likelihood cease when the opposition achieves limited but concrete changes in government policy or attitude? Will the government use even more force to crack down? How far can gradual reform go? Nineteen eighty-nine left these questions wide open with the deep wound inflicted by the double impact of an intolerant government and the movement's uncompromising leadership.

The price for radical reform remains terribly high. The dramatic ending of the 1989 movement demonstrated how high that price can be and cast a shadow over future possibilities. When a mass movement rises again, there will be no room for naiveté. What could not be accomplished last time does not necessitate its realization next time around. History tends to repeat itself, and no matter how fantastic it may seem, things can always be worse.

This complexity of the 1989 movement in the Chinese national psyche, along with the Anti-Rightist Campaign in the 1950s and the Cultural Revolution from the mid-1960s to mid-1970s, has made the already tortuous path of China's modernization even more uncertain. Embedded in the complexity of post-Communist transitions in Central and Eastern European countries and the former Soviet Union since the end of the 1980s, the triumph of the institution of liberal democracy and market economy is not so certain as some have claimed and as many tend to believe. The "end of history," as some enthusiastically believed after the fall of the Berlin Wall, remains an inspiration, and far from reality.

This is not to say that the chance that China will finally get on the liberal democratic track is slim. On the contrary, the opening up of China in the reform period, the experience of the 1989 movement, the collapse of the world Communist camp, and the great expansion of the global market have all provided favorable conditions for democratization in China. What this does say is that the process is not an easy one and cannot be taken for granted. China's liberal democrats face even more complex situations, for the Chinese population has more complex examples to learn from, therefore raising more complex expectations.

While liberal opposition in China and in exile has the dream of promoting a free society of responsible individuals, how to accomplish the goal, and to start with, how to assess China's current situation continue to be difficult tasks. Contrary to the accusations by those in the Beijing regime and to some China experts in the West, we fully understand the torturous path of China's modern history. We have empathy for the pain that all the people in China endure. We are alert to the complex domestic and international security issues China faces and, subsequently, the political and social stability that is important for a balanced development.

We differ with the Beijing regime on the point of stability. Stability should not be mere stagnation, and progress does not necessarily lead to chaos. We believe that stability should be for the good of the country, not the party in power, and that stability is only achieved if a prospering China also develops respect for human rights, rule of law, an accountable democratic government, and responsible and peaceful participation in international affairs. Only then will we have lasting stability.

We differ also from Beijing and the apparent majority opinion in the Western political and commercial establishments on the virtue of China's economic development. We welcome the greater freedom in job allocation, travel, access to information, civic association due to the economic growth, and most of all, the expansion of the free market. However, when economic growth strengthens a regime, that increases the military budget and increases the budget for police surveillance, but also continually decreases the investments in education, in arts and culture, in social justice, and in government's public accountability, this represents a negative growth in the overall quality of life. Pure economic growth as such does not necessarily mean it is sustainable, nor does it mean it is a balanced development.

On the same note, we do not believe that China's problems have to be dealt with in a one-time, revolutionary fashion (though we respect people's right to do so). We support all the healthy reform measures including new Premier Zhu Rongji's anticorruption campaign and administrative streamlining. We believe that if gradual reform can reach the necessary depth, the price people have to pay for the transformation could be lower than that for a revolution. At the meantime, we clearly see the limitation of the current reform and its avoidance of genuine political institutional change. Though we appreciate the complexity of the problems China is facing, and understand that such a complexity is not only a political one, we believe that without a genuine political reform, balanced development can not be achieved.

The year 1997 witnessed some of the most turbulent events in China's past years: the death of the paramount leader, Deng Xiaoping, which ended the rule of the Communists' first generation of revolutionaries; the June 4 commemoration in various parts of the world, which has reached record highs since 1990; Hong Kong's handover, followed by persistent international monitoring and the local struggle for a more democratic and a freer society; the Communist Party's 15th Congress, which launched the biggest moves yet toward privatizing ailing state-owned enterprises; the open letter from Zhao Ziyang, the reform-minded former general secretary of the party, calling for reevaluation of the June 4 Tiananmen massacre; the visit to the United States by Jiang Zemin, China's new boss, and his eager moves to garner international approval for his reign including the release of Wei Jingsheng; the release of the Hong Kong human rights report and the signing of the United Nation's Covenant on Social, Economic and Cultural Rights; and Beijing's most recent gesture to the Taiwan government on negotiating the name of a would-be-unified China, opening possibilities for a constructive dialogue, which had been suspended since the end of 1995 when China fired missiles over the Taiwan Straight.

These changes have taken place along with the relentless efforts of China's liberal opposition forces inside the country and abroad. The Democracy for China Fund, which I co-founded in 1989, is proud of having played a major role in the shaping of these events. Our contributions include voicing dissent against the Beijing regime; our hopes and designs for a liberal and democratized China for the general public both in China and in the free world through international media; our participation in the establishment and effective operation of Radio Free Asia, which is in its second year and will continue to expand; liberal organization gatherings in and outside China, along with publication of liberal journals, book series, and production of television series that promote liberal ideas and discussions about China's current and future problems; and the joint efforts to apply pressure on Beijing from the outside world on the issues of human rights improvement and political reform, which have been kept alive by the Democracy for China Fund, the U.S. government, the Western NGOs, and the members of the opposition movement inside China, who have been fighting for the end of the Communist dictatorship despite severe punishment by the Beijing regime.

The Democracy for China Fund has not only survived the low tide of the movement under the impact of the Beijing regime's repression and the lack of determination of governments in the free world, but also we have managed to expand considerably in the last three years, particularly in 1997. We realize that due to changes over the past months, Jiang Zemin has become a variable in the future of China, instead of what has been generally regarded as a transitional factor. It is our understanding that the future of China does not depend on Jiang's leadership but on various forces in China, including how effective the liberal opposition is in pushing forward its agenda under a weak leadership. Looking ahead to a new millennium, we are more hopeful than ever for a liberal democratic China.

Nine years have gone by since the bloody crackdown the night of June 3–4, 1989. Once again, the Chinese have paid a price in blood for reform—that night and in the mass arrests and forced exiles that followed the massacre. Today, there are still over an estimated 3,000 prisoners in China who have been imprisoned in connection with the 1989 movement, and hundreds remain in exile, most of whom are not allowed to return to our homeland or even to enter Hong Kong.

So much loss, and so much pain have once again captured a generation in the bitterness that so many generations in Chinese modern history have tasted. And yet, it is the duty of we who survived the massacre to rise above the tortuous past for a better tomorrow.

Nine years of time at least should give us the distance for a better understanding of the meaning of 1989 in Chinese history. Like the May 4 Movement in 1919, the 1989 movement means not only its particular historical events but also a historical movement broadly defined. What a movement can leave us by and large depends on what we can discover in the process of our reflection.

Looking back at the last two decades of China's change, we can see a history of liberalizing development. Such a development centered around humanitarianism, greater human rights, democracy, and rule of law since the end of the 1970s and most of the 1980s. In the post–1989 years, Chinese liberals have gone through exploration and soul-searching in the face of the June 4 crackdown, the clasps of the Communist bloc and the difficulties the new democracies have experienced, the decline of the confidence in the universality of liberalism in the West, and the pragmatic policy orientation of the Beijing government managing to cope with post–1989 changes while maintaining its power and limited ideological control. The June 4 massacre ended the legitimacy of the Communist rule in China in the heart of Chinese people. For many, it was a relief that their free thinking do not have to be under the banner of "supporting CCP, supporting socialism." From this point on, for many more people, the legitimacy of the regime has to be negotiated on economic terms and occasionally nationalistic terms; otherwise it has to be maintained by sheer coercion. In these years, we have witnessed many liberal reformers from the 1980s finding refuge in cynicism, some discovering their new intellectual home in cultural conservatism, and others preaching "neo-conservatism," which in fact provided new justifications of the legitimacy of the current regime that once lost its claim over the Chinese urban population in the days following the massacre of June 4.

We have also seen the relentless effort to call for continuing comprehensive reform by some of the liberal reformers; the forcefully elaborated left-wing liberalism that focuses on social justice, and clearly asserted right-wing liberalism that concerns itself with private property and limited government; and we have witnessed the emergence of a firm and open opposition in China and in exile promoting constitutional democracy in its two camps—gradual and radical. These forces have actively taken the initiative in the newly opened aspects of China, especially with regard to mass media, publishing, and education. And a year after the death of Deng Xiaoping, their joint forces surfaced to become what is called a new "Beijing Spring."

Seeing the 1989 movement in this light, we can proudly claim that the broad 1989 movement is a movement that established liberalism as an appealing political alternative for China's future.

Liberalism is a product of the West that was introduced into China around the turn of the century. But liberty is not the rights exclusively reserved for the West. No society in the world founded itself with a complete guarantee of liberty. In today's world, as part of their modern development, the more liberal countries increased the degree of freedom and defined the core meaning of liberalism. After World War II, the West finally came to establish a polity with the purpose of protecting the basic set of liberties—sometimes known as negative liberties, as compared to positive liberties—including freedom of life, freedom of thought and religion, freedom of speech, and freedom of pursuing one's own happiness without interfering with another's basic freedom.

The struggle for freedom has become an organic part of Chinese modern civilization. The 1989 movement is a clear demonstration that even under a Communist totalitarian regime, a massive movement highlighting individualism, calling for greater democracy and rule of law, can emerge from within. Basic liberty, and its corresponding political democracy, free market economy, and constitutional rule of law, belongs to humanity; its universal validity transcends the differences of civilizations; and under the modern condition, its realization is possible in all parts of the world.

One hundred years ago, Chinese reformers had their short but glorious days working constructively with the Emperor Guangxu in the 1898 Wuxu Reform movement. We wish the reform of a century ago had forecast a beautiful future for China, one when we can leave behind the ghost of Tiananmen, when we can lift from the heaviness of the bloody ending of the Wuxu reform, when we can live in the dream of a better future without forgetting our tortuous past. That will be the day of China's nirvana. We pray for the liberalism movement symbolized by the 1989 movement to guide our journey from tyranny and disaster to embrace freedom and dignity.

In preparing this edition of the book, I've reread some of the eyewitness accounts of the 1989 movement and this book. Once again, I realized the complexity of the event. Writing history may need intellectual and emotional distance, but I find that a luxury that I did not have till today. Yet I still believe this book can make its contribution to a student of China in the West by virtue of its first-person account of what it was like to grow up in Beijing in the 1970s and 1980s, and what it was like to be part of the 1989 movement.

I do, however, continue to take pride in the straightforwardness and honesty that I tried to maintain with Marianne Yen in the writing of the book eight years ago. The autobiographies of Chinese and politicians are often inadequate as material sources for objective recording of events. By comparing other eyewitness accounts with my own, and through direct and indirect input from other major participants of the event, I find that what I experienced at various moments was not, as might be expected, merely a single part of the entire picture, but also that the extent of the broad picture was not always accessible to me from where I stood. This was especially true during the latter part of the movement. This inevitably affected the weight I assigned to various events and the relevance of my involvement. However, I take comfort in knowing that after revisiting the writing several times in the past years, I find there were no factual errors. I did my best to provide an analysis of the movement without the luxury of perspective that time allows. While my analysis today might differ to some degree, my self-reflection and criticisms remain the same.

June 4, 1998

Contents

Map of Beijing   xx

Preface   xxi

Part I   Beginnings

1. Avenue of Eternal Peace   3
2. Billy Clubs and Violins   31
3. Blue Dove and Misty Poets   58
4. "Young Leaf in Spring"   85
5. Beijing University   107
6. Year of the Dragon   132

Part II   Movement

7. Hu Yaobang Is Dead   165
8. The Spirit of May Fourth   196
9. Dialogue Delegation   223
10. Gorbachev Is Coming   255
11. Martial Law and the Goddess of Democracy   286
12. Bloody Sunday and Farewell   317

Epilogue   335
Acknowledgments   343

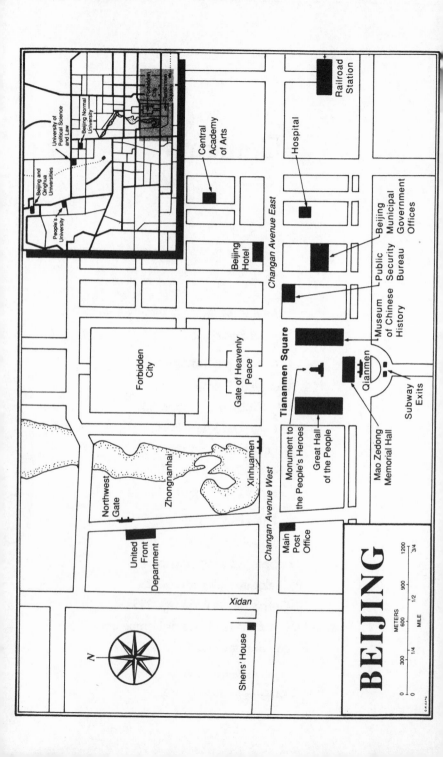

BEIJING

Preface

Coming from hope. Going to hope.
Adrift upon a sea of hope.
I look back on the mists of home,
    on the shadow eyes
    and half-turned smiles,
    on waves and waves of time.

Time sings to me:
    "The boundless sea
    becomes the field you plant upon."

The song becomes a poem
I store safely in my trunks.

                   "Exile"

Last year on this day I left the place of my birth, the place where I lived for the twenty years of my life in Beijing.

When I got to America, China suddenly seemed to me more beautiful and magical. Because of her beauty, because of her pain, and because of that night — June 3–4, 1989, which will never be forgotten by all who love China, by all who love freedom and peace — every drop of time that I had in China is now that much more precious to me.

So many people, of different skin color and cultural backgrounds, have opened their eyes to China's ancient civilization and the tragedy of its modern times. Their concern has strengthened the hope and deepened the faith of this child, this boy who loves to dream.

Once an American friend said to me, "Shen Tong, you must not miss your home very much, because the world is your neighborhood now." In this great international family that I now live in, there is only one door that remains closed to me — the door that leads to my native country, China.

The story I want to tell is the story that lies behind the closed door. There is my childhood, the silent Changan Avenue that holds our history and our future. There is my family, that splendid earth, and my people. There is my dream and my friends who wait in prison for that dream to come true.

That dream belongs to the young, who love to imagine.

That dream is the struggle of a generation of Chinese, who, like a larva waiting to be transformed, yearn for the strong and beautiful wings of a butterfly.

S.T.
June 11, 1990
Boston

PART I

BEGINNINGS

· 1 ·

Avenue of
Eternal Peace

MY NAME IS Shen Tong. I was born on July 30, 1968, a time when all of China was awash in a sea of red. It was the height of the Great Proletarian Cultural Revolution, and the Red Guards — in a movement called *honghaiyang,* red ocean — had painted city streets and walls red throughout the country. My given name, Tong, is a word used to describe the redness of the sunrise. Many children born in 1968 were named Tong because the word was also used to describe Chairman Mao Zedong, the supreme leader of China. But my parents didn't give me this name for its connection with Chairman Mao. They chose it because Shen Tong sounds like the word *prodigy.*

I was born on an army base in Zhangjiakou, a small town northwest of Beijing. My parents worked for the People's Liberation Army and were attached to a school that trained members of a group that was the precursor of the secret police. My father taught Korean, and my mother worked as a medic in the army hospital.

My father, whose real family was named Liu, was born in the town of Qidong on the banks of the Yangtze River in Jiangsu Province, about a two-hour boat ride from Shanghai. When he was born, the Liu family already had seven children and could not support another. They left my father, wrapped like a bundle, in a local restaurant. It was not uncommon for poor families to leave newborns in public places, hoping that kind strangers would take them in. A postman named Shen found my father and took him home. Grandfather Shen had a daughter but had always wanted a son, so he treated my father as his own. The Lius knew that Grandfather Shen had adopted their baby, but Grandfather Shen never knew my father's real family. In 1968, the year I was born, the Liu family traced my father to the army base and established contact with him, and as a result my father nicknamed me Yuan Yuan, choosing the character *yuan* that means "reunion." My sister and I were the only children I knew of with three sets of grandparents.

When my father was a boy in the 1940s, China was at war with Japan, and he was a member of the Anti-Japan Children's League, set up by the Chinese Communist Party. He and the other children carried wooden sticks with bayonets attached and strings of red cloth hanging from the end. They served as road inspectors, checking people's identification cards. My father was very proud that he and his friends had rooted out several Japanese agents that way. Many Chinese children of my generation, myself included, learned to hate the "Japanese devils" at an early age because of the stories our fathers told us about fighting them before and during World War II.

My father attended the best high school in Shanghai, and in 1956 was preparing to go to Fudan University in that city to study journalism. Writing was his first love, and he wanted to work for the New China News Agency, China's official news service. But two agents from the government's Foreign Affairs Department came and asked him to study Far Eastern languages at Beijing University (Beida) because, they said, the country desperately needed language instructors. My father was full of idealism about the newly established People's Republic and full of faith in Chairman Mao's promise to build a New China. The war with Japan had left many cities in ruins and millions in poverty. After years of civil war, the Communist Party in 1949 had finally driven the Guomindang, led by Chiang Kai-shek, to exile on the tiny island of Taiwan, off the coast of mainland

China. The whole country looked to the Communist Party for leadership, and young intellectuals at the time were eager to take an active part in restoring China to greatness. Many Chinese who were studying abroad went back home to lend their expertise to the country. So when the government asked my father to study languages, he readily agreed to go to Beida, where he majored in Korean.

My father wrote a lot of poetry in college which he saved in a suitcase. I saw the yellowed pieces of paper the few times he went into the suitcase to organize it. At Beida, his friends considered him the campus poet and called him Pushkin. Because he had skinny ankles and was a good distance runner, his other nickname was Shanyang, mountain goat.

In 1957, my father's first year at Beida, the Communist Party leadership asked the people to criticize the Party's shortcomings in a campaign known as the Hundred Flowers Movement. Many well-meaning intellectuals, encouraged by this openness, came forward with honest opinions of what was wrong. But when the leaders felt that the criticisms had become too blunt and widespread, they launched the Anti-Rightist Campaign to punish those who had spoken out. Each department at Beida was directed to come up with a list of students who could be labeled rightists. Because my father had spoken up, his name was on one of these lists. Luckily, the Far Eastern languages department had more names of rightists than the government required. My father's name didn't survive the list-trimming, and for that arbitrary reason he escaped persecution.

When my father graduated from Beida, he chose to work as a language instructor for the People's Liberation Army, because this was the most honorable way to serve the country. After Liberation, the army commanded the love and respect of all citizens. To be a member of the PLA was a highly prestigious position, as one then joined the ranks of the revolutionary heroes.

At the army base in Zhangjiakou, my father met my mother, who, according to him, was one of the most beautiful girls in the whole regiment. Many men pursued her until they heard that one of her brothers had fled to Taiwan with the Guomindang. In the political climate of that time, the Guomindang was the most dreaded enemy of the People's Republic, and anyone associated with it in any way was suspected of being a traitor. My mother was marked politically and could not even join the Communist Youth League, a social group the Party organized for teenagers. Because of that, many men in the army were afraid to go near her. By marrying my mother, my father jeopardized his career — a courageous decision, and one typical of my father, who spent his whole life trying to do the right thing in his own quiet way.

My mother was the youngest of seven children. She was born in Jiangsu Province to a large family that had belonged to the scholar-official class in the Qing Dynasty. By the turn of the century, however, the family had lost much of its wealth and prestige. Her father, who was head of the Beijing Telegraph Office for twenty years, had refused to work for the puppet government set up by the Japanese during the war and fervently supported the budding Chinese Communist Party. When the Communists took over in 1949 they asked him to resign from his post so that they would not have to pay him a pension. It was a great humiliation for an old man to suffer, and my grandfather felt betrayed. He died of illness soon after he was removed from his job.

My mother was fifteen when her father died, and rather than be a burden on her family, she left home to attend a military nursing school in Tianjin. She diligently saved her food coupons and mailed them back to her family during the famine of 1960–63, when more than 43 million died of starvation and people killed each other for a bowl of rice gruel. After my sister, Shen Qing, was born, in 1966, my mother's mother, whom I call Nai-nai, came to live with my parents at the army base.

That same year the Cultural Revolution began. Grandfather Shen became one of its earliest victims. Chairman Mao urged the Red Guards, most of whom were high school and university students, to carry on the proletarian revolution by rooting out all of the antisocialist elements in society. The Red Guards went after landlords, rich peasants, counterrevolutionaries, bad elements, rightists, and capitalists with such zeal that many people were wrongfully accused. The mayor of Qidong victimized Grandfather Shen out of spite. Shortly after Liberation, the government had appointed this man to be the new village mayor, to implement the redistribution of land from the rich to the poor. The mayor, an uneducated peasant, was very corrupt and incompetent, and Grandfather Shen, who was an honest and righteous man, felt that he had to criticize him vocally. For this reason the mayor labeled him a rich peasant, although he was actually a poor postman rather than a farmer. Thus he became a target for the Red Guards during the Cultural Revolution.

Both my grandparents, then in their sixties, were to be paraded in the village square wearing dunce caps and humiliating placards, but they committed suicide the day before by standing their bed on end and hanging themselves on the bamboo bed frame. Their bodies were found the next day, when the Red Guards came for them. My father, who received the news of his parents' death in a letter from village officials, knew that they had killed themselves to save face.

In 1968 the People's Liberation Army began participating in the Cultural Revolution. Nainai, who took care of me while my parents were at work, told me many stories about the political chaos at the time of my birth. The regiment my parents belonged to was commanded by Marshal Lin Biao, but the rank-and-file soldiers were split up into factions based on different political ideologies. These factions engaged in *wudo*, armed struggle, fighting one another to become the true revolutionary vanguard. There were so many splinter groups that it became difficult to tell who was fighting whom. One of the radical factions once surrounded the barracks where my parents lived and pelted anyone who set foot outside with stones. Since my mother was pregnant with me at the time, Nainai had to do all of the food shopping, braving the stone-throwers daily on her way to the market. She once showed me an army jacket that was rid-

dled with bullet holes and stained with maroon blood; she said
that my father had lent this jacket to a friend, who had suffered
ten gunshot wounds but survived to return the jacket.

Right after I was born, my parents and many others in their
regiment left the army to return to civilian life. My parents were
both from Jiangsu Province, and had planned to settle in nearby
Shanghai. But when they visited friends in Beijing, they were
told that it was easier to find work there than in Shanghai, which
was already overcrowded, so they decided to stay and apply for
jobs as well as housing. In China, everyone belongs to a work
unit, and people live in the city where they work. Jobs are
assigned by the government and often do not correspond to an
individual's skills. My parents were given jobs as laborers in a
chemical factory.

During the Cultural Revolution, the Communist Party promoted the slogan that it was better to be Red than expert. Workers with little or no education were considered more fit to run
the country than members of the educated and skilled middle
class. People like my father were to learn from the workers. So
for three years my father moved drums of sulfuric acid, earning
40 yuan a month (one yuan is now worth about 25 cents). He
was paid less than the average worker because the factory did
not recognize his years of teaching as work experience. Like
other intellectuals, he was given a menial job that would reform
him. The head of the work unit at his factory, a man from the
worker class, gathered the intellectuals together weekly and lec-
tured to them. Some of the workers abused their power, and
because of this my father suffered many indignities. His supervisor routinely borrowed 10 yuan from him, but never paid him
back. Although my family was poor, my father could not refuse
to give him money or insist on being repaid, because the supervisor wrote his political evaluation. My father regarded his three
years at the chemical factory as a form of punishment, because
he was humiliated by not having meaningful work and by not
being able to use his abilities fully. Like many others, my idealistic father was often disappointed with the New China.

Eventually he found a job at Beijing's largest paint factory, hoping that he could make use of his knowledge of Korean. He went to a dozen different work units to ask if they could use someone with his language skills. He made a lot of friends that way, but other workers resented him and thought he was too ambitious. Some of the workers thought he was stupid, because the pay was the same no matter how much or how little you worked. My father might have been better off if he had spent his days chatting with his coworkers and ingratiating himself with his superiors, but he never got very good evaluations, because he didn't try to form positive relationships with others at the factory. He was a product of the ivory tower of Beida and could never bring himself to ask his superiors for a raise. My mother was the one who stayed on friendly terms with the supervisors, and she asked them for more money on my father's behalf.

My mother worked at the factory's clinic as a doctor, even though she had only been trained as a nurse. During the Cultural Revolution, when the whole educational system shut down and professionals were sent to the countryside to do manual labor, qualified medical personnel were in short supply. My mother often came home with stories of how illnesses were misdiagnosed or mistreated at the clinic. One of her colleagues was a woman who had never received any formal medical training but who had been assigned a position as a doctor. When a worker came in one day complaining of ringing in his ear, this woman held his head close to her own, listened intently for several seconds, and said, "I don't hear any ringing. There is nothing wrong with you."

Like jobs, housing is allocated by the government, and we were assigned a dilapidated house in an alley near the corner of Xidan and Changan Avenue, the largest thoroughfare in Beijing. Our house was a fifteen-minute walk from Tiananmen Square and consisted of two rooms constructed of cracked bricks and mud. It was built long before Beijing was modernized, so when the streets were repaved, it fell below street level. To enter the small courtyard in front, you had to walk down three steps.

When it rained, the tile roof leaked and the courtyard flooded. My father and the neighbors would roll up their pants and scoop out the water in the courtyard with buckets, and eventually our neighbors dug two tunnels to divert the flood water.

At first my sister and I lived in one room with our parents, and Nainai slept in the other room, which was the family room during the day. When we grew older, my sister and grandmother shared a room and I lived in a seven-foot extension we built into the courtyard. This gave me less privacy than before, because the new front door was in my room, which also served as the family room during the day and the dining room in the evening.

I never felt that my family was poor, even though our household income was always below the average. As a child, I often thought we were better off than other people because my mother was a good seamstress and my sister and I were relatively well dressed. During the Cultural Revolution, people wore Mao suits like uniforms. These were often ill-fitting and always navy or gray. The clothes my mother sewed for us were not made of expensive materials, but they fit well and had a dash of color.

Nainai started teaching me at home when I was three. She hadn't had a formal education herself but had been tutored at home in the old style. Having her as a teacher, I learned many more things about China's history and culture than my friends who went to the state-run kindergarten did. Nainai was very strict and every day gave me lessons in reading and writing, arithmetic, and drawing. She taught me to appreciate traditional Chinese culture, reading me stories from the classics, such as *Romance of the Three Kingdoms*, a historical novel about warring Chinese kingdoms in the fourteenth century; *Journey to the West*, a mythical tale of a Tang dynasty monk's travels to India for the Buddhist scriptures; and *Dream of the Red Chamber*, an eighteenth-century novel about an extended family in feudal China. During the Cultural Revolution, these classics were considered part of the Four Olds — old ideology, old culture, old customs, and old habits — which the Red Guards wanted to eliminate from society. Nainai taught me these things because she believed that to build a new China we did not have to throw away everything that was good about our country's history and culture.

Nainai was a fairly good painter and was a friend of some of the famous contemporary artists in China, including Zhang Daqian and Qi Baishi. She had a collection of their paintings as well as of ancient Chinese landscape paintings. I didn't realize as a child how valuable her collection was, but seeing her unroll the delicate scrolls, I knew that the paintings were precious objects, and this instilled in me an appreciation for art. Nainai also taught me to write Chinese characters with a brush and ink and to memorize Tang dynasty poetry and Chairman Mao's poems. I could recite twenty to thirty poems one after another, although I didn't know what I was saying. When my parents came home from work, I'd perform for them by rattling off as many poems as I could remember. After a while Nainai began to worry that cramming so much poetry into my little brain might damage my intelligence; I heard her tell my mother several times that she was going to ease up on my lessons.

By the time my parents came home every evening, Nainai had dinner ready for us. My father thought it was important for us to eat together and talk with one another at the end of the day, and he got very annoyed whenever my sister and I didn't come to the dinner table right away. Dinnertime was when we had all of our family discussions. Unlike typical Chinese parents, my parents consulted Shen Qing and me about everything. If they were considering buying something for the house, for instance, they asked us what we thought of the idea.

After dinner every night the five of us sat by the light of four desk lamps and read. My father usually read books of poetry or Korean literature. On his bookshelves were many Chinese translations of Western poetry, including the English poets Byron and Shelley and the Indian poet Rabindranath Tagore. My mother read medical texts, to teach herself what she hadn't learned in nursing school. Nainai liked to read classical Chinese novels. My sister and I shared a lamp, and we both had our own books too. My favorites were the Grimm fairy tales and the stories of Hans Christian Andersen, which were very popular then. Long after Qing and I had gone to sleep, my parents and Nainai continued to read, late into the night. I often woke up in the middle of the night and saw their silhouettes lit by the desk lamps.

Most of the people in my neighborhood worked in factories or stores. The government had not yet instituted the one-child-per-family policy, so there were plenty of children living in my alley. The neighbor who shared the courtyard with us was a factory worker with eight children. His wife worked in a handicraft factory painting eggshells. All of his children were much older than I, and they took turns playing with me and taking care of me when Nainai wasn't home. They taught me how to swim in a nearby river when I was about five. I remember it because I jumped in the water totally unafraid, but then found that I couldn't keep myself afloat and started to go under. I thrashed around, then grabbed a little girl my age who was being held by her father. He dragged both of us out of the water. I was really embarrassed.

I got along best with my neighbor's seventh child, a boy who was eight years older than I. I called him Qige, seventh brother. In the summertime we walked up and down Changan Avenue wearing only our swimming trunks. He took me along when his gang of friends had fights with other neighborhood teenagers, which usually started when one group accused the other of cheating at marbles. Qige assigned two of his friends to be my personal bodyguards, and they would lift me up and carry me whenever their side lost and was running away. When Qige turned fourteen, he started body building with weights and barbells; I pretended to train with him, but of course I couldn't pick up any of the weights.

Although many of the neighbors never knew my parents' names, everyone knew me, because I ran around the alley striking up conversations with all the grownups. Everyone always referred to our house as "Yuan Yuan's house," and whenever a call came in for my family on the only telephone on our block, whoever answered the phone would call for Yuan Yuan's family. Nainai let me go off on my own because everyone knew me and I couldn't possibly get lost. I always wanted to be helpful to everyone, and whenever a neighbor needed something, I'd run home to see if we had it in our house. I gave away chairs, food, and lots of other things before my mother put an end to it. She was reluctant to criticize me at first because she was pleased that I was so generous, but when things got out of hand, she finally told me that if I continued giving away our possessions, we would have nothing left.

After Nainai finished the day's lessons, I often went to the local grocery store and talked with the saleslady. I brought some of my storybooks with me and read to her. When the store wasn't crowded with customers, she let me sit behind the counter with her, which made my friends who went to kindergarten very envious.

If the saleslady was busy, I'd walk over to the movie theater and chat with the ticket vendor. It must have been a lonely job to sit all day behind the ticket booth, because the vendor's face always lit up with a broad smile when I came along. I'd tell him some of the fables my grandmother had told me. I'm sure he had heard them all before, when he was a kid, but he always seemed very interested. He also let me into the theater whenever I wanted, but I usually didn't go in, since watching a movie I was too young to understand was not as much fun as talking to him. When I told my sister that I could get into the movies for free, she didn't believe me. I took her with me to the theater one day and simply announced to the ticket vendor, "This is my sister," then waltzed in with her.

Another one of my favorite places to spend time was the barber shop. The barbers talked to me as if I were a grownup, and I liked that. Once, when I was getting a haircut myself, I sat on the high chair and began to entertain everybody with a story.

"Do you know the one about the cat and the mouse?" I asked the haircutter.

"No," she said. "Why don't you tell me?"

Keeping my head motionless while she cut my hair, I launched into the story. "A cat and her kitten were tending a granary. A little mouse waited until the big cat went away and walked up to the kitten. 'I'm your third uncle,' he said to the kitten. 'Funny, you don't look like my uncle,' the kitten said. 'Well, I am and you should let me in,' the mouse said."

By now all of the barbers and customers were listening to my story, surprised that I could bring such a simple tale to life. Seeing their interest, I continued with even more animation.

"The kitten let the mouse in, and the mouse ate so much that its belly was large and round and its mouth was full of grain," I said, puffing out my cheeks. "The mouse practically had to roll out of the granary. When the cat came back and heard what had happened, she told the kitten that the visitor was a mouse and not Third Uncle. The mouse came back the next day. 'Remember me?' he said to the kitten. 'I'm your third uncle.' The kitten didn't fall for the trick this time and chased the mouse away."

When I finished, the barber forgot to charge me for the haircut.

Besides telling stories, I liked to sing. I had a good voice and wasn't afraid of crowds, so my mother took me to the factory whenever her work unit staged a variety show. I'd stand on a little stool on the makeshift stage and sing my heart out. I made my mother very proud, because her colleagues thought I was brave to perform in public.

Most of the songs I learned as a child were political, because everything was politicized during the Cultural Revolution. The arts were under such tight government control that songs, modern Chinese operas, and films were all about Liberation and the revolutionary heroes. One of the songs was part of a campaign called Learn from Lei Feng, a short, squat soldier from the countryside who had died in an accident and who the government decided to turn into a national symbol of the modern revolutionary. The song went, "Learn from Lei Feng's good example, loyal to the revolution, loyal to the Party," and every child was told stories about his spirit of sacrifice. Lei Feng was so frugal, one of the stories said, that he continued to use his toothbrush even when the bristles had all worn away. The story that moved me most was about how Lei Feng worked in the fields in the wintertime even though his hands were chafed by the cold, biting winds. In the winter months the skin on my hands was always dry and cracked and hurt me very much, so I could well imagine how difficult it must have been for Lei Feng.

One of my mother's brothers, whom I called Fourth Uncle, also taught me many songs. He had worked as a butcher in a prison colony in Tianjin until my mother helped him get a job at her factory so he could live near us in Beijing. The songs he taught me were not children's songs but complicated tunes written for grownups, and my mother was convinced that Fourth Uncle was ruining my voice with them.

I wanted to be like the grownups, so I often helped my parents and Nainai with chores. Once a week the market sold live chickens, and people lined up at dawn to buy them. Buying chickens was very important, since only about forty were available each week. Under China's planned economy, the government gave out ration coupons for almost every commodity you could think of: cooking oil, rice, pork, textiles, cotton, and coal and vegetables in the winter. These coupons, which could be traded or sold for money, became a second kind of currency. Because chickens were so scarce, though, there were no coupons for them; you just had to stand in line and pay high prices.

I volunteered to wait in line and fussed until my parents agreed. My mother set the alarm for me the night before. When it went off at 4 a.m., the whole house woke up except me. My mother finally managed to wake me up, and I insisted that everyone go back to sleep, because I wanted to do the job by myself. My parents climbed back into bed and pretended that they were asleep while I dressed and went to the market. It was dark out when I first got there. All of the storefronts were closed, and people were forming a line on the sidewalk outside the butcher shop. Someone at the head of the line handed out small

pieces of paper, and we each wrote our number according to
where we stood in the line. It turned out to be a good idea that I
had gone, because some of the grownups, probably thinking
that my parents had forced me to stand in line, felt sorry for me
and let me go ahead of them. By the time the market opened at
eight, Nainai had come with her straw basket to buy the chickens.

I was friendly with all of the kids in the alley, but Nainai must
have sensed that I preferred to be with adults, because she
encouraged me to go out and play with the other children when
they came home from school. I was known as *haiziwang*, king of
the kids, because I always came up with the ideas for our play.
Often we dug sandtraps in the dirt in front of my house and
played army. As far back as I can remember, I wanted to grow up
to be a member of the People's Liberation Army like my parents.
I didn't know any boy who didn't want to be a PLA soldier. We
had no other heroes to look up to. There were no Luke Sky-
walkers, no cowboys, for us to admire; the PLA soldier was all
there was. My mother even made me a PLA uniform with a fur
collar, which I wore whenever I played war with the kids in the
alley.

All of us little kids knew that the Japanese devils, the American imperialists, and the Guomindang were China's enemies.
When we played war, they were always the bad guys. The PLA
soldiers were the heroes who defeated the enemy. Because I had
the uniform, I usually took the part of the PLA. But one time all
of the other kids were fighting to be PLA soldiers.

"That's no fun, if we're all PLA," I said. "What's the big deal?
I'll be the Guomindang."

My father heard me and hurriedly pulled me into the house.
"Do you know what the Guomindang is?" he asked me very
seriously. "They are the worst kind of people. You cannot fool
around and say you want to be the Guomindang."

I was too young to understand fully the paranoia the adults
felt about the Guomindang. After Liberation there had been
persistent rumors that Chiang Kai-shek's forces on Taiwan were

preparing to invade mainland China, and the Chinese government was determined to rid the country of any possible Guomindang influence on the mainland. As a result, anyone associated with the government in Taiwan was in serious trouble. For example, one night I heard loud knocking on the door of our courtyard. "It's the police; we just want to ask you some questions," someone called out. Then I heard one of our neighbor's sons say, "Mother, Father, I'm going with the policemen to have a little talk. I'll be right back." But he never returned. I heard the grownups say that he was accused of trying to buy arms from the Taiwan government and jailed as a counterrevolutionary. Apparently a group of people were arrested for running guns from Taiwan and one of them implicated him. When the police came that night, they found a letter from Taiwan in his room. I'm still not sure what he did exactly. I just remember his parents crying for hours whenever they came home from a prison visit.

My neighborhood friends and I ran freely in our alley, but I had to be with a grownup to go on Changan Avenue, because there was so much traffic. Only on special occasions did I realize that Changan Avenue — the Avenue of Eternal Peace — was the most important boulevard in China's capital. Living a few meters away from it, I saw world events take place right outside my front door. Whenever a foreign dignitary visited Beijing, he drove from the Great Hall of the People in Tiananmen Square down Changan Avenue past my house to the National Guest Hotel in a western suburb. Each neighborhood had a committee, and ours always organized a people's welcoming party whenever there was a state visit. The government gave out flags of the visitor's country to the neighborhood committees, which distributed them to us and told us to line the avenue as the cars drove by. We'd holler, *"Huanying huanying, reli huanying,"* "Welcome welcome, an enthusiastic welcome," and wave the flags in the air. We chanted the same thing in the same tone of voice no matter who it was. We were out on the street because we had been told to go, but we had no feelings at all about these dignitaries.

When President Richard Nixon came to Beijing in 1972, there was unusual excitement. I knew it was a big deal because people actually wanted to go and welcome the American president.

"Aren't the Americans our enemies?" I remember asking some neighbors.

"The American devils have surrendered," I was told. "They're breaking their ties with Taiwan and now want to be our friends."

Since the Americans were now our friends, I too waved the Stars and Stripes enthusiastically while Nainai held me up to watch the limousines come down Changan Avenue.

When Japan's Prime Minister Tanaka came to Beijing several months later, my whole neighborhood went out dutifully to wave the Japanese flag. I went along at first, and then it occurred to me: *It's the Japanese devils! How can we welcome them?* I ran home, put on my PLA uniform, and rounded up four of my friends. We took our toy rifles and went to fight the Japanese. We had barely gotten out of the alley and onto Changan Avenue when we were stopped by a real soldier. I only came up to his knees.

"What are you boys doing?" he asked in a gruff voice.

"The Japanese are coming. We have to fight them," I said, looking up at the giant in front of me.

"You can't fight the Japanese," he said, to my surprise.

"Why?" I asked.

"Because we are now friends with Japan," the soldier said matter-of-factly.

I was dumfounded. "How can we be friends with the Japanese?" I said. "We can't let them get away."

The soldier was losing patience with me. "Go home," he said, waving his large hand in front of my face. "You are affecting international relations."

I led my troops back home, suddenly feeling scared. I didn't know what international relations were, but they sounded serious. The soldier was carrying a real rifle, which looked too heavy for any of us even to lift.

As soon as I entered my courtyard, I saw Fourth Uncle and

quickly told him what had happened. "He said we are affecting international relations," I reported nervously.

But my uncle didn't share my concern. He seemed more worried about the fact that I was wearing a PLA uniform. He thought I might get into trouble for impersonating a soldier.

"Remember," he said, "if you're on the street and the soldiers approach, run home as fast as you can. If they stop you and ask you where you got the uniform, tell them that your parents gave it to you because they were both members of the PLA."

"But what about the Japanese?" I asked.

"Oh, don't worry about the Japanese," he said. "We're not fighting them anymore."

Just the night before, Fourth Uncle had taught me a new song about bayoneting a Japanese and throwing him into the river. I was so confused.

Despite the changes in China's relations with the United States and Japan, my friends and I didn't change the way we played war. The Japanese, the Americans, and the Guomindang were still the bad guys.

One month before I was to begin first grade, Premier Zhou Enlai died. It was January 8, 1976, and I was happily anticipating starting school and being with my friends every day when suddenly everyone around me was sad and upset because of the premier's death. They were also worried about what might follow. I had heard my parents and my neighbors say many times that 1976 was the Year of the Dragon, which meant that something calamitous was likely to happen. The death of Zhou Enlai, whom many Chinese considered the most morally upright and politically moderate of the top Communist Party leaders, unleashed the first spontaneous mass movement China had experienced since the 1949 revolution. Thousands of people filled Tiananmen Square to pay tribute to the beloved premier and to vent their anger at the radicals responsible for the Cultural Revolution. This protest was violently crushed by the government in what was to be the last bloody act of the Gang of Four, the four

high-ranking officials who had been in power for the past decade.

I did not really understand the events of that year until I was
much older, but I vividly remember the day Zhou Enlai died.
When the death was announced over the radio, my neighbors
ran from house to house to make sure everyone heard the news.
The old ladies cried bitterly as they handed out black cloths so
that each family could make armbands. Grownups wept openly
in the streets.

On the day of the funeral, a procession of limousines came
down Changan Avenue, and the streets were mobbed. It was
incredibly cold, and clouds of steam rose from the mouths and
nostrils of the mourners. I learned later that a million people had
stood for hours in the below-freezing temperature to bid farewell to the beloved premier.

Everyone in my alley went to see the procession. My parents
were at work, so I went with my grandmother, my sister, and the
neighbors to see what was going on. There was a sea of blue and
gray quilted jackets; so many people were lining the avenue that
I couldn't see anything, and I was afraid I might be trampled. I
saw some of the older kids climbing up onto the tops of cars, so I
looked around for something to stand on. I found a delivery
person's tricycle beside a building, and I tried to balance myself
on its tiny triangular seat. A nice man held me steady so that I
wouldn't fall, but I could just barely see over the heads of the
people in front of me. Soldiers were lined up along the avenue to
prevent hysterical people from rushing into the path of the
limousines and taking a last chance to touch the premier.

I saw a long black car move slowly by. It was different from
the others in the procession: this one was decked with a large
wreath of flowers from which hung two white ribbons with
black Chinese characters. I could tell from the reaction that it
must hold the premier's coffin. The crowd began to surge forward, and one woman tried to break through the barricade of
soldiers to throw herself on the hood of the car. As the soldiers
carried her out of sight, she was wailing loudly.

Not far behind the limousines, an open car held a camera that was filming the people crying along the way.

I could not balance on the tricycle any longer and climbed down, coming face to face with some people who were kneeling on the ground. Their eyes were red and their cheeks were wet. Their faces were contorted with pain. I was very moved by this, but I was puzzled.

"Are they making a movie?" I asked the man who had helped me down from the tricycle. He didn't answer.

"There's a camera on the last car," I told him.

"Yes, yes," he said impatiently. He was craning his neck for a better look.

All of my neighbors are in this crowd, I thought. *What are they doing in this movie?*

People around me were overcome with sadness, but I was not sure I understood why. I had heard that Premier Zhou was a good man, but I didn't know what his good deeds were.

"Uncle, was Premier Zhou a great man?" I asked, tugging the elbow of a stranger standing next to me.

"Of course he was," the man said, wiping his teary face with his coat sleeves.

"What made him so great?" I continued.

"He was the premier," he said, not even bothering to look down at me.

"What does it mean to be great?" I asked again.

The man heaved a long sigh. "He was a very good speaker," he answered curtly.

I pushed my way through the crowd to an old woman from my block. I tried the question again. "Auntie, was Premier Zhou a great man?"

Dabbing her eyes with a crumpled cloth, she said, "I will tell you. Once Zhou Enlai received a foreign dignitary and the two of them shook hands. After the handshake, the foreigner took a handkerchief and wiped his hand. Premier Zhou smiled, took his handkerchief, wiped his hand, and threw the handkerchief into a spittoon."

After a few seconds I realized that there was no more to her story. I nodded as if I had understood and moved on.

I must have annoyed a lot of people as I squeezed my way through the crowd to ask my simple question. But none of the adults got angry. They were patient with me because they thought I should know what kind of man Zhou Enlai had been.

"Why was Premier Zhou a great man?" I asked yet another grownup.

"Because he always knew what to say," the man answered. With animation, he told me this story: "When a foreigner met Premier Zhou, he asked, 'Why are the Chinese so thin, and why do they cower with pained expressions on their faces? We Westerners are tall and sturdy and walk with pride in our chests.' Premier Zhou answered, 'Because our country is on the rise and we are climbing a mountain. You are very proud and your civilization is on the decline. That is why you sit back like fatted calves waiting for your own demise.' "

Another man chimed in: "Yes, he was a clever speaker. Once he was asked whether China still had prostitutes. He answered, 'Yes, we still do — in Taiwan Province.' "

I walked away from the two of them as they chuckled over Premier Zhou's joke. I didn't understand what it meant or why it was funny. I kept moving through the crowd, looking for a better answer. *Zhou Enlai must have been a very special person for all of these people to have come to pay their last respects,* I thought. *I must find out more about him.* But right then everyone else was more interested in watching the procession than in answering my questions.

I approached an elderly man, who was sure to know.

"Uncle, how great was Premier Zhou?" I asked.

He thought for a moment and said, "After Liberation, Zhou Enlai was on the same level as Chairman Mao and Marshal Zhu De. But he declined to be the supreme leader. He never sought to be the top man. He was truly a servant of the people. Even though he was a first-rank government official, deserving of the highest salary, he never accepted the money. He chose to take lesser pay. That is how great he was!"

At last a story made some sense to me. *But,* I thought, *why does a premier need to be paid any money at all? Doesn't he already have everything?*

After the funeral cortege passed out of view, the crowd began to break up and head for home. When I got to my front yard, all of the kids in the neighborhood were already there, listening to the radio programs memorializing Premier Zhou. My mother was home from work and had put little wooden stools out for us to sit on in a circle. Some of the other children began giggling and playing around. I thought, *This is not the time to laugh.* After the incredible display of emotion I had seen that day, I too had begun to feel a sense of loss and sadness. I was upset by their disrespectful behavior, so I stared them down, not saying a word, hoping they would pick up from me the seriousness of the occasion.

After the radio program, my mother gave us white paper and white cloth and told us to make flowers for Premier Zhou. It is a tradition for mourners to wear white flowers and black armbands. Making flowers was the highlight of the day. I liked the paper best, because I could make accordion folds and have the flowers fan out like white chrysanthemums. Some of the boys didn't know what they were doing and made a mess of everything, so that their mothers scolded them and slapped their clumsy hands. My mother stood at a distance, but I could see that she was quietly admiring my handiwork. Afterward she directed us to do something unusual: we put on our black armbands and took all of the white flowers we had made to Tiananmen Square.

The largest public square in the world, Tiananmen Square had always seemed overwhelming to me. With the Gate of Heavenly Peace on the north side, the Museum of Chinese History to the east, the Great Hall of the People to the west, Zhengyang Gate to the south, and the Monument to the People's Heroes in the center, it is a place of grandeur and history. In the days following Premier Zhou's death, it was suddenly transformed with white. It seemed that everybody in Beijing had made flowers. Hundreds of flowers were on every tree, every flagpole, and every lamppost. White floral wreaths brought by the residents of Beijing and by people from all over the country were piled high at the base of the Monument to the People's Heroes and lined the perimeter of the hundred-acre square.

That image made an indelible impression on me, and later, when I was in junior high school, I wrote an essay about it. "My parents took me to Tiananmen Square after Premier Zhou died," I wrote. "Thousands of white chrysanthemums floated in a sea of people wearing deep blue coats. The day was extremely cold. I wore the cotton padded jacket that my mother made for me. The chill wind made my nose red like a rabbit's, and my breath froze. Rising above all of the flowers and the bobbing black heads was the genteel image of Premier Zhou. I could see his kind face smiling at us from the light blue sky."

Toward the end of March I went with my family almost every day to Tiananmen Square to see all of the *xiaozibao*, small-character posters with writings and slogans on them, that had been put up by the people of Beijing. After dinner my father took me with him, and on Sundays he interrupted my play with other children to ask me to go with him.

Thousands of people seemed to be making their way to the pedestal of the Monument to the People's Heroes to read the *xiaozibao*, but there were very few children in the square. Many people were copying the *xiaozibao*. My father must have copied everything he could, because he had several notebooks full of the writings. He told me they were very good poems, but I was too young to ask him about them, although I knew that he had written some poetry himself and that literature and writing were important to him. Since the Cultural Revolution had begun, all of the books published and sold in bookstores had been politically "correct," which meant that the contents were meaningless propaganda. My father and thousands of other Beijing residents furiously copied the writings on the monument because this was a way in which they could read contemporary Chinese works of real literary value and because the poems were an expression of the dissatisfaction they all felt. Every night Fourth Uncle came over, and he and my parents exchanged what they had copied that day.

On some days young poets stood on the steps of the monument and read their poetry aloud. On Sundays people just milled about, as if strolling through a busy marketplace. But my father never moved from the pedestal. He spent every minute of his time reading the posters and writing in his notebook. I got tired of standing next to him and waiting. I wanted to go home and play with my friends, and I wondered why he wanted me to be there.

What I didn't know then was that the poems and essays being written and posted daily were not only endorsements of Premier Zhou and his wish to modernize China but veiled attacks on the radicals who had disrupted China's progress by continuing the Great Proletarian Cultural Revolution. To praise Zhou Enlai was to criticize the Gang of Four. The poems my parents so painstakingly collected were expressions of defiance that grew out of the anger and frustration caused by ten years of chaos and repression. My father knew he was taking part in history. Although he didn't say so at the time, I now know that he wanted me to be there to witness it.

Eventually my parents started to go to the square after dinner, to read the posters that had gone up earlier that day. They often did not come home until ten or eleven o'clock. I can't say I minded that much, because without them at home I could stay up as late as I wanted. It was even more fun when I was allowed to stay up late and go with them. Some dim streetlamps lit up the square, but many people brought flashlights to help them read the *xiaozibao*. Tiananmen Square, usually empty and quiet at night, was now full of people who walked and talked freely to one another. It felt like a big Chinese New Year's party.

It became a nightly event to go the square, and the chatter

became more and more animated as the *xiaozibao* writers became bolder in their criticisms of the radicals. I was caught up by the excitement around me, but my father, my mother, and Fourth Uncle acted as if they were on a serious mission. They never left the monument to talk to anybody. They each took a side of the pedestal and intently copied the writings. When we came home, they exchanged notebooks. Soon they had compiled a stack of booklets copied from the *xiaozibao*.

One night I noticed something new as soon as we approached Tiananmen Square. A huge wreath of flowers like a halo lay atop the towering Monument to the People's Heroes. It was hard for me to imagine how anyone could climb up there to put the wreath in place.

"Look, Mother, those flowers on the monument weren't there before," I said, pointing skyward.

My mother told me the wreath had been placed there for the festival of Qingming, which was a few days later, on April 5. Qingming is the Chinese Memorial Day, and since Liberation it has been designated as the day to remember not only our ancestors but in particular the revolutionary soldiers who gave their lives.

On the night of April 4 my father was working late, but my mother and grandmother wanted to go to the square after dinner. While Nainai was clearing the dishes, Fourth Uncle stopped by. He said that he had heard a rumor in the factory that the government was going to clean out the square soon. "They already started removing the flowers," he said.

As soon as we got to the monument we heard the voice of the mayor, Wu De, booming over the public address system. He was warning everyone in the square to leave or they would suffer the consequences. My mother was telling Nainai that she thought we should head home when suddenly she clutched my right hand and pointed to the north side of the square. She had caught sight of the People's Militia, who were running in columns from all four sides of the square to block the perimeter. My grandmother immediately grabbed my left hand, and we started to run north toward Changan Avenue, to get home. Other people were starting to move quickly too, but by the time we reached the avenue the militia had closed ranks and blocked the way. Before I could look up to see the men standing right before us, two of them moved apart for a few seconds to let us through. We ran all the way home, never turning around to see what was happening behind us. I couldn't run fast enough. My feet flew off the ground as my mother and grandmother hurriedly pulled me along. It might have been a dangerous situation, but I was too young and too excited to be scared. We were running so fast that I didn't have a chance to ask my mother why.

The three of us didn't say a word the entire way home. When we walked into our house, my father and Fourth Uncle were anxiously waiting for us. My adrenaline was pumping and I was out of breath, but I was in the safety of my home with my family around me, so I felt no danger at all. The adults talked excitedly late into the night. I did not detect any fear in my parents' voices, and I didn't think about what might be happening back at the square. Exhausted, I quickly fell asleep.

The significance of that night was completely lost on me, at age seven. On the night before Qingming, a night that I remember only for the brief thrill of running at full speed for home, the government dispatched the militia to remove all the portraits of the late premier and all the wreaths laid by the people to memorialize him, including the one crowning the Monument to the People's Heroes. The next day, when the people of Beijing found the square stripped and started to riot, the militia dealt with them violently. Thousands were arrested, and many died.

The next day and for weeks thereafter the radio broadcast that a counterrevolutionary movement in Tiananmen Square had been crushed, and said that anyone who had collected the subversive writings should turn them in to his work unit and that no punishment would be levied against him. The radio said that the people who had copied the writings on the monument were counterrevolutionary collaborators. If they did not voluntarily turn over the subversive writings, they too faced arrest and imprisonment. The broadcasts urging people to turn themselves in were relentless. They seemed to be the only news on the radio for days.

I knew that my parents were the people the radio announcers were talking about. That first night, when they came home from work, we ate dinner in total silence. Fourth Uncle came over afterward, and all of the adults were very solemn. My grandmother cleared the table while my parents quietly locked the door and closed all the windows and shades around our house. The room was lit by the yellow light of a single bulb. No one said a word. I knew enough not to interrupt the silence. I remained quiet, and my sister stayed in the other room, reading. I stood to the side and watched. When the table had been cleared, the adults sat and whispered.

"Handing in the books is out of the question," my father said in a low voice. "We have to destroy them, burn everything."

"Burning is dangerous," my mother replied. "It is too warm to be starting a fire in the stove. The neighbors would suspect if they saw ashes."

They sat staring at the precious booklets. My father fingered the pages delicately, as if he had second thoughts about destroying them.

"Brother Shen," my uncle finally said to my father, "perhaps we can dissolve the pages in water."

"That is a very good idea," my grandmother agreed. "I will get trays and fill them with water."

Nainai took out every pot, every pan, every tray, every bowl we had in the house and filled them with water. The four grown-ups spent the entire night tearing the pages of writing out of the booklets and dissolving each individual sheet of paper. I don't think they noticed me standing there, but I was fascinated by this. I was leaning against a wall, watching what I felt was a dangerous operation.

They were afraid that one of the old women from the neighborhood committee would come by unexpectedly while the pages were slowly dissolving. Those women were out looking

for people wh
My parents di
trays in a hurr
hear the fear in
how to conceal

The sheets wr
to destroy compl
but traces of ink
impatient because
the last page was
mixture and poure
threw the solution
in with the night s
tomorrow won't be

30

the stage, but the hero was unm
hair, which was prohibited at
next to me while he was sp
is his hair.
Years later I lear
counterrevolutio
ing the Great
That April
camp.
lab

My grandmother ...without saying a word. My parents never talked to my sister and me about what they had done. I knew from the repeated announcements on the radio that they would be in trouble if they were found with counterrevolutionary poetry, and I could feel their fear, so I instinctively did not breathe a word about this to anyone. We were a family. We had to protect ourselves. But my parents took a great chance by not warning us to be quiet. If we accidentally mentioned what we had seen to a neighbor or a teacher, they both could have been threatened with official action. Luckily, my sister and I somehow knew that this was our family secret. I also knew in my heart that my parents were not bad people, as the radio said.

In school, the teacher told us about a young man who became a hero on Qingming, the day the counterrevolutionary movement was crushed. She said this young man, who had very badly cut long hair, had seen one of the ringleaders of the demonstration trying to escape and had cleverly copied down the license number of his bicycle. The hero reported this immediately to the Public Security Bureau — the secret police — and was held up as a model citizen by the government. After the teacher's story, we lined up and marched to a large auditorium to hear the hero speak. All sorts of government officials were on on

stakable because of his long
hat time. I played with the boy
aking. All I can remember about him

ed that the police had never caught the
ary on the bicycle, who was accused of storm-
Hall of the People and trying to air his grievances.
he had been on parole from a reform-through-labor
After the incident was publicized, he went back to the
r camp. No one thought that he would be in a labor camp,
and the camp guards never suspected that someone under their
noses was the most wanted person in Beijing.

· 2 ·

Billy Clubs
and Violins

AFTER THE CRACKDOWN OF the Tiananmen incident, Deng Xiaoping, who was the vice premier at that time and had been one of Zhou Enlai's allies, was purged from his government posts, because the radicals believed that he had been behind the demonstrators' calls for changes within the Party and the country. I went to all of the parades on Changan Avenue that denounced him as a rightist. The government organized hundreds of people to march up and down the streets with drums and cymbals and firecrackers, as well as banners with slogans opposing him. Crowds gathered on the avenue yelling, "Down with Deng Xiaoping!" My friends and I followed them and mimicked their chants. "Down with Deng Xiaoping!" we shouted, raising our fists in the air like the grownups.

After the rallies Changan Avenue was littered with used firecracker papers, banners, and pennants, which my friends and I went after as if they were free toys. Our courtyard was full of multicolored flags and pennants with slogans written on them. I could read one or two of the words on each, but I had no idea what the writing was about. We liked the banners because they were colorful and were attached to wooden sticks. The grownups sometimes gave us leftover fireworks too. We had a great time at these events.

The government staged rallies whenever a high-ranking official was purged, to show that the Party had popular support. All of the adults were accustomed to these orchestrated demonstrations, and my parents didn't think much about letting me go to them. When they came home from work and saw the slogan-filled banners I had collected, they didn't say anything. They knew that I was just having fun and was too young to know what the rallies were about.

Around this time one of my mother's brothers, Third Uncle, received word that he would be sent to the northeast to work in a coal mine. He was being transferred because he didn't get along with the head of his work unit. As in my father's case, his relationship with the supervisor played a large role in how well he was treated at work. Third Uncle had a daughter, Lili, who was six years older than I, and an infant son. Our family was very upset that he had to go so far away with such small children, and we were also afraid that he would never be able to move back to Beijing, because the government required everyone to live where he or she was assigned to work. My mother came up with the idea that my cousin Lili could live with us. As long as Third Uncle had a child registered as a Beijing resident, he would always be able to use that as a reason to come back to the city.

After much discussion, Lili stayed with us while the rest of her family moved north. My parents treated her like their own daughter and we called her Dajie, Big Sister, but she never got along with our family. She was probably always thinking about her parents and wondering why they had left her behind. No matter how well my parents treated her, she never felt comfortable.

Once we had another person living with us, our small house became even more cramped. Sometimes my father and I went to spend the night in the room my uncle's family had vacated, which was just eight blocks from our house. My father liked the quiet, because he could read in peace. After he came home from work he rode there on his bicycle, and I followed him on a tricycle I borrowed from a friend.

One night while we were at my uncle's I woke up from a sound sleep because I felt very cold. "Dad, I'm freezing," I said, forcing one eye open. I was in my father's arms, and he was standing in the middle of the street. People were all around us, and the houses seemed to be moving from side to side.

"I couldn't wake you," my father said. "I shouted 'Earthquake!' several times and you didn't budge. I had to carry you out."

That earthquake, which shook Beijing on July 28, 1976, measured 7.6 on the Richter scale. Its epicenter wiped out the city of Tangshan, about 150 kilometers east of Beijing, killing an estimated 250,000 people. Some people were killed in Beijing too; in fact, several people in my neighborhood were crushed when their houses fell on them. I didn't know what an earthquake was until I went back home and saw the collapsed houses. No one in my family was hurt, but the neighborhood suffered a lot of damage. Everyone was busily salvaging their belongings and preparing for the aftershock. It was mass confusion.

When my father and I went back to the house, he and my mother were relieved to see that we were all all right. I didn't feel scared, because my parents remained very calm. I even heard Mom tell Dad how, while everyone was panicking to get outside, Nainai had dressed herself, combed her hair, and locked all the cabinets in the house before going out. All of our neighbors stood in the alley, calling to her to hurry, but Nainai took one last look around to make sure everything was in order. By the time she finally went outside, the earthquake was almost over. Only after my mother told this story did I notice a trace of fear on her face.

The day after the earthquake, Changan Avenue became almost a shantytown. All the people who lived along it had moved out of their homes and into the street. The most important avenue in the nation's capital was turned into a sea of makeshift tents, erected from the bamboo sticks that were usually used to hang laundry with sheets of plastic and bedding draped every which way over them. Families moved beds and furniture into the tents, thinking they might be there a while, because several violent aftershocks were expected. Over the next few days it was very windy and the rain came down in buckets. After a week, people found all sorts of materials they could use to build better tents. Some even replaced the bamboo sticks with metal rods. Others found ways to insulate their tents with layers of material.

We lived in the middle of Changan Avenue for a couple of weeks, and it was probably the most fun I had ever had in my eight years. The avenue near our house is six lanes wide, and all of it was ours to play on. My friends and I ran from tent to tent visiting each other. People were afraid to go back to their homes to cook in case another earthquake hit, so we all stood in long lines at the food stalls, buying steamed bread and pork buns. My sister and I were happy because it was like eating out every night.

One afternoon while I was resting on the bed from all the running around I did, I saw a scary-looking man with mussed hair and a torn raincoat walking his bicycle slowly over to our tent. As soon as he approached us, Nainai exclaimed, "Isn't that your fifth uncle?" Fifth Uncle worked as a well digger in Tianjin, which is close to Tangshan. He had offered to take me there for a holiday that summer, but although it was only a two-hour train ride away from Beijing, for some reason my parents hadn't let me go. The house where Fifth Uncle was staying had collapsed in the earthquake and he had had to crawl out from under the rubble. He had ridden his bicycle for days to get to Beijing and find us on Changan Avenue.

"Uncle, you're filthy," I said, not knowing what he had been through.

Fifth Uncle just dropped himself on the bed and fell asleep from exhaustion.

When he woke up that evening, he told us that thousands of people in Tianjin were homeless and roaming the streets, scavenging for food. A man on the farm where he was living had slaughtered a horse, and people had fought for pieces of the meat. Fifth Uncle had cooked his share, and that was the only thing he had had to eat for days. He took the leftover horsemeat from his pouch and I asked to try a piece. Living in a tent and eating from food stalls had made me feel adventurous. As I chewed on the tough and stringy meat, I suddenly thought about what could have happened to me if I had gone to Tianjin for a visit.

Even after we moved out of the tents on Changan Avenue and back into our house, we were preparing for another earthquake. The radio warned of more aftershocks that could affect any part of the country. All of China seemed to be living in a state of emergency, waiting for the aftershocks that never came. Some of my neighbors slept with their doors open so they could run out in a hurry. My parents took large pieces of metal shaped like staples and nailed them into the corners of the house in the hope that they would prevent the walls from caving in. They stacked my sister's bed on top of my bed, and we both slept in the lower one. My father stored some dry goods and crackers underneath this bed in case the family was trapped inside the house, and told us not to eat them because they were our emergency rations.

One night my sister and I could not resist, and we took some crackers out of the tin. Lili, who was sleeping with Nainai, saw us on her way to the outhouse. She told my father the next day, and I remember his reaction because it was the first time he had ever gotten angry with us.

"That food is for everyone in case of an earthquake," he fumed. "How can the two of you think only about yourselves? Do you think the family doesn't give you enough to eat, so you have to steal from the tin?"

My sister and I stood with our heads lowered and nothing to say. Neither of us ever really got along with our cousin after that. Lili left us not long afterward; she missed her parents so much that they agreed to let her join them.

In August I began the second half of first grade in tents built in the schoolyard. All day the teacher read stories to us instead of having regular reading and writing classes, because we didn't have desks outside. We heard stories about the brave people of Tangshan and about the courageous PLA, who had rescued people trapped in their homes. I especially liked a story about a boy our age whose whole family had been buried under their house. The soldiers didn't have any equipment but used their bare hands to dig these people out. The boy underneath the house said to one of the soldiers, "Big brother, rest a while before you dig again." Trapped under the rubble, he was more concerned about the soldier's welfare than he was about himself. It was such a great story. The teacher told us to go home and write poems to send to the people of Tangshan, showing our support for them and for the PLA soldiers who had been so brave. With my father's help, I wrote a twelve-page poem based on the boy's story.

A few weeks after the earthquake, on September 9, when our lives had barely returned to normal, Chairman Mao died. That day I was taking a walk with Qige, and we heard people on the streets telling each other the news. It didn't register with me at first; then all of a sudden it hit me. "Oh no, Chairman Mao died!" I said to Qige. He nodded his head and repeated, "Chairman Mao died," as if in disbelief.

I didn't need to ask how great Chairman Mao was. He was the greatest. From the time that I could speak, nearly everything I read and every song I sang praised Chairman Mao — "The East is red / The sun has risen / China has produced a Mao Zedong," or "I love Beijing Tiananmen / Tiananmen rises toward the sun / Our great leader Chairman Mao / Exhorts us ever forward" — or had lyrics based on his writings. We copied Chairman Mao's sayings in school to learn the Chinese characters. We even did our physical exercises while reciting his famous quotations. It was a common practice for people to stand before Chairman Mao's portrait in their home at the end of the workday and talk to him about what they had contributed that day to the revolution. My parents had a portrait of Chairman Mao and a book of his quotations, but I never saw them talk to the picture.

My family made a floral wreath for Chairman Mao and hung it outside our front gate as a sign of mourning, but somehow people weren't as emotional as they had been after Premier Zhou's death. My parents were aware of the economic failures and the political persecution that Chairman Mao's policies had brought to the country, but even so, they, like most other Chinese citizens, thought Chairman Mao was the greatest leader China had ever had. At the time of his death, people temporarily forgot about all of his mistakes and remembered only the glory days. They could also feel that something was changing in the country. In early July Marshal Zhu De, a military hero of the Revolution, had also died, so 1976 saw the deaths of three great revolutionaries.

My sister, who was ten, seemed unusually subdued after she heard the news. I saw her and a friend sitting on a corner of the bed talking somberly.

"Now that Chairman Mao is dead there will be no more New China," Qing said. "We'll be going back to the old society, and we probably won't be able to go to school anymore."

"We'll become child laborers at the haircutters'," my sister's friend said.

"I think I can get a job at the tea store," my sister replied. "I like the smell."

I didn't share their concern. I knew I was too little to be put to work. If I couldn't go to school, I thought, I would just stay at home with Nainai.

Many people could not imagine China without Chairman Mao, because he was such an important part of our everyday lives. Everywhere you looked, you were reminded of his contribution to modern China. Billboards reading LONG LIVE CHAIRMAN MAO could be seen on the city walls. On top of one of the municipal buildings was a sign that said REVOLUTION DEPENDS ON MAO ZEDONG THOUGHT. For young people a generation older than my sister and me, Chairman Mao's death was a devastating event, and high school and university students jammed Tiananmen Square on the day of his funeral. I sat home with Nainai that day, listening to the radio broadcast of the memorial service. It didn't seem very interesting to me, because it sounded identical to the one I had heard when Premier Zhou died.

Soon after Chairman Mao's death, big tractors began digging up the south side of Tiananmen Square to construct a mausoleum, the Chairman Mao Zedong Memorial Hall. When they broke ground for it there was a big ceremony, which I watched on television. Every time my mother and I rode the Changan Avenue bus along the northern side of the square, I could see the construction site in the distance. The workers put up wooden walls to keep people out, but there were always knots of people trying to peek through the cracks. While the mausoleum was being built, everyone talked about how long it would be before it was finished and we could view the chairman's body. The lines would be tremendous, everyone said, but it would be well worth the wait to get a glimpse of the great man.

The country was undergoing a sea change, moving out of a very dark chapter in its history. In October the Gang of Four were arrested, an act that signaled the beginning of the end of the Cultural Revolution. Again, those in power organized many parades on Changan Avenue to criticize the radicals, who were being blamed for the horrors of the past decade. A massive rally held in Tiananmen Square was attended by a million people, because the Gang of Four, led by Chairman Mao's widow, Jiang Qing, were universally despised by the people.

The Campaign to Criticize the Gang of Four went on for more than a year, but my friends and I were more interested in a people's campaign to improve China's sanitation that went on at the same time. The neighborhood committees were mobilized to wipe out the Four Pests — mosquitoes, flies, roaches, and rats. The old ladies went from house to house, giving each family tins of insecticide and rat poison and demonstrating how best to use them. A spin-off of the sanitation campaign was a drive started by the women to catch a black slug they said was used in Chinese medicine. At night the old ladies fanned out all over the neighborhood with flashlights, looking for these slugs.

As the Cultural Revolution ended and the country slowly became more open to the West, the government eased up on its control of literature and music, making the arts available to the people. During this time classical musicians began to give concerts in Beijing, and my parents took me and my sister to a few of them. These outings were really special for us, because we had our own seats. Very few children's parents took them to concerts, and the ones who did always made the children sit on their laps. People in the back of the auditorium who were looking for a place often thought that my seat was vacant because they couldn't see my head over the back of the chair.

These rare outings taught me to love and appreciate classical music. During the performance my eyes would move from one instrument to another, because I was fascinated by the sounds each of them made. When I was a little older, the Japanese conductor Seiji Ozawa came to Beijing and gave three concerts, which immediately sold out. Since tickets were impossible to get, I stood outside the concert hall, hoping to get a glimpse of the performance whenever the door opened. The ticket taker, who had been watching me, was moved by my enthusiasm and eventually let me in. I stood in the back of the concert hall and caught part of Ozawa's thrilling performance.

While I was still in first grade, the coaches of Beijing's athletic teams came to the grammar schools looking for young talent. Both the Ping-Pong coach and the martial arts coach wanted to have me on their teams. They remarked to my parents that my eyes were round and dark and full of fire. "They said that means you must be a quick thinker and have good reflexes," my mother told me. My parents decided that I should practice Ping-Pong and not the martial arts — Ping-Pong was a very popular sport, especially since China had participated in tournaments with American teams — so I began training for Ping-Pong every afternoon after school. I had to take two buses to get to the gymnasium for practice, and Nainai was very proud that I could get there and back on my own. We first practiced swinging the paddle without the ball to learn the proper technique. After a week we lined up facing the wall of the gym and hit the balls against the wall to learn control. The sight of a dozen pint-sized Ping-Pong players clumsily hitting the little white balls against the wall must have been quite hilarious, but at the time we took these practices seriously. I trained for Ping-Pong for two years, but I never became a great player.

Sometime during the school year I discovered that what really interested me was scientific experiments. My sister, who was in third grade, had a schoolbook called *Scientific Common Knowledge* that gave the instructions for some simple projects, and I started trying some of them in our courtyard. I built model airplanes with materials my parents brought me and odds and ends collected from home, gluing pieces of wood together and pasting colored paper on them. I won a prize in a school science competition for one of my experiments, in which I filled one bowl with saltwater and another with fresh water and placed an egg in each. The egg floated in the bowl with saltwater and sank in the other bowl. I used a tube to siphon saltwater into the bottom of a third bowl, which also contained fresh water. In that bowl the egg floated in the middle, partly buoyed by the saltwater. The other children thought I was performing a magic act.

I was adjusting well to going to school and being away from home every day. I began to develop a life of my own. In the morning I rounded up the kids in my alley to walk to school together. After school I rode the bus to Ping-Pong practice. When I got home, I conducted experiments while the other neighborhood kids gathered around to watch. Occasionally I'd leave my science project and play war in the sandtrap in the alley.

I encountered my first disappointment in school when the teachers selected the first group of first graders to be inducted into the Young Pioneers, an organization founded by the Chinese Communist Party for children aged seven to fourteen. For a child, entering the Young Pioneers was like joining the Communist Party for adults. It was an honor to serve the people. In the spirit of the Party's hero Lei Feng, Young Pioneers picked up litter on city streets, collected seeds and sent them to the farmers to plant, and helped old ladies with errands.

Even though my grades were the best in my class, my teacher said I wasn't disciplined enough yet to be a Young Pioneer. I often talked during lessons, and I didn't always sit with my hands behind my back. Our rule in class was "Hands behind back, feet together, eyes on Chairman Mao." I always made fun of the rule, asking my friends, "If we follow the rule and stare at the portrait of Chairman Mao, how can we read and write?"

I was finally made a Young Pioneer at the end of first grade. The school held an assembly, and each of us walked onstage to receive a red scarf, which we would wear every day. I was very proud that I could now be a part of this group and do good things for the country.

About halfway into my second year in school, in September 1977, one year after Chairman Mao's death, the mausoleum that would hold his embalmed body was completed. I recall it vividly, because the most exciting thing happened.

"I'm going to see Chairman Mao!" I screamed, running down our alley so that everyone in the neighborhood could hear.

At school the principal had announced that representatives of every sector of society — workers, peasants, soldiers, and students — would make up the first public group to view Chairman Mao's body in the mausoleum. To represent the students, Beijing's schools were selecting a few outstanding pupils from each grade. I was chosen to represent my second-grade class because I was now team leader of the Young Pioneers. It was such an honor to be one of the first in China to visit the memorial hall and see Chairman Mao — even though he was dead — that I felt my chest would burst. Everybody wanted to see him, whether they liked him or not.

My neighbors were very proud, even for themselves. "Yuan

Yuan, you are so lucky!" said a lady down the street. "Be sure and tell us all about it when you come home."

While the neighbors were making a big fuss, my father didn't say anything. Not until the night before I was to go to the mausoleum, while my mother and Nainai cleaned and pressed my Young Pioneer uniform, did he ask me to sit by his side while he talked to me.

"You're very excited about tomorrow, aren't you?" he asked.

"I'm going to see the great Chairman Mao," I said. "Only a few people from my school get to go."

"Do you understand that the mausoleum has been built for one man but the Monument to the People's Heroes was built for all the thousands of Chinese citizens who died during the war against Japan and the Revolution?" he asked.

I didn't know what he was driving at, and the puzzled look on my face didn't make him explain. But I now know that my father, in his subtle way, was expressing his disapproval that one man, Chairman Mao, should be placed above all of the Chinese citizens who sacrificed their lives for the country. He had trouble reconciling his admiration for Mao Zedong with the suffering that Mao had caused.

That conversation was typical of the way my father and I talked about things. He always gave me information and allowed me to think and draw my own conclusions. When I was a boy, I did not always fully appreciate the significance of what he said or did. But everything clearly made an impression, because as I grew older, I could recall these conversations vividly. The process of thinking for myself was an important part of the way my father educated me.

That night I went to bed full of expectations. When I woke up the next morning, my clothes were laid out neatly for me: a white shirt, navy blue pants, a red scarf, white socks, and black shoes. Because I was the team leader of my grade, I wore three stripes on my sleeve.

Those of us chosen as representatives lined up in the school-yard and walked to Tiananmen Square in total silence. The sun was bright; although not very hot, it made me feel tired and sleepy all the same. By the time we got to Xinhuamen, the entrance to the Zhongnanhai compound where the high-ranking Party officials live, a long line had formed. In front of us were groups of workers and peasants, chosen by their work units, and regiments of soldiers from the People's Liberation Army.

As we stood waiting to enter the mausoleum, I considered what I was about to experience. *I must feel something very strong,* I thought.

When we finally entered, all of our eyes turned skyward. The memorial hall was a huge palace with a high ceiling. Very quickly we walked past a glass coffin, which seemed quite far away from the roped-off area we were ushered through. I had to stand on tiptoes to see over the heads of the children in front of me. I didn't get a good look, but the person inside the coffin didn't look familiar. He had such red cheeks. He looked too healthy to be dead. "This must be a wax dummy," I whispered to the boy in front of me. "The real body is probably behind the curtains."

But before I realized it, we were already walking out of the mausoleum. I was let down, because I hadn't felt a thing. Then all of a sudden it dawned on me that I had just seen Chairman Mao and I should be very sad. I put on the somberest face I could and walked with my head bowed all the way back to school. I blamed myself for not getting a better look.

"How was it?" Nainai asked me as soon as I got home.

"Chairman Mao has a lot of wrinkles," I said. "His face is so red he looks too healthy. It looks like they put paint on his face."

From my scant response, Nainai sensed that I was very disappointed.

Everyone asked me about my experience, but I didn't know what to say. As I described what I saw, I was a little afraid that others would think I was disrespectful. How could I describe Chairman Mao that way? His body was stiff, I kept saying, he looked like a dummy.

The next time I went to see Chairman Mao was on an outing in eighth grade. That time I was telling jokes to the girl next to me and was scolded by the teacher the whole way there. The line was not as long; it started at the Monument to the People's Heroes. It was a hot day and I was tired of standing in the heat. "There's nothing to look at," I said to the girl.

In 1978 the school year changed from the Soviet system of beginning in February to the American system of beginning in September. I had received very high marks the year before, so I skipped third grade and went straight to fourth.

Around this time Deng Xiaoping was restored to power, the Gang of Four were put in jail, and the radical elements of the Communist Party were in retreat. As Deng and his followers within the Party battled the hardliners over the direction of the country, the people of Beijing hoped to hasten the changes by speaking out.

Shortly after I celebrated my tenth birthday, one of the most important events in the movement for democratic reform in China took place at a bus stop about a five-minute walk from my house. It became known as the Democracy Wall Movement, and it lasted from the fall of 1978 to the spring of 1979. Wei Jingsheng, the most vocal dissident of this movement, was later a hero for my generation, and many of the young poets and writers who emerged at this time also had a profound effect on me.

My family was especially aware of the movement because the center of action was the brick wall behind a bus stop near the corner of Xidan and Changan Avenue. The wall, which is about three meters high and one hundred meters long, was dubbed the Democracy Wall because hundreds of *dazibao*, big-character posters, denouncing the radicals and arguing for more democratic freedoms seemed to cover it overnight. Thousands who had been falsely imprisoned during the Cultural Revolution were finally released that fall and participated in this protest.

My father took me to the Democracy Wall whenever he went, usually after dinner or on Sundays. The area was already crowded as buses picked up and discharged passengers, but during those few months, hundreds more gathered to read the *dazibao*. It reminded me of the scene at the pedestal of the monument just after Zhou Enlai's death.

Almost a third of the wall was filled with *xueshu*, testaments written in blood, which symbolized the people's sufferings. I watched in amazement as people stood before sheets of white paper pasted on the wall, biting their index fingers to write and, whenever the blood ran dry, biting their fingers again so they could continue writing. That made the bloody characters thick in the beginning, thin as you read along, and thick again. My father told me that these people were writing the stories of their persecution during the Cultural Revolution, describing how they were wrongly accused and detailing the tortures they had endured. Many horrible stories covered the wall. Some people had been put in solitary confinement, without trial, for ten years; others had been beaten for refusing to confess to trumped-up charges and were now permanently paralyzed.

I also saw names written in large characters that were pasted on the wall upside down. These names, which were crossed out with red *x*'s, were those of officials accused by the *dazibao* writers of carrying out the injustices during the Cultural Revolution.

Some of the observers who stood in front of the *dazibao* seemed uneasy. They stood close enough to read the writings but far enough away that others would not know for sure whether they were reading. You could tell which of the *dazibao* were outspoken or controversial, because the people reading them seemed uneasy, as if they were afraid to be seen to participate in anything that could be considered antigovernment.

My father and I always started at one end of the wall, and he read the *dazibao* as we worked our way to the other end. He stood close to the wall with his hands folded behind his back, peering through his thick eyeglasses. Sometimes he copied down things as he read. What interested him most, as before, was the poetry.

One of the poems that he copied from the Democracy Wall

used the character for *yuan* that meant "the common people." My father decided at this point to change the character of my nickname, Yuan Yuan, from the one meaning "reunion" to the one meaning "the people." He idealized the common people and taught me never to look down on peasants and workers, often saying, "Remember that your father came from a village of farmers." By changing the character of my nickname, he wanted me too to have the enormous respect he had for the common people.

If I wandered away from him to look around, I could always find him by walking along the wall. While I waited for him, I ran around the bustling bus stop. Even when the weather began to get cold, hundreds of people wearing padded jackets and fingerless gloves continued to copy the writings into little notebooks.

One Sunday when my father and I went to the wall, I was drawn to a noisy crowd gathered around a young man. Maneuvering myself through the legs of the grownups, I pushed my way to the front and found myself standing at the feet of the young man, who I could tell was an artist because he had his oil paintings hung on a metal wire strung between two trees behind him. He was wearing a very plain, colorless Mao suit and was standing on a slightly elevated platform. His tousled hair looked as if it had never been combed, and his face was dingy, as if he hadn't washed it in days. He gestured with one hand while he spoke. The other hand held a steamed bun, which he ate between sentences.

Directly behind him was a thick oil painting, which he had just started explaining to the crowd. I had no idea what the picture was about until he talked about it. It was so impressionistic that you couldn't be sure of what it represented. He said it was a painting of Tiananmen Square. There was a yellow moon that was broken in pieces. Where the moon had fragmented, blood-red liquid seemed to ooze out.

"I want the image to convey the idea that the sky is grieving; even the moon is brokenhearted," the artist said. He went on and on about what his painting meant, but I stopped really listening and only stared up at him. I was mesmerized by this young man. He seemed very idealistic and dramatic to me. He was talking about his art and had forgotten all about himself. He was speaking so passionately that he didn't even bother to swallow his saliva, and white foam collected on the edges of his mouth. As he spoke, he accidentally spat out bits of his bun, which hit my face.

People were shouting questions at him as he was trying to explain, but nothing satisfied them. He listened to the questions, then launched into longer explanations. He wasn't really answering the questions as much as using this moment to speak his mind. It was the first time I had seen anyone talk so honestly about his own ideas in public. He stood out as a unique individual.

For several months, whenever I passed the bus stop there were crowds of people at the wall. But one afternoon my father and I walked there and found that the *dazibao* were all gone. Where the wall had been were now metal stands covered with advertisements for all sorts of imported products. I never asked my father why the wall had been covered up, and he never spoke to me about it. I didn't fully understand the importance of the event until I was much older.

The Democracy Wall Movement ended in the spring of 1979, when Deng Xiaoping cracked down on the *dazibao* writers for directing their criticisms at him. Playing on Deng's policy of the Four Modernizations, a plan first devised by Zhou Enlai in 1974 to move China technologically forward by modernizing agriculture, industry, science, and defense, Wei Jingsheng, the most active participant in the movement, had written an essay calling for a fifth modernization — democratic freedom. His essay said that the Four Modernizations would not be possible without democratic reform. For his outspokenness, Wei was arrested, falsely accused of selling state secrets to foreigners, and sentenced to fifteen years in a labor camp. He is still serving his long prison sentence, but he has become a hero for all who work for democracy in China.

Though my father took me to the wall and read the *dazibao* that criticized the government, he too was uneasy about participating. He told me later that during the months of the Democracy Wall Movement, he watched from a distance as a group of people tried forcibly to enter Zhongnanhai, where the top Party officials live, to air their grievances. "One needs to be concerned enough to become more educated but know enough to stay away from disaster," my father said. He spent his whole life trying to perform this political balancing act.

One day my father came home with a big smile on his face and announced to us that in three months he would be going to Korea to work as an interpreter. Ever since he had gotten the job at the paint factory, in 1971, he had been applying for an opportunity to use his language skills. We were all very happy for him, because he could finally make use of his university education and work as a professional, not a laborer. It meant that our financial situation would be much better, because he would receive his regular pay plus a sum of money to live on in Korea. For three months my mother and Nainai shopped for food they thought he would not be able to get in Korea and fussed over what he should pack. The government gave him money to have new suits of clothes made so that he would look presentable when he went abroad. In the excitement, my family never sat down and talked about the fact that he would be away from us for four years.

I heard my mother tell my father many times that he should take good care of himself and watch what he ate. Other than that, I never saw any exchange of affection between them. In this respect, my parents were not unlike other Chinese parents, who never show their love for each other physically in front of the children.

On the day my father left for Korea, we ate lunch together and went to the train station to see him off. No one was crying. We were all happy that he had this great chance to go abroad. He seemed ready for the adventure. Before boarding the train, he took each of us aside.

"Yuan Yuan, study hard," he said to me. "Try your best to learn how to ride the bicycle." My family had just bought me a bicycle, and I was struggling with it. "Listen to your mother, and write to me often."

My father said all of the things that he felt it was his duty to say, and no more. I waved goodbye as the train pulled away, not realizing what being without him would be like. I was about to turn eleven that summer, in 1979. I didn't know then that the next four years — my passage from boyhood to young adulthood — would be a time when I needed my father the most.

I began to spend a lot of time with the men who were members of the *lianhefangwei*, our neighborhood watch group. These groups existed to help the official police, who rarely came into our alley. Every neighborhood had a brigade like this, made up of twelve to fifteen men who policed the area, catching criminals. The official law enforcement groups didn't supervise them, so they often beat up people indiscriminately to amuse themselves. For this reason they were also known as *bangzidui*, billy-club brigades. No one dared to complain about their feudal-style justice; most of the people they picked on were afraid of arrest and imprisonment, so they put up with an occasional beating rather than go to the police.

Almost all of the men in my neighborhood watch group were in their thirties and forties. They were salesclerks in the local stores or laborers in nearby factories, and each of them had been temporarily assigned by his work unit to staff the neighborhood watch group, either because he was not a productive worker or because he had a bad relationship with his unit leader. Some of the men never went back to their original jobs.

The brigade station was a one-story house across the narrow alley from our home. The members gathered there to cook, eat, make telephone calls, and talk, and they took turns sleeping there when they were on night duty. The men in the billy-club brigade knew that my father was away, so they treated me like their son. They often asked me over for meals, and they taught me how to play Chinese chess. On lazy afternoons I sat with them and listened to their idle chatter, perking up my ears whenever they exchanged gossip about my neighbors.

In the summertime they sat on stools in the alley in their undershirts, smoking and talking about themselves.

"I have fifty-five channels on my TV and I watch bare-assed dancing every night," one of them boasted.

"The day I met Chairman Mao . . ." another would cut in.

On most days of the week the brigade men sat around drinking tea and reading the newspaper, but on the days designated for *daqingcha*, big cleanup and investigation, they put on their red armbands, went out on foot patrol, and rounded up whatever hooligans they could find. "Time to take to the streets," their leader, a rotund former policeman, would announce — usually after he had finished reading the day's newspapers. Some evenings when they went on raids they took me along.

The brigade went after all of the criminal types in our neighborhood — drunkards, youth gangs, prostitutes, and street vendors. Once they surrounded a drunk and took turns kicking him in the face as their way of sobering him up. When the drunk's false teeth suddenly flew out of his mouth and fell on the ground, the men seemed frightened. The drunk quickly retrieved his teeth and popped them back into his mouth. The brigade men all had a hearty laugh and thereafter left him alone.

The brigade also liked to seek out prostitutes. In China prostitutes don't walk the streets; they are simply women in a neighborhood who are known to give sexual favors in exchange for money. Whenever the men cornered one, they would lift her dress with their billy clubs, at the same time criticizing her for wearing something indecently revealing.

One night they brought in a young couple who had been taking a nighttime stroll. The young man, probably a college student, was angry that he and his girlfriend had been detained and threatened to report the brigade members to the police. Before he finished protesting, one of the men gave him a severe beating. The girl, in a panic, screamed out that her boyfriend was the son of a high-ranking government official. The brigade men suspected that it was a lie, but they stopped and let the couple go.

If you were a friend of the brigade members, you could get away with anything. A tourist came into the station one day and reported that he and the ticket vendor of our local theater had had an argument. The vendor had thrown a cup of hot water in his face, scalding him. The brigade members filled out a phony report to placate the tourist but never did anything about it.

Because their station was small, whenever the men rounded up a bunch of criminals, they brought them over to our court-yard to beat them. All the kids gathered around to watch, as if it were street theater.

The outhouse in our front yard was often used as a detention room. One afternoon I was doing homework when I heard high-pitched squealing. I looked out of my window and saw the brigade men pushing two young women into our yard, then opening the outhouse door and pushing them into the small, stinky stall.

"Do you admit you're guilty?" one of the men shouted.

The women were crying and trying to explain at the same time. I couldn't figure out what they were guilty of.

"Don't give me any excuses," the brigade member barked. Then he took a tree branch, opened the door to the outhouse, and started hitting them.

The young women made their problems worse by trying to reason with the brigade men. Often the best way to get out of a beating was to confess quickly and apologize profusely, because the men were only concerned with a criminal's attitude. If they grabbed you, then you must be guilty. It was better to give in than to argue. I knew it was wrong for them to rough people up, but at the same time I couldn't take my eyes off them while they hit and kicked the unlucky victim. I wanted to say something

against this, but as a child I had learned not to question authority. The brigade men represented the law, and the law was
always right.

Sometime later they locked up a hooligan in our outhouse, but
he managed to clamber out of a small opening on top of the stall
and jump onto our roof to escape. "He got away, he got away!"
the brigade men cried. All of the teenagers on our block were
enlisted to catch the criminal. I watched them climb up onto our
roof, yelling, "Get him, get him!"

My mother finally told the brigade men not to bring their
business to our yard again. "It's a bad influence on the children,"
I heard her explain politely.

"There are so many criminals, and we don't have room for
them at the station," the men protested. But they used our yard
less often after this.

My mother didn't like me to stay late at the station playing
chess with the brigade men, but she didn't really protest. While
my father was away, she pretty much let me be. I guess she
thought I should have male influences in my life, and not stay
home all day in a house full of women.

One of the brigade members was a young man named Weimin who had just returned to Beijing from a commune. Whole
groups of young people, known as *zhishi qingnian,* knowledge
youth, had been sent to the countryside during the Cultural
Revolution to work on farms and learn from the peasants. Weimin had been sent to the most desolate commune in Northeast
China, because he came from a wealthy family and his father
had been labeled a rightist during the 1957 Anti-Rightist Campaign. This made Weimin a *gozaizi,* son of a dog, as the children
of class enemies were called.

In the late 1970s the *zhishi qingnian* returned and were reab-
sorbed into the cities. Most of them had not had a formal education and were able to find only menial jobs. Weimin was a
salesclerk in a bookstore until the head of his work unit assigned
him to the billy-club brigade because he was supercritical. Since
his return to Beijing, he had taken the college entrance examina-

tion several times and failed. He had also applied for a ,
New China News Agency and been rejected. I can't believe ..
was because he was not good enough. Although he was only in
his twenties, he was the most cultured person I knew.

Weimin was not crass and boisterous like the other brigade
men. Whenever the brigade took to the streets on cleanup days,
he sneaked away and came to my house to talk with me. He
didn't approve of the other brigade men and never went with
them on patrol. He would rather take me on walks than look for
troublemakers. I thought he was rather handsome. His nose had
a high bridge and his eyebrows arched. His eyes sparkled, but
there was a certain sadness about them. And he played the
violin.

He had learned to play as a small child, when he had lived in
a big house with his rich family. When I told him how much I
had loved the classical concerts my parents had taken me to, he
started giving me lessons. What a thrill it was to handle his
beautiful mahogany violin, even though I could only eke out the
most awful sounds. He taught me for two years, but then I gave
it up. My family could not afford to buy me a violin, and the
neighbors no longer wished to suffer through my practice. But
over the course of those two years, my violin teacher became my
best friend.

My mother was very glad that I was spending time with
Weimin, because she thought he was a good influence on me.
On weekends he often took me on outings. Our first trip outside
Beijing was to a village where his grandmother lived. I was
twelve years old and taking my first trip without my parents. My
mother packed me some clothes, which we put in Weimin's
mustard-colored army-issue canvas bag. I noticed that he had
stuffed a very large flashlight into the bag. The bus we took was
extremely dilapidated, and I sat by a window that had no glass.
As we drove out of Beijing, we passed many shops. Then the
roads became dirt, and the bus shook every time we hit a hole.
The farther we got from the city, the cleaner the air became.
Leaning out of the open window, I could smell the horse manure

in the fields. It seemed like such a long ride.

"Are we there yet? Will it be soon?" I kept asking Weimin.

That night, after we arrived, we folded our pants up to our knees, took off our shoes, and walked into the flooded rice paddies to catch frogs. Weimin wanted to take them to his grandmother, who knew how to cook them. Armed with the big flashlight and with earthworms skewered on metal wires, we waded into the paddies as quietly as we could. He shone the light on the frogs; they froze, and we grabbed them and put them in our sacks. When we couldn't see the frogs, we dangled the worms just above the water until they jumped up and bit.

When I came home, I told my family all about this adventure. Nainai was interested in how Weimin's grandmother had prepared the frogs, but my sister was disgusted by the worms.

Another weekend we went to see the Summer Palace, which is eleven kilometers northwest of the center of Beijing. Famous for a marble ship built on Kunming Lake, the Summer Palace was commissioned by the empress dowager of the Qing dynasty and built with money intended for the Chinese navy. Swimming was not allowed at the time, but Weimin and I sneaked into the water at night and made our way from the shore to a small island floating in the middle of the lake. Wearing only our swimming trunks, we combed the island by moonlight, searching for odd-shaped rocks. The lake water glittered under the dark sky.

On the nights when Weimin was on night duty, I slept over at the brigade station. I had known him for about a year before he told me stories about his years laboring in the countryside. He had been only fifteen when the government assigned him to the commune, and he had often been mistaken for a girl in the men's latrine because he had still had a boy's high-pitched voice.

The commune was in a wilderness area, and he was sent out to dig the hard earth and collect manure. There was no heat or hot water, and it was difficult to bathe in the winter. Weimin said that when the women needed to bathe, which they did every month when they had their periods, they risked freezing to death. He said he was always half starved and he constantly thought of home and fantasized about women. Many of the men, he said, spent their nights masturbating. A village girl had come to his room one night to bring him something and he had wanted her very much, but he hadn't known what to do. When she left, he went to bed and pretended that she was still with him. He left some room under his quilt for her and imagined that they held each other tightly. He didn't seem to know what else he was supposed to do.

I in turn told Weimin about my feelings for Dongyun, a girl who sat near me in my seventh-grade class. She was the first girl I had a crush on. There was nothing special about her, but she was special to me. I told him how jealous I was of the boy who sat next to her in class. Weimin didn't give me any advice. Although he often talked about women, it seemed he knew very little about them. I think he was still a virgin then.

Although Weimin was no substitute for my father, I could tell him all of my private thoughts, some that I might have been too embarrassed to tell my father. For me, he was both an older brother and a friend.

During the years Weimin spent on the commune, one of his childhood friends went to the United States and studied the violin with Yehudi Menuhin. Weimin thought that if he had had the same opportunity as his friend, he might have become a great violinist, a thought that always depressed him. Once when Menuhin came to Beijing, we went to meet Weimin's friend, who gave us tickets for every performance and let us into all of the orchestra rehearsals. Before he left Beijing, this man gave Weimin a gold violin string. I saw that my friend was happy for a moment, but the gesture reminded him of his lost opportunity and he soon became sad again.

Although I stopped taking violin lessons, Weimin did not stop teaching me about music. He introduced me to the great Western composers, especially Mozart, Beethoven, and Tchaikovsky, and told me the stories of their lives. We listened to Beethoven's violin concerto over and over again — I can still hum every note and anticipate every crescendo. I began to love not only this music but the tragic lives of these three heroes. I too wanted to do remarkable things and die young, to have the same feeling of tragedy and greatness.

Weimin also thought that I should see exhibits of great art. Around that time I was reading Bible stories, because I saw Dongyun reading them in school. I noticed that many of the famous works of Western art were based on the myths in the Bible, so when Weimin and I went to art exhibits displaying masterpieces from Versailles and the Louvre, I told him, "This one is about Jesus' birth; the three men are kings who have come to bring him gifts," and "This is the last supper before he dies." He was impressed, and I felt good that I had something to contribute.

A salesgirl at the bookstore where Weimin had worked was after him to marry her. He always told me that he didn't like her, but he accepted her, just as he accepted all of the other unpleasant things in his life. My neighbor's youngest daughter was also in love with him, and I knew that he loved her too. He showed me some of the letters she had written to him, including one that told of a dream she had had in which they were a couple. The salesgirl read this letter too and told the girl's mother that she was engaged to Weimin and that her daughter should no longer write such letters. After that Weimin was too embarrassed to come to my house, in case he saw my neighbor and her daughter. We slowly lost touch.

I wrote many essays in high school about him. One, called "Moon Night in the Rice Field," was about our adventure catching frogs. I also wrote a fictional story, "Entrust," based on our friendship. The story began:

> I came home from school one day and was cleaning my room when I found my violin under a pile of papers. I dusted it off, opened it, and admired the dark mahogany wood of this precious instrument. I began to recall a story seemingly from a past life. A boy and his violin teacher were walking home late one night after a concert. The street was empty except for them. Their

shadows lengthened and shortened as they walked past the yellow rays of the streetlamps. The strains of Beethoven's violin concerto floated in the air about them. The boy noticed that his teacher's eyes were aglow, and saw that it was the reflection of tears. The teacher stopped and opened the violin case he had clutched under his arm. He picked up the instrument and slowly began to play. The strange melody was the most beautiful the boy had ever heard. It was as if the music poured forth from the light of the moon. The teacher's only audience was the boy, the streetlamps, and the moon. The boy saw that one of the strings of the violin was golden. The night air carried the melody to faraway places. Exhausted, the teacher returned the violin to its case. "The golden string was given to me by my violin teacher," he said to the boy. "Life has not been fair to me, but I am certain that it will be fair to you. I entrust to you this violin."

I wanted very much to show Weimin this story, but I never had the chance.

· 3 ·

Blue Dove
and Misty Poets

I WAS THE SHORTEST BOY in my seventh-grade class. Our teacher made us line up in order of size, so I became best friends with all of the other short boys, because we were always together. We called our group Square Root of Two because that equals 1.41, which was about our height in meters.

One of the shorties, Rong Dong, became my blood brother. One day after school we were playing in his backyard, exploding firecrackers in a bottle. When the bottle shattered, we said that made us blood brothers. Then we decided to seal our brotherhood by drinking a cup of wine mixed with our blood. But neither of us knew where to get the wine, and we didn't really want to drink it anyway. Instead we used a cup of water. We tried to puncture our fingers to draw blood, but we didn't want to hurt ourselves. Finally I was able to get a drop of blood out of my finger, which I quickly dipped into the water. The two of us drank the cloudy liquid and sealed our brotherhood.

Our teacher designated Rong Dong and me class monitors because we had the best grades, but he soon found out that we were also his naughtiest pupils. Chewing gum was strictly against the rules, but whenever the teacher turned his back to us, I began chewing as loudly as I could. I thought I was so clever. Rong Dong and I once made such a racket in class that the teacher threw us out. "And get rid of the gum on your way out," he called to me. He made us stand in the schoolyard all morning, but we amused ourselves by drawing battle lines for ants in the dirt. The next day the teacher assigned two other students to be the class monitors.

One of our favorite places to play was the White Pagoda Temple, a Yuan dynasty Buddhist temple that had been closed during the Cultural Revolution and was later made into a museum. Nothing was left there except a thirteenth-century pagoda, and hardly anyone ever visited it. The entrance was always guarded, so we climbed over the walls to get to the temple grounds. We liked to run our hands over the wind chimes in the courtyard and listen to the beautiful music they made. Inside was a large statue of a Buddha with the palm of his hand turned up. We would stand on the Buddha's palm and climb to his head. It looked like there was a piece of jade on his forehead, but when we climbed up, it turned out to be only painted stone.

All this time we would be listening for the guard. One afternoon he caught us.

"What are you two doing here?" he barked. "You don't think I've been watching you? I know what you've been up to."

He must have known all along that we were there.

"What school are you from?" he asked as we scurried out. "What grade are you in? What class?" he said, running after us. "I'm going to report you to your teacher."

We knew he was just trying to scare us. We got on our bicycles and raced home.

On the days we played at my house, Rong Dong and I spent hours looking at my stamp collection. My father started this collection by sending me beautiful stamps from Korea, and soon I was spending all of my free time buying stamps and pasting them into neat little books. After school I went to the black market, an open-air public trading place on Changan Avenue, and traded some of the Korean stamps for ones from other countries. The stamp vendors stood behind tables selling their collections as crowds of people moved from table to table. I carefully browsed through each collection, looking for stamps I liked.

I soon discovered that the vendors were out to cheat everyone. I didn't have much money, so instead of taking money from me, they cheated me out of my more valuable stamps. After a couple of bad experiences, my attitude changed, and I started stealing from them. When the vendors weren't looking, I swiped a stamp or two.

By the time I was in the eighth grade, I was so addicted to stamp collecting that I eventually had to borrow five yuan from a well-known bully in school, a boy who was about my age but who was bigger and stronger than most of us. He acted like a mob boss; I heard that he sometimes burned people's faces with cigarettes. Although I was deathly afraid of him, I wanted the money desperately to buy stamps.

When the bully demanded his money back and threatened to hurt me if I didn't pay him, I borrowed two yuan from a gym teacher I especially liked. Then some students told the teacher that I already owed the bully five yuan, so he would probably never be repaid. When he saw me in the hall at school, he grabbed me by the collar and said, "If you think you can get away with stealing my money, you just wait and see." I was scared, and I felt bad because he was one of my favorite teachers.

When my homeroom teacher found out about all this, he called my mother in for a conference and questioned her about my five-yuan debt and other little things. My mother didn't understand what was happening. The teacher was about to become a Party member, and he was disciplining a number of students to show how serious he was about our ideological education.

Still the bully was after me for the five yuan I had borrowed. One night I decided to do something crazy. Waiting until my family was asleep, I sneaked out and went down to the local store. The old man who tended it was asleep on his chair with a newspaper on his lap. I went inside, looked around, grabbed a box of drinking glasses, and ran for home. I knew I could sell the glasses for five yuan and pay the bully back, so I hid the box under my mother's sewing machine and went to sleep, feeling that my problems were solved. The next morning I forgot about the glasses until my mother found them and I had to admit what I had done.

My mother was so disappointed in me. "Yuan Yuan," she said, with tears in her eyes, "do you want to continue school? If you don't want to, we will help you find odd jobs."

"No, I want to go to school," I said sheepishly.

My mother let out a heavy sigh. I felt very ashamed. After this, even my mother began to distrust me.

My reputation for being naughty was the major factor that kept me from becoming a member of the Communist Youth League, the step after the Young Pioneers toward eventually becoming a Communist Party member. Youth League members got together to clean up People's Park or sweep the city streets. Everyone admired them because they were serving the people in the spirit of the patriot Lei Feng. It was a real badge of honor to be in the league, and I was disappointed in myself.

Even though I wasn't a member, I participated in many of the league activities anyway. It was a way to be near Dongyun, the girl I had a crush on. Each week the members took turns writing in the league diary, recording what they had done and what they had learned from their experiences. One week's entry read: "Shen Tong is truly a model youth. Even though he is not a league member, he participates earnestly in our work. He cleaned cobwebs from the ceiling and was not afraid of dirt or sweat." I was surprised to read all these nice things about me, but even more surprised when I found out that it had been Dongyun's turn to write in the diary. I was ecstatic!

Dongyun's house was on my way home from school, and I often tried to walk home with her. We never talked, because she was afraid to associate with me openly; instead she walked five steps ahead of me. One day I decided to visit her at her house after school, an unusual act that meant something serious between a boy and a girl. I called to Dongyun from the street, and she finally came out, although she wouldn't allow me to go into her yard because her parents would not approve. That was fine.

I was thrilled that she had come out to talk with me, since she totally ignored me in school, acting as if I didn't exist.

We stood outside her gate and chatted. I told her about the novels I liked to read and dropped the names of a few European authors, but she said, "I don't like Western novels. I only like Chinese novels." Just as I was telling her about the classical concerts Weimin had taken me to, her face turned white and her body froze. Her father had come out and seen us. She immediately ran inside her house, and she didn't look back when I called after her.

Her father, a dour-looking man, walked over to where I was standing. "You shouldn't come and see my daughter. It is not right," he said sternly. "You should be studying instead of talking nonsense."

I knew what he meant by nonsense: he thought we were talking about love. But he didn't even know his own daughter. She would never dare talk about love. Our conversation was just small talk.

The next day in school, disaster struck. My homeroom teacher told me to go with him to the administration office. A lump formed in my throat when I walked into the office and saw Dongyun's father and older brother standing there. I tried to avoid their icy stares, but I could see that they were both furious. The brother, who looked about twenty, said he wanted to beat me up. After my teacher calmed them both down, Dongyun's father said that after I had left the previous day, his daughter had cried all night and refused to eat. He had asked her what was the matter and she wouldn't say. She just cried. Her whole family thought I must have done something awful to her. To make matters worse, her father was in charge of youth education — or, more accurately, thought control — at some large institution. He was convinced that my behavior proved that I was morally corrupt.

I cowered in a corner of the room, shaking inside. This was very serious. I started thinking about the different punishments I might receive. The whole incident could go on my school record and keep me from graduating with honors. And there was the possibility that I would be expelled. I was really scared.

Finally Dongyun's father and brother left the office, and my teacher turned to me. "I think I know what happened," he said. "I don't have anything to say to you. Let's just forget it."

My knees buckled and I gave a sigh of relief. I didn't dare tell my friends what had happened. Although I knew I hadn't done anything wrong, I still felt twinges of guilt. A truly good student would not have gone to see a girl at her house.

After this I lost interest in Dongyun. I decided that I had to get rid of two things that had been plaguing me: money and women. This may seem like a funny thing for a young kid to think, but I took it very seriously.

By the time I was in the ninth grade, I began to look at the billy-club brigade differently. I had never thought it was right that they beat up on people, but now I felt an urge to do something about it. However, they considered me a friend, so I didn't have the courage to approach them directly. Whenever I saw them do something that I thought was unjust, I wrote a letter to the newspaper describing what I had seen. My mother read every letter I wrote, but she wouldn't let me mail them. She said, "What you have written is true, but you cannot say these things. When you are older, you will understand why." I also wrote about the excesses of the billy-club brigade in my school compositions, but each time my teacher crossed out what I had written with a red pencil. She never said why. I think this was the first time I really encountered censorship, even if it was in a very small way. This was when I missed my father the most. He might have been able to help me understand why people in power could get away with anything and why ordinary people couldn't challenge them.

Even though I wrote my father a lot of letters during the four years he was away and received many more from him, it was not the same as talking to him in person. I found that I was still writing to the father I had known as a child, and that kept me from saying a lot of the things I wanted to say. My father was not writing to that child; his letters were to an adult. He spoke to me man to man.

Once I sent him a pillowcase I had embroidered with the design of a cat. His next letter to me was almost as long as a novella. It covered twenty pages and told the story of a man whose son had given him such a pillowcase. Falling asleep on the pillowcase, the man dreamed that the cat came alive and that he and the cat went fishing. During their trip the man told the cat about his innermost feelings. For the rest of the letter, the man talked about himself — my father's way of telling me what he was thinking.

In another letter he wrote: "I have often heard the farmers say, 'If in spring you neglect the fields, in autumn the fields will neglect you.' This is the springtime of your life. Your fate rests in what you make of this season. Tomorrow the sky may greet you with scarlet-lined clouds, your path may be strewn with floral wreaths. Your father beseeches you to struggle for your tomorrow. The road of life is open and wide. Spring is the season when flowers blossom into myriad colors. For my son, may all your hopes be fulfilled and may your studies progress a hundredfold." I had never written to him about the trouble I was having in school, but he seemed to know that I was going through a difficult time. He always encouraged me and urged me to try to do better so that he would be proud of me.

My father was due to return home in the spring of 1983. My emotions were mixed: I wanted to see him, but I was afraid of how he would react when I had to tell him about all the bad things I had done while he was away. I was a little nervous when we went to the train station to pick him up on the day of his arrival. I tried to imagine what he looked like now. When he got off the train, I recognized him immediately. He was loaded down with shoulder bags full of gifts for us.

Later, after we got home, he sat me down and said, "Yuan Yuan, I want you to tell me what happened."

I started from the very beginning, telling him about the money I had spent on stamps, the stolen glasses, and the debt I still owed to the bully — everything. My mother kept interrupting. "That's not what you told me," she said, remembering all of the half-truths and outright lies I had told her. My father asked her to be quiet and let me continue.

He didn't react at all the whole time I was talking, and I was frightened. I expected him to tell me how ashamed he was of me and to say that I had betrayed his trust. But he wasn't even angry. He calmly said to me, "As long as you admit your mistakes, I will not punish you. I will go tomorrow to talk to your teachers and ask them not to keep pressuring you. But you must study hard and behave yourself." He then gave me five yuan so I could settle my debt with the bully.

I wanted to cry, not only because I loved him so much but because I realized how much I had missed him.

I gave my father my stamp collection. I had almost two thousand stamps, and he was very touched that I was giving him my most prized possession. But my action was also a way of giving up the hobby. Like money and women, it had caused me nothing but trouble.

My father went back to his old job at the paint factory but spent the next several months looking for something better. He finally found a position as an administrator in the foreign ministry of the Beijing municipal government.

I was happy when school started that fall. This was my first year in high school, which in China begins with the tenth grade. All the students were separated into sections based on their grades, and I was placed in the section with the best students. My new teachers either didn't know about the trouble I had been in before or didn't care, so I was able to start over and be thought of as a good student again.

Now that my father was home, I was determined to behave myself. I directed my energies to my schoolwork and to learning more about the poetry my father loved so much. I started reading translations of Byron, Shelley, Tagore, and Kahlil Gibran, books that had always been on my father's bookshelf but that I was discovering for the first time. I also listened to classical music on the FM radio, becoming dreamy from the combination of poetry and music.

I thought drawing would make me more sensitive and focused, and my father agreed. He introduced me to a friend who taught me how to sketch with a pencil. When my father saw that I was serious about this, he signed me up for lessons at the Central Academy of Arts, where the classes were very rigid and the teachers demanding. We started by sketching the sculptures of Michelangelo and Leonardo, and I spent a lot of time happily drawing the eyes, nose, and mouth of Michelangelo's David.

When I moved on to painting, I had a vision in my head of a blue dove. No matter what I was doing, this image stayed in my mind. I dreamed about the dove flying around in my head like a sign, a lucky charm. I decided that all my clothes would be blue. Every day I wore a blue shirt, blue pants, blue socks, blue shoes, blue gloves, blue scarf, everything blue. If my mother made me clothes of another color, I refused to wear them. I later read somewhere that the color blue expresses a person's desire to emphasize his own personality, to strengthen his own character.

For the two years I was enrolled at the Central Academy of Arts, every Sunday morning I woke up early, ate a quick breakfast, and rode my bicycle to Beijing's Exhibition Hall. I spent the entire day at the museum, getting home just in time for dinner. There I saw the paintings of the French impressionists on loan from the Louvre, Van Gogh's sunflowers and his self-portraits, and once the photographs of Ansel Adams. Although Weimin had taken me to the museum when I was younger, I enjoyed it much more now that I went alone. I walked around admiring the paintings, absorbed in my own thoughts. It was my own little secret.

When an exhibit of Italian Renaissance art came to Beijing, I was feeling lazy and couldn't decide whether I wanted to see it. My father said, "Why don't I go with you?" Encouraged by his interest, I sprang out of bed and off we went. As soon as we entered Exhibition Hall, I recognized the music blaring on the speaker system: one of Mozart's sonatas. I excitedly told my father what the music was and waved my hands in the air as if conducting. A smile came over his face. I told him everything I knew about Mozart, and as we went through the exhibit I told him what I knew about the paintings and the artists. He listened and asked questions. I was happy to share my secret with him.

"Each exhibit is like a book," my father said as we walked home from the museum. "Reading books is not the only way to learn. Each exhibit you see is the equivalent of reading a book, if you try to understand the spirit of the art by your study of each painting." This was his way of encouraging me. He knew that I was not as good a reader as my sister, who had been reading translations of *War and Peace* and *Anna Karenina* since she was in the third grade.

My father wanted me to read more books, so he made a bargain with me. A new bookstore in Beijing had more of the scientific books that interested me than any other store in the city. He promised to pay me half the selling price of every book I finished reading at the bookstore, so I started going there every day after school. I settled myself in a corner where no one ever bothered me and read for two hours each afternoon. Over the course of a month, I was able to finish two entire books. One, I remember, was on supernatural phenomena, and the other was a book of common scientific knowledge. I read slowly, because I had heard somewhere that Newton once said, "When you read, look beyond the words," and I was trying to take his advice to heart.

My father and I always operated on an honor system. When I told him I had completed two books at the bookstore, he gave me the money as promised and never checked up on me. Similarly, when I told him that I felt old enough to drink alcohol, I promised to drink only reasonable amounts of beer, because it was harmless. My father said, "If you do as you say, I will approve of your drinking." Even now I will drink only beer, because I gave him my word.

At my father's suggestion, I read biographies of Isaac Newton, Benjamin Franklin, and Albert Einstein. Their stories showed me that these men were writers, philosophers, and thinkers as well as scientists. Now that I was learning about art, literature, and music, I decided to broaden myself by studying science.

In China, most students who are good in both the sciences and the arts choose to study science. Studying the arts is considered either a futile exercise or a dangerous one; there is little artistic freedom, and there are virtually no jobs in those fields. My father wanted both my sister and me to study science, but was disappointed when Qing declared herself a student in the arts. He was very relieved when I chose science.

The books I was reading reminded me of my early experiments, and I started conducting more sophisticated ones than I had done as a child. One experiment that I found in my sister's scientific textbook involved using electricity to separate the hydrogen from the oxygen in water. It looked simple, so I tried it. First I filled a porcelain bowl with water and set it in our yard. Then I looked around for the electricity. I decided that the current from our light sockets was probably not enough, so I detached a cable from the electric pole outside our gate and brought it into our yard. As soon as the wires touched the water, the bowl shattered into a million pieces and a flash of fire came out of the electrical socket nearest me. Our cat, Panda, let out a bloodcurdling "Waaaa!" and ran away. I heard a commotion outside our gate: the neighbors were all out in the street, wondering why the electricity was off. They must have followed the trail of the electrical cable, because I looked up to see a group of women peering into the courtyard. There I was, squatting over a million pieces of porcelain and a small puddle of water.

That was the first time I blacked out the neighborhood. There were two other occasions. After the third try, my neighbors found a way for me to redirect some of the electricity via a special wire, so I wouldn't blow out everyone else's electricity if the experiment failed. Except for an occasional sarcastic "Oh, that boy!" and "He's so clever, isn't he?" my neighbors were good-humored about it. After each blackout my mother said, "Yuan Yuan, you shouldn't do this." But my parents never made any real effort to stop me, because they wanted to encourage me to learn.

In high school I was part of a close-knit group of eight — four boys and four girls. Rong Dong, my blood brother, was one of the boys. Another boy, Wu Dakun, became my best friend.

I was drawn to Dakun, who sat behind me in class, because he had such an honest face. We started spending time together after school, going to the movies and museums and talking about art and music, and later about more philosophical topics, such as life and how best to live it. He was very patient and reflective, different from my other friends. I was never able to have conversations like this with anyone else my age.

It is not uncommon for people in China to write each other letters even when they see each other often. Once in high school I wrote Dakun a letter that said: "We are like rocks in the river of life. I want to be forever a sharp rock that has not been made smooth by life's currents. I don't want the ups and downs of life to make me dull and weak, eventually settling me to the bottom of the riverbed. I want to retain my jagged edges and be swept into the ocean." Dakun wrote back: "I think there is a good chance that I will become the rounded, flat rock that you so despise. I'm not sure that I have the will or strength to fight the currents."

My parents liked Dakun right away, the first time he came to our house. My father shook his hand and greeted him as if he were a colleague. Then, because he had to tend to some business and could not stay to talk with us, he apologized to my friend. This was so unlike the behavior of any other parent Dakun had ever met that he quickly became very fond of my father and envious of my relationship with him.

Dakun rarely spoke to his own father, who was extremely severe with him. For example, one day when he was in grammar school, his family was going to his uncle's house for a visit. At first Dakun's father would not let him go because he hadn't finished one problem in his math homework; then he relented on the condition that Dakun ask his uncle, who was a high school teacher, to help him solve the problem. When they returned from the uncle's house, his father asked him if he had done the problem. Dakun said he had forgotten to ask his uncle.

"My father took me into his room, locked the door so my mother couldn't come in, and hit me," Dakun told me. "I will never forget that as long as I live. Your father would never do such a thing."

I tried to talk to him about his father, but he was never able to make their relationship any better. I think that as he grew older, he stopped trying.

Dakun and I spent a lot of time together, but we also did things with the other six in our group. After school, all of us would go to Dakun's house, listen to music, and talk until late in the evening. There was a persimmon tree in Dakun's yard, and when the persimmons were ripe, the boys would climb up and hit the branches with bamboo sticks so the girls beneath the tree could catch the falling fruit.

One time our cat, Panda, ran away from home for six days, and the eight of us went looking for him. I was afraid he would never come back, but Nainai wasn't worried at all. "He'll be back," she assured me. "He knows where his next meal is." During lunch recess, the girls combed the neighborhood while we boys jumped across the flat tin roofs of the one-story houses, looking for him. Some of the houses were only shacks with roofs made of wooden slats. Needless to say, the people in these shacks came out and cursed us, because we made a lot of noise landing over their heads. Dakun must have put his foot through someone's wooden roof, because some men came after us with sticks. We made a mad dash back to school without having found the cat. But one day, just as Nainai had predicted, I returned from school to see Panda happily licking clean the fishbone on his plate. I ran to tell Dakun and the others that I had found the cat, or rather, that he had found me.

One of the girls in our group, Liu Yan, liked me a lot and secretly wanted me to be her boyfriend. None of us knew that, especially me, since I had given up on girls after my run-in with Dongyun's father and brother. On New Year's Eve of 1984, though, Liu Yan invited us all to a party at her house, which was empty because her parents were away visiting relatives. The eight of us sat around the dinner table making dumplings. Then, after we ate, Yan went to her parents' bedroom and asked me to come in for a minute. She closed the door, leaving the others laughing and talking in the next room.

She sat on the bed and I sat on a chair opposite her. We stayed that way for a long time. She didn't say anything, and I wondered, *What's going on?* In those silent minutes, I suddenly thought about all the long letters she had written me, telling me what a good friend I was. I remembered the times she and Dakun had lingered at my house, going home very late at night. I was just about to figure out what was on her mind when she broke the silence.

"Shen Tong, I love you," she whispered.

I had never noticed how pretty she was, but she definitely seemed beautiful to me then. She put her head on my shoulder and I held her hand. We kissed for a very long time. It was the first time I had ever been that close to a girl, and I realized that we had both been feeling the same thing for each other, only I had never thought about it or acted on it. I hadn't paid attention to any of her signals. Besides, I thought it was wrong to have a girlfriend. In China, these relationships are frowned upon. Most parents feel the way Dongyun's father did — that fifteen-year-olds shouldn't be involved in romance. That's why the eight of us never paired off into couples.

Suddenly there was a banging on the door. "Hey, what are you two doing?" the others called out. Before we had a chance to move, they barged into the bedroom and dragged us back to the party.

After that Liu Yan and I started dating secretly. I went to her house when her parents weren't there, and we kissed and hugged on her bed. When I was with her, I had a very dreamy, romantic feeling. Even so, we both felt tremendously guilty because what we were doing was wrong. I told her, "You should be very strict with me and not let me kiss you and touch you so much." We all had exams coming up in the spring, and I thought I shouldn't be spending so much time with her. But we always seemed to end up in People's Park, kissing behind the bushes — the only place that young people in Beijing could find privacy.

In the spring semester of eleventh grade, a film company from Guangzhou Province came to my school looking for students to play parts in a movie for television. This was a time when there was a campaign to give teachers more recognition, and the film was part of that. It was about a teacher who always stood up for her students, which offended many of her superiors. When she was being fired, four of her students, who had nothing in common except their love for her, got together and came to her defense.

The teachers in my school selected me and a handful of other boys, including the principal's son, to go to the audition for this movie. They also picked a number of girls they thought were the prettiest. First we went into a room where the casting crew looked us up and down and talked to us to see how we presented ourselves; then, after they eliminated several students, they videotaped us while we read portions of the script. We waited a long time for the results, because the tapes were shipped to Guangzhou, where the movie's director made the decisions.

I didn't think I had done very well at the audition, but one day my teacher walked up to me and said, "Shen Tong, they want you to start filming right away. You no longer have to come to class." I had been cast to play one of the four major student parts. I don't know why they chose me. Most of the other students in the film were from drama schools. I played an extremely good student who was very earnest. He wore the number 10 for his soccer team, which meant that he was the best player. The other characters were a troublemaker, a poor student who was also a soccer player, and the president of the class.

The movie was scheduled to be broadcast on Teacher's Day, September 10. The cast and crew assembled at a hotel in downtown Beijing, and the other students and I got an interesting glimpse of behind-the-scenes theatrical life.

The director of our film had been a child star in the 1950s, known for her role in a movie called *Red Child,* which was about a girl who helped the Communist guerrillas during the Chinese civil war. When that movie had been released, she had had her picture taken with Chairman Mao, so she was really famous.

Many of the set designers also worked for a television series based on the novel *Dream of the Red Chamber,* the most popular show at the time. The directors of that show were always looking for pretty girls to cast, and all around the set were stacks of pictures of actresses who had sent in their résumés. The set designers would toss the pictures around, saying, "Here's one for you. Here's a nice one for me," and talking about how easy it was to have sex with these women because they were desperate to get on the show. In fact, the chief set designer, who was fat and greasy, was dating a girl who played a servant in *Dream of the Red Chamber,* and it was pretty clear to us why she was seeing him.

On the days we filmed, the older actors gave us tips on how to act, treating us like little children. Most of my scenes were done in one take because I just did what came naturally. The only time I had to put on an act was when my character was supposed to hurt his ankle during an important soccer game. I hobbled on the sidelines, cheering my teammates on, and jumped up from the bench in frustration, unable to play, when my team was losing. The actress who played the teacher had to massage my ankle in that scene. One of her lines was "Your feet really stink."

As a bonus, the cast and crew were treated to private showings of American movies at the hotel. It was always a 007 movie.

I couldn't understand what was going on because my English wasn't good enough, but I could see that it involved a bunch of scantily dressed women running around and James Bond sleeping with all of them. For some reason, I was very turned off by these movies. It wasn't that I thought they were pornographic or that I was embarrassed by them. In another setting, with my friends from school, I might have enjoyed them. But I had come to believe that the people I was working with on the film weren't very interesting, so I didn't like watching these movies with them. After two showings I stopped going.

By the time we completed the filming, it was already July. My sister had completed her first year at Beijing University and asked me to live on campus with her and her boyfriend, Qiu, for the summer. I was about to begin my senior year of high school and my preparations for the college entrance examination, so they thought it was a good time for me to see what life was like on the Beida campus, and I was thrilled to get a chance to be around the college students I looked up to.

I stayed with Qiu, who was the resident haircutter in his dormitory. His friends had helped him set up a makeshift shop in a corner of the dormitory hall by building a wall to make a separate room. At one end of this long, narrow room was a large mirror with a chair in front of it. At the other end, separated by a night table, were the two beds where we slept at night. Qiu hung a sign on the wall that said MIMI FALANG, Mimi Hair Salon. I never asked him how he got the name. He cut everybody's hair at school, and once or twice he even gave some of the Beida girls permanents. He didn't charge any money, because, he said, it was his way of serving the people. Some of his customers gave him packs of cigarettes as a way of thanking him.

That summer, to make extra money, Qiu was also selling a three-volume collection of poetry, *Xinshichao Shiji*, or *New Age Poetry Collection*, which had just been released by one of the publishing houses on campus. I became one of thirty students who sold this collection at Beida. At first I was just helping Qiu, but when I started to read the poetry, I wanted everyone else to read it too.

The book collected the work of a generation of writers who had grown up during the Cultural Revolution. These poets, whose work had first become public during the 1976 movement in Tiananmen Square and had resurfaced on the Democracy Wall in 1978, were now in their late twenties and early thirties. When the government had crushed the Democracy Wall Movement, their poetry, which the Communist Party considered "spiritual pollution," had gone underground again. Although some of it had been written during the Cultural Revolution, it had never been collected and published.

Chinese poetry written before the Cultural Revolution painted lovely pictures of landscapes and celebrated the beauty of nature. During the 1960s and 1970s, however, poetry became so filled with political slogans and revolutionary imagery that it lost its lyricism. But this group of writers, known as the Misty Poets because their images were impressionistic and full of sorrow, had a style completely unlike that of any Chinese poets I had ever read. The poems, which often expressed the poets' suffering during the Cultural Revolution and which came to be known as "scar literature," were beautifully written and also had deep meaning. The poets looked inside themselves for inspiration. They were individualists, a trait I cherished but had seen only in Western poetry.

For the first time I began to learn about contemporary China and about life outside my own sheltered environment. I could feel the pain, the loneliness, and the power in this poetry. It was about youth, something I could identify with. Before I read the *New Age Poetry Collection,* I was hooked on Western poetry. But now I was reading pure Chinese poetry that had the same resonance as Byron, Shelley, and Tagore. Western poetry was beautiful, but it had nothing to do with my own world. My copy of the poetry collection was very important to me, and when I showed it to Dakun and Rong Dong, they each bought a set.

I proudly brought the books home to show my father. He had

always been the one to give me books and introduce me to new writers, but now I had a collection of poems I knew were dear to him, since I had stood with him at the Democracy Wall seven years before as he intently read the works of the Misty Poets. He said very little to me about the collection, perhaps because he was concerned that the poems might still be considered illegal. But I noticed that he kept the books under his pillow for a very long time, which told me that he read them every night before he went to sleep.

That summer I discovered for myself why these poems meant so much to my father. I saw in them the power of ideas. No matter how hard the government had tried to crush them, they kept coming back. I discovered through these poems that art and literature could be active. Through their writing, the Misty Poets told people about themselves and about what was wrong in China. That summer showed me that I was ready to do more than just cultivate myself; I was ready to act, to put my ideas — whenever I figured out what they were — into practice. One of my favorite passages, which best expressed how I felt at the time, was from a poem by Gu Cheng:

> I am a willful child
> I want to paint the earth full of windows
> To let all of the eyes that are accustomed to darkness
> become accustomed to light.

Selling the poetry collection was one of the ways I made friends on campus that summer. Another way that I really enjoyed was sitting in on student discussion groups. I was awed by the way everyone lived, the way they acted, and their attitudes. The best students from all over the country, they not only talked about politics, they discussed history and philosophy. They even debated the Cold War between the United States and the Soviet Union. Their conversations were different from any that my friends and I ever had; everyone was very well informed, and they had theories about everything.

One night I tried to participate in a discussion with a group of Qing's friends about the political situation in the Middle East. I was just hearing about many of these issues for the first time, but when there was a lull in the conversation, I decided to jump in anyway.

"In the Bible, it says that one day the Jewish people will reclaim their homeland in Palestine," I said. "It's amazing how the state of Israel was founded. The biblical prediction seems to have come true."

No one made any comment. Everyone just looked at me. I felt foolish, and I didn't know if I had said something wrong. Someone changed the subject to the latest books everyone was reading on campus: many were reading translations of Sartre and Camus, and the women were reading Simone de Beauvoir's *The Second Sex*.

Summoning up my courage, I decided to jump in again. "I've read very few books compared to all of you," I said. "There are many books I haven't read yet. There is so much I don't know."

Suddenly they all stopped talking and lowered their heads. After a few minutes everyone looked up at me. One of them said, "I'm surprised you would say that. Very few Beida students will admit they don't know everything."

In August the Guangzhou film studio sent all the student actors from Beijing to Guangzhou to dub the soundtrack of our film. Even though it was the first time I was leaving home alone, I didn't want my parents to take me to the train station. My time at Beida had made me feel like an adult, and I was ready to see the world and do things on my own.

I shared a cabin on the train with two drama school students and one of the chaperones. As the trip wore on, they began telling dirty jokes while I read my poetry collection. I like dirty jokes too, but theirs weren't funny, just crude. When they ran out of jokes, they started reading movie magazines and gossiping about Hong Kong starlets as if they knew them personally. One of the drama students wanted to show off, so he began telling us about all the girls in his school who had gotten pregnant and needed abortions. I didn't know what his point was.

Finally they were all talked out, and it became very quiet in the cabin. I climbed onto one of the top berths and lay down. The student who had been talking so much about his pregnant classmates came over to me. "What are you reading?"

I showed him the poetry collection. "Why don't you have a look at it?" I said, handing him the book. "It's very good."

I closed my eyes and went to sleep. When I woke up, around midnight, I noticed that he wasn't in the cabin. I found him sitting under a light in the narrow corridor of the train, reading the poetry collection. He had read a lot of it already.

A snack cart came around selling cold drinks, peanuts, and cigarettes. I bought a beer for each of us and a pack of cigarettes. No one was in the corridor but us. The light was dim. It was quiet except for the rickety noise of the train rolling across the countryside. We both looked out the window. I offered him a cigarette, and we smoked quietly for a while.

"You were right. I like these poems," he said, looking down at the well-worn pages.

"Have you seen the one I underlined?" I said.

I had underlined a poem by Bei Dao titled "The Answer." This poem had become a symbol of the 1976 movement in Tiananmen Square, the event that had so touched my parents when I was too young to understand.

> Baseness is the password of the base,
> Honour is the epitaph of the honourable.
> Look how the gilded sky is covered
> With the drifting, crooked shadows of the dead.
>
> The Ice Age is over now,
> Why is there still ice everywhere?
> The Cape of Good Hope has been discovered,
> Why do a thousand sails contest the Dead Sea?

I come into this world
Bringing only paper, rope, a shadow,
To proclaim before the judgment
The voices of the judged:

Let me tell you, world,
I — do — not — believe!
If a thousand challengers lie beneath your feet,
Count me as number one thousand and one.

I don't believe the sky is blue;
I don't believe in the sound of thunder;
I don't believe that dreams are false;
I don't believe that death has no revenge.

If the sea is destined to breach the dikes,
Let the brackish water pour into my heart;
If the land is destined to rise,
Let humanity choose anew a peak for our existence.

A new juncture and glimmering stars
Adorn the unobstructed sky,
They are five thousand year old pictographs,
The staring eyes of future generations.

The drama student agreed that it was one of the best. "I also underlined some of my favorites," he said. "I hope you don't mind." He had been so absorbed in the poems he had forgotten it was my book.

I told him about my love of poetry, about the rhythms of language and the hidden meanings behind many of the words and phrases. I could see that he knew what I meant.

Neither of us said anything for a long time.

"A man should do something worthwhile in his lifetime," he finally said. "Most of us get up when the sun rises, go to sleep when the sun sets. And in between, we carry on meaningless activities." He wasn't lecturing me. It sounded as though this were the first time he'd ever thought of this. I hardly recognized him. He was a completely different person from the one who had been cracking lewd jokes in the cabin all day.

When the lights in the corridor went out and we could only see the glow of our cigarettes in the darkness, we stubbed them out and went back to the cabin to sleep.

The next day I wrote in my diary: "Every person has the truth in his heart. No matter how complicated his circumstances, no matter how others look at him from the outside, and no matter how deep or shallow the truth dwells in his heart, once his heart is pierced with a crystal needle, the truth will gush forth like a geyser."

When I returned from Guangzhou at the end of August, as students were returning to Beida for the fall semester, a movement was brewing on the college campus. Japan's Prime Minister Nakasone had made an official visit to a temple in Tokyo where the remains of Japanese soldiers who had died fighting in China were buried. This action was an outrage to the Chinese people. The Chinese government lodged a complaint with the Japanese government, but the students thought that wasn't enough. They wanted to make a much stronger protest.

Dazibao went up all over the campus, some of them even advocating breaking relations with Japan. One said that Japan was rewriting its history textbooks and whitewashing the massacre of Chinese civilians during the war. Many others warned that Japan's economic stranglehold on China, caused by heavy investments in our country and an unfavorable balance of trade, was slowly gaining strength. The authors of the *dazibao* believed that many high-ranking Chinese officials had been bribed by Japanese executives in exchange for millions of dollars' worth of contracts. One poster described a deal in which a Chinese official was duped into signing a contract for what turned out to be 300,000 defective television sets; he had rushed into the deal because the Japanese had promised him three sets for free.

The *dazibao* writers compared Japan's current economic invasion of China to its military invasion during the 1930s. For this reason, the student movement was called *xin jiuyiba*, the New September 18, commemorating the day in 1931 when the Japanese army invaded China's northeast territory.

Every night after dinner Qiu and I carried flashlights to the Beida campus to read the *dazibao*. We paid the most attention to the posters that urged political as well as economic reform. I was impressed by the energy and idealism of the writers' words. How could our officials be so corrupt? How could they sell out our country to the hated Japanese? I walked around campus absorbing everything I saw.

The Beida students were very courageous. Whenever security officers came to tear down the *dazibao*, and whenever student or faculty spies working for the government took pictures of the people reading them, activists wrote their own names prominently on the bulletin boards so that everyone would know that they weren't afraid of being reported. Even so, some of the students grabbed the spies' cameras and pulled out the film. I didn't understand at first, because I thought the whole idea of posting *dazibao* was to let everyone see them. But the students told me that the authorities used the photographs to identify the writers. Someone could always be coerced into divulging the source of a *dazibao*. In fact, the authorities could trace the authors of every *dazibao* ever posted; even if a poster was put up at night when no one was around or the handwriting was disguised, they would interrogate so many people that someone, somewhere, would lead them to the author. There are university employees who make a full-time job of identifying the authors of the most radical posters.

When the head of the Beijing Communist Youth League came to Beida to read the *dazibao*, a whole group of students chased him away and threatened to beat him up. He ran into a girls' dormitory and hid there until his car came for him. In another case, a student who worked for an official school organization became angry when he found out that he was criticized in one of the *dazibao*, so he tore the poster off the wall. A group of students surrounded him and shouted at him. He tried to run away, but they wouldn't let him go until they had given him an earful. "If you disagree with what is written, you can say so in your own *dazibao,*" someone told him. "You can't rip it up, because by doing that you are denying us the right to speak."

I had heard the issue of free speech raised many times before by the Beida students. It had always been an abstract idea for me, but when I saw the students putting themselves in danger in order to tell the truth, I understood for the first time what freedom of speech was all about.

After a week of posting *dazibao,* the students wanted to place a wreath on the Monument to the People's Heroes in Tiananmen Square to memorialize those who had died during Japan's occupation and as a symbolic gesture protesting the action of the Japanese prime minister. They organized a huge contingent of students to march to the monument on September 18 to express their outrage at government corruption. My sister was very involved in the planning of the wreath ceremony. When I visited her and Qiu at Beida a few days after the march, she told me that the police had surrounded the campus and prevented many students from leaving. Tiananmen Square had also been completely blocked off by the police. In the end, Qing had been one of only five hundred students to break through the police barricades to lay the wreath.

"Why is the government against the students laying a wreath of flowers?" I asked.

"They're afraid that it will lead to an antigovernment protest," my sister said.

"But it's really a protest against the Japanese," I said.

"Every student movement, no matter what its origins, eventually becomes a movement against some form of official corruption and government oppression," Qiu said. "The government knows that better than anyone. Because so many things are wrong in this country, any spark could set off a prairie fire."

"I think we've all been photographed by the secret police in the square," Qing added. "My friends said they saw enlargements of the photos when the police went to each department at Beida to identify the students."

"If you're in one of those pictures, you'll never be able to join the Party," Qiu said to my sister.

"I don't care about that," Qing replied. "But one of my friends was just made a Communist Party member. She was still on probation. The police showed her teachers a photograph of her in the square, but fortunately her teachers lied and said they didn't recognize her. If they hadn't protected her, she would have been expelled from the Party."

I left Beida feeling depressed. The university students were clearly right. Not only had the government stopped them from carrying out a patriotic gesture, but now it was harassing them. I was angry.

I went home and told my father about the conversation I had had with my sister at school. To my surprise, he wasn't as outraged as I was. "You should be concerned about your country and understand what's going on," he said in a calm voice. "But don't participate in anything."

"Why?" I asked, not believing my ears. "Don't you think the students are right?"

He didn't answer. He thought for a few moments and said, "If you participate, I will be very disappointed."

He walked away and went about his business. I couldn't believe he had just told me not to get involved. He had always allowed me to choose and had given me an education that had no bounds. This was the first time he had ever tried to place restrictions on me.

A couple of weekends later, Qiu came to look for my sister at our house. Two of his friends had just been arrested.

"Who are you talking about?" Qing asked anxiously.

"The two who formed a group called the Young Marxists," he said.

After the movement was crushed, these two students posted a notice at Beida saying that they were forming the Young Marxists as an alternative to the Chinese Communist Party. The same night their *dazibao* went up, the authorities tore it down and arrested them. One of the charges against them was selling the *New Age Poetry Collection*, which the government now declared an illegal publication.

"I sold the poetry collection too!" I exclaimed.

Qiu told me to hush. "You have to be careful when you participate in these movements," he said. "You can't do too much or be too visible. I never participated directly. I always watched from the sidelines. When the two of them were arrested, they were so stubborn. As they were being led away, they were still arguing with the police. After they were beaten, they both recanted and admitted their crimes." One of the Young Marxists was sentenced to three years in prison, the other to five years.

Qiu wasn't trying to scare me. He just wanted me to know what it meant to fall into the hands of the police. His fear is shared by almost all Chinese. In 1988 Qiu went to Japan to study, but he kept in touch with us through letters. After the 1989 movement, however, he refused to correspond with me. I called him once from Boston, but he just said, "If you continue to be active, don't bother writing me or visiting me."

· 4 ·

"Young Leaf in Spring"

AT THE BEGINNING of my senior year in high school, I decided to conduct my own survey about life in China as a first step toward becoming more active. The *New Age Poetry Collection* made me realize how little I knew about the people of China, so after school I walked around Beijing looking for people who would talk to me about their lives. One of the places where I found the most interesting people was a noodle shop in a downtown neighborhood.

"Excuse me, comrade," I would say to a man slurping a bowl of noodle soup. "I am a high school student. May I ask you some questions?" Usually, if the man nodded, I sat down. If he waved me away, I went to the next table.

Whenever I saw a nice-looking woman, I made my way over to her. "Excuse me, miss, I am a high school student thinking of going to college. May I talk with you?" The women always giggled first and then agreed to talk. "Are you married?" I'd ask. "Is your marriage satisfactory? Do you have any children?"

No one ever seemed to think my questions were too personal. Some people laughed at me and walked away, but most agreed to talk with me. In fact, a few of them even seemed to enjoy it.

I was against China's war with Vietnam, which had begun in the late 1970s with fights over the Chinese-Vietnamese border and by 1979 had escalated into all-out warfare. By this time the war had settled down, but sporadic fighting continued. I was curious to know what people thought about this conflict, but I found that I was the one who did all the talking, because most Chinese had no opinion at all or were afraid to express one. I told people that I thought it was all right for a country to use its army to protect itself but wrong to worship violence. They all seemed much more comfortable talking about themselves than they did about politics.

Around this time many of the soldiers who had fought in the war were coming back to Beijing and being hailed by the government as heroes. They gave patriotic speeches about the fighting to factory workers and university students. Wherever the heroes went, the government organized crowds to shower them with wreaths of flowers.

"Why don't we go and find out what happened to some of these soldiers?" I said to Rong Dong one day, thinking that they would be perfect subjects for my survey.

"Where are we going to find them?" he said.

"A lot of them were wounded," I said. "They must still be in a hospital."

It took us a long time to find out where they were staying. Finally I got the name of the hospital where one of the most famous soldiers was living. The two of us and Ziping, another friend, sneaked by the nurses, went into his room, and introduced ourselves as students. He was twenty years old and from a rural village in Shandong Province. One of his legs had been amputated.

"What grade are you in?" he asked us.

"We're all seniors," I answered. "We'll probably be going to university next year."

"We're fighting in the south for you, so that you can go to college," he said. "You must study hard."

Instead of really talking to us, he was just spewing propaganda. I didn't tell him I was against the war, because it seemed awkward to say that to someone who had been so badly injured by it.

When we left the hospital, Rong Dong was very excited that

we had seen this soldier. He couldn't wait to get back to school and tell everybody. I shared his excitement about having met a famous person, but I was saddened by the soldier's personal loss and by the fact that he had suffered because of an unnecessary war.

Soon after that we had a lecture competition at school, and I told the story of how I had found the soldier and sneaked into the hospital to meet him. That speech was one of six selected to be given to the other grades at a general assembly, which was scheduled for December 9. My sister had told me that the Beida students were organizing another demonstration in Tiananmen Square for December 9, the anniversary of the day in 1935 when university students forced the Guomindang and the Communist Party to forge a temporary alliance to fight the Japanese.

The government heard about the Beida students' plan, and to prevent it from happening they were sending all high school seniors to the square to hear patriotic speeches. This way the square would be too crowded for the student activists to get in. I wanted to be there, but I couldn't go because I had to give my speech at the assembly. I was the only senior who wouldn't be there. This upset me so much that I even asked my teachers if I could skip the speech, but they said no.

Many of my classmates didn't want to go to Tiananmen Square. They didn't understand why they were being sent there, and they complained about the cold weather and said they didn't want to stay out so long. But I knew what the university students were doing and I wanted to be present, even if I was part of a ploy by the government. I thought something momentous might happen, and I didn't want to miss it.

When Dakun came back from the square on December 9, he told me that the teachers had made them all sit and listen to propaganda speeches memorializing the spirit of the Communist Revolution. "Nothing happened," he said. "It was so cold that everyone just wanted to go home."

Few of my high school classmates knew or cared about political movements, but I had seen political activism at work in the few weeks I had spent at Beida with my sister and her friends. I was also reading a number of political magazines from Hong Kong, many of which were illegal in China. My girlfriend, Liu Yan, first showed me these magazines, which her parents got at the publishing house where they worked. They reported the real news, including things that happened in China that the government tried to keep secret. For example, I had not heard about the uprising of Tibetans in 1959 and the PLA's subsequent massacre of many innocent people until I read about it in one of these magazines. This was also where I first saw the term "prince's party," a reference to the children of high-ranking Party officials who used their family ties for unfair political and financial advantage. Some of the articles described the political breakdown of the Chinese army and the alliances of army generals and their regiments. At the time I didn't completely understand the significance of what I was reading, but I soaked up the information.

It was through an article in one of the Hong Kong magazines that I learned the full story of Wei Jingsheng and the Democracy Wall Movement. The magazine published the complete transcript of Wei's defense against the government's charges and showed that the accusation that he had sold military secrets to foreigners was a lie. This article made me angry at the government's fabrications; Wei Jingsheng had been punished simply because he had spoken out about the need for reform.

At dinner that night I got into an argument with my father about Wei Jingsheng. My father still held to the government's story that he had given away national secrets.

"Don't believe it," I said. "The government is full of lies."

"Yuan Yuan, you mustn't say things like that," my father said.

"Look at yourself," I huffed. "You've been tricked and cheated by the Party. They forced you to study Korean and then put you to work in a factory."

"The Party never forced me to study Korean," he said defensively. "I made my own choice."

"In 1957 they asked people like you to criticize the Party and then punished you for speaking up," I said.

My father fell silent.

I was going through a rebellious stage, questioning my father about his loyalty to the Party. I repeatedly asked him why he still wanted to join the Party when it had always made his life difficult. He reminded me that the Communist Party had put China back on its feet after years of foreign invasion and civil war. He seemed to say that there was no alternative. This is where we parted. The more I read and the more I saw, the more I began to feel that communism was not the only way.

Dakun and I went to see the movie *Gandhi,* about the life of the Indian leader who preached and practiced nonviolence. Chairman Mao had said, "Power comes from the barrel of a gun." Gandhi's life story showed me that what Chairman Mao had said was not necessarily true. There was a better way.

After seeing the movie I went to the library and read everything I could about Gandhi. As I read a translation of his speeches, I was drawn to something he had said: "A crystal goal can only be reached by crystal means." That simple idea made me understand why I was disappointed in the Communist Party.

Young Chinese Communists seventy years ago had a deep commitment to an ideal, a commitment that enabled a small band of guerrillas to transform the nation completely. Their goal was to build a better China, to liberate the masses and give power to the people. Over the years, however, the Party leaders lost their idealism and resorted to all kinds of corruption and violence in order to build a Communist China. I had always been taught that Chinese Communists believed that before each person could really be free, the whole world must be made communist. But Gandhi believed that freedom began with the individual and that it was impossible to have a New India until each Indian transformed himself. I was now convinced that the same was true for China.

In January I began preparing for the college entrance examination. All high school students in China have to take this grueling three-day exam, which tests everything they learn in high school. The test is in essay form and covers seven subjects, ranging from calculus and chemistry to history and literature. Doing well on the exam is the only way to be admitted to university. Only one third of the students who take the test are accepted for college, and Beida takes only 5 percent of those who apply.

If you aren't accepted by a university, you often have a lot of trouble getting a job. Some people go to trade schools, join the military, or study to take the test a second time. Most of us refused to consider what our futures would be if we didn't go to college. We had to get in. The pressure was on.

Dakun and I moved into an empty room in his parents' house so we could have a quiet place to study. Both our families were elated because we were taking our exam preparation seriously, and my parents thought that Dakun was a good influence on their son, the romantic. The room was not very big, with just enough space for two desks. On the wall in front of my desk I wrote in large English letters the word *smile*, to remind me to enjoy myself while I reviewed my courses. I was going to write *laugh*, but I didn't want to get too carried away. Next to *smile* I hung a plain calendar to mark down the days left before *dakao*, the Big Test.

Dakun and I set up a daily routine of waking at eight, going to school, running in the afternoon, and studying until two in the morning. I then rode my bicycle home to sleep, and started it all over again the next morning at eight.

As I reviewed each subject, with my books strewn on the desk in front of me, I discovered a connection between what I had been learning in school and what I had been teaching myself about classical music, art, and Western literature. I had been like a computer storing reams of data, but I had never taken the time to process all of the information. In the quiet of our cramped little study, I began, for the first time, to think.

My brain seemed to shoot off in every direction. I thought about all sorts of things. Why is the English word for the first person, *I*, always written with a capital letter? To me, it showed the Westerners' respect for self. I was easily inspired by anything and everything I read. I came across a fascinating debate between Albert Einstein and Niels Bohr in a physics book. Einstein believed it was possible to understand truth even if one couldn't verify it, but Bohr argued strongly that truth did not exist unless one could prove it. I couldn't decide which of them I thought was right, but their discussion certainly made me think.

I began to debate everything, as Einstein and Bohr had done. One thing I did agree with was Einstein's assumption that all human beings are basically good and that each person has the potential to do great things.

When Dakun and I weren't studying for the Big Test, we were busy organizing after-school activities, because we had been appointed president and vice president of our class. Both of us noticed that one of the girls in our class, Xiaoying, never came to any of our parties and never talked to anyone other than the teachers. Some of our classmates thought that she was arrogant, but we could tell that she was really just shy. Dakun thought that we should try to help her socialize. "I can't imagine what we could do," I said, but I agreed to go along with him.

Dakun and I talked to Xiaoying in school, trying to get her involved in some of the after-school activities. For Chinese New Year, I bought her a card with a picture of a beautiful winged fairy standing on a snow-capped mountain. I wrote two simple lines of prose on it:

One who has her back to the streetlamp casts her dark shadow in her own path.
    Two strangers in a strange circumstance can become very good friends.

The first line was a subtle way of telling her that she was only hurting herself by being such a loner. The second line was my way of asking her to come out of her shell.

It wasn't easy with our study schedule, but Dakun and I tried to see Xiaoying at home every week or two. One afternoon she finally let us into her tiny room, and the three of us sat around and talked (although Dakun did most of the talking). We were all sitting very close, and when my knees accidentally touched hers, I began to feel something more than friendship toward her. Every now and then I glanced at her shy face as Dakun rambled on about this and that.

When I finished studying that night, I rode by Xiaoying's house, which was on my way home. I noticed that she was sitting out on the sidewalk under the streetlamp, studying.

"What are you doing out here?" I asked her.

"My room is very small and stuffy," she explained, too embarrassed to look at me. I waited a few seconds, then moved on.

After that, I started taking that route every night, and Xiaoying was always there, studying under the streetlamp. I always waved at her as I rode by, and sometimes I stopped and exchanged a few words with her. I thought this was going very well.

Each week when we went to see her, Dakun busily recruited her for one activity or another. One day while he was talking I saw a notebook on her desk, open to a page in the middle, so I started to read it. "I know he's coming soon, so I can't raise my head," it said. "It seems like I have been memorizing these English vocabulary words for hours, but I still don't know them by heart. Here he comes. There he goes. I will never learn these words!"

One night I had a fever and couldn't study any longer, so I went out for a walk. I went by Xiaoying's house to see her, but she wasn't there. Later, around midnight, my mother woke me to say, "Yuan Yuan, there is a girl here to see you."

I looked out the front door and was startled to see Xiaoying standing in the courtyard.

"My parents told me you had come looking for me," she said with great effort. I could see she was beginning to regret having taken such a bold step.

"It was nothing urgent," I said. "I wanted to know whether you wanted to help Dakun and me plan a party for school."

Qige, my neighbor's seventh son, was eavesdropping, but he

walked away as soon as we saw him. Xiaoying told me that when she had first entered our yard, she had seen him standing in the darkness and had called out to him, "Excuse me, lady, does Shen Tong live here?" She had mistaken him for an old woman. We both laughed. For the first time, she seemed at ease.

I thought my preparation for the college entrance exam was going well, but all my philosophical thinking put me in a poetic mood. Whatever emotions I felt at any given moment made me want to write down my innermost thoughts. At those times I wouldn't even eat dinner or talk to my family.

Dakun and I were studying together so much that we began to get in each other's way. When he read, he put his index finger on each word and said it out loud to help him absorb the meaning. I, in contrast, often let out an "Ah!" or banged on my desk, or both, whenever I read something interesting. I was even known to throw books if I made a particularly startling discovery. I always tried to be quiet whenever Dakun protested, and he agreed to read to himself when I was in the room. But I continued to make noises that drove him crazy.

Just as my parents suspected, he was thoroughly disciplined — and he was very strict with me and didn't let me take any breaks. One day after school the two of us were lingering in study hall. Dakun was bent over a book, but I was playing with a handheld computer, hoping he wouldn't notice.

"Give me that toy," Dakun demanded when the clicking noise of the game gave me away.

I ignored him. I thought he would just go back to his reading. But to my astonishment, he grabbed the computer out of my hands and ran. I chased him all the way to his house and throughout the neighborhood. After a while I gave up on catching him and went home for dinner. Later, when I went to our study room, I found him with the toy sitting on his desk.

"What did you do that for?" I asked.

"It's for your own good," he said righteously. "You have to study."

"I don't need you to tell me when I should study," I fumed. "I like to do things at my own pace."

Our argument quickly turned into a shouting match.

"You are so bad!" Dakun hollered.

"Do you think you're better than I am? You are sloppy, your books are all over this room, and you never start the wood stove. I always have to do it to keep the place warm," I blurted out. "Furthermore, you're such a slow reader, and when you read no one is allowed to make any sounds!"

"You think you're so special," Dakun said, his face turning red. "Just because you're smart, you expect the same of everyone else. Look at you in class — you know the lesson already, so you talk to Rong Dong and distract him. After class the poor fellow has to go to you for help with the homework. If you don't want to study, that's fine. When we're all at university and you're not, then what will you do?"

I suddenly stopped arguing and felt deeply touched. It dawned on me that my best friend really cared for me.

Dakun noticed that my eyes were misty. "There's no use getting emotional now," he said, his voice softening. He must have thought that his scolding was upsetting me.

"You're right, Dakun," I replied, not bothering to explain myself. "I will try harder."

During the second semester of my senior year, while I was studying for the Big Test, my father was in the hospital. I woke up one morning in February to hear my mother pleading with him to stay in bed. Apparently he had spit up blood, but he was insisting that he was going to go to work. He had been spitting up blood for a number of mornings in the past few weeks, but he wouldn't see the doctor. This morning my mother was frantic, because there had been a lot of blood. Under pressure from all of us, my father remembered that the town he was from in Jiangsu Province had the highest rate of lung and liver cancer in China, and so he at last agreed to have tests. I could see that he was worried.

The diagnosis was tuberculosis, and he was a hospital quite far from our house. Dakun and I visit day, and I sat with him while we read books tog these, I remember, was *Leaders*, by Richard Nixon.

Sometime in April my father wrote me a letter to give me some encouragement for the last big push before the test. He wrote me several letters while he was in the hospital, but this one was fifteen pages long. It was one of the few precious things I took with me when I escaped from China.

Even though I am in the hospital and not at your side, I very much understand because our hearts are connected. It is as if we are a tree, one part connected to the other. I am the bottom of the tree, the root, wanting to speak to the new and tender leaf. A long time in the white hospital bed makes even the trees outside my window seem white. I wish my pen and my words were snow-flakes too, to bathe the young leaf in spring.

In 1956, when I studied for the college entrance examination, the number of places exceeded the number of candidates. We were like sheep running from the pen to feed on the plentiful grasslands. But for you, the competition is keen. You are so many marathoners greasing yourselves for the long run on a narrow, uphill road.

When I was in junior high school, I wanted to attend the Shanghai Shipbuilding Academy because I had always dreamed of sailing and adventure. My childhood dream never came true. When I was making plans in senior year of high school to study journalism at Fudan University, the people from the Foreign Service came and persuaded me to study Asian languages at Beijing University. So that was what I decided, and it affected my whole life.

I don't regret what I did. But the moral of this is, when you are young, you are often unsure of yourself and lack a clear idea of your goals. When I was young, my ideas were ordinary. I did not have a vision of my future. I followed the instructions of my elders. I never questioned them. I never weighed the pros and cons. I went whichever way the wind blew and wherever the water flowed. We were simple students then. We took our books and studied regardless of the seasons. I did not study well and had the weakness of not abiding by my own ideas. All of this is a result of my lack of independent thinking. When you are young, if you do not correct that mistake, by middle age you will become exhausted from trying to rectify a lifelong habit.

You have your own idea of your studies and of society. This is a very good beginning. When you are studying, hundreds of people may advise you like hundreds of birds singing all at once. But use your own eyes, your own mind. Be the master of your own destiny.

Although my father worked for the paint factory and then the municipal government because he thought my mother deserved a better life than a low-paid teacher could provide, he always wished he had continued his studies and spent his life as an academic. "I have been drifting too long," he once said to me. "My wish for my retirement is just to have a quiet place to read."

After almost four months in the hospital, he recovered his strength and was able to come home. I was relieved to have him back in our house, and I spent the last few weeks before the Big Test studying hard to please him.

The week of the college entrance exam, which began on July 7, was known as Black Week. The night before it began, every family who had a child taking the exam went through the same ritual: deciding what the student should eat and when, not too much or too little, not too much fat and not too much lean; letting the student drink some tea, but not enough to make him anxious; being sure there were no pressures on the student from the family, and no television; deciding when the student should sleep and for how long, what time he should get up, what he should eat for breakfast. My family made sure that I ate precisely an hour and a half before the test so I wouldn't be hungry but wouldn't waste energy digesting the food.

After breakfast they went with me to the test site. My sister's boyfriend, Qiu, led the way; then came my father and me; then Nainai and Qing; then my mother, who brought lunch pails and ice cream. For them, it was like going on a picnic. It was a lovely day, with clear blue skies and puffy white clouds. Just as we were leaving, though, the skies suddenly turned black. As we got to the schoolyard, the wind was howling, and it began to rain and hail. Everyone was running for shelter. When my mother arrived, a few minutes after the rest of us, she told us that a student riding his bicycle to the exam had veered into the middle of the street and been hit by a truck. I guess he was so nervous about the test and frightened by the sudden hailstorm that he lost control of his bicycle.

Those of us who made it safely to the exam looked pale and ghastly. The proctors checked our identification cards and then handed out the papers in complete silence. Tension replaced the oxygen in the room, and many of us could hardly breathe. Then the chief proctor yelled, "Begin!" and we wrote like mad.

By the time the morning session was over, the weather had become sunny and warm again. My family was waiting for me outside. Even my teacher from junior high school had come to see how I was doing.

"How did it go?" my father asked, patting me on the back.

I shrugged my shoulders nonchalantly.

"You must be very tired and hungry," Nainai said. "Come, eat the buns I made for you."

My family was surrounding me, doting on me. I noticed that the same thing was happening to hundreds of other test candidates all over the schoolyard.

We ate lunch, then I went home for a nap before the afternoon session. As soon as I hit the pillow I was asleep.

"Come on, come on, it's test time, it's test time!" my father bellowed as he yanked me out of bed. I didn't want to get up. Still groggy, I heard my parents say to each other, "Other students have to be coaxed into taking a rest. Why does Yuan Yuan sleep like a log?"

This lasted for three days. At the end of it I was so tired I didn't even care anymore how I had done.

Four days after the exam I took the train to Jiangsu Province to see my father's blood family, the Lius, and to go sightseeing in the south. Since my sister had taken the same trip after her college entrance exam, it had become sort of a rite of passage in my family. I stayed with my father's brother in Qidong, a small town on the bank of the Yangtze River. The first thing my uncle did was take me to see the graves of Grandfather and Grandmother Shen, my father's adoptive parents, who had been buried unceremoniously during the Cultural Revolution. It was a shock to see the two heaps of dirt in the middle of a field. There was nothing to look at, no gravestones or photographs. Weeds had grown all around. My uncle and I stood there silently. *Someday,* I thought, *I'm going to give them a proper burial.* We stayed for only a few minutes.

I went fishing with a cousin who was my age, and we had a great time. He was catching such huge fish that he decided we should stay out all day, but he suffered a heat stroke, so his family took him home and treated him with traditional Chinese medicine. My aunt made him lie down on his stomach, then rubbed an ointment on his back before scraping his skin with a porcelain spoon until dark red lines appeared. "That relieves the heat," she explained.

While he recovered, I played with my younger cousin, who showed me how to make one of the local delicacies. He caught an ordinary sparrow, killed it, and wrapped it in a cocoon of black mud and straw, then put this mudball into the fire to bake. When the mud had hardened, he removed it from the fire and peeled off the dried outer covering. The sparrow's feathers came right off with the mud. As the hot steam escaped, I could smell the roasted flesh of the bird, which smelled surprisingly good. I watched my cousin savor the meat. He offered me a bite, but I didn't have the stomach for it.

After this, both cousins took me out to catch crayfish, using chicken intestines as bait. As soon as the crayfish grabbed the intestines with their claws, we pulled up. We caught almost two kilos that day.

One day while my cousins and I were walking around town, a villager approached me. "I hear you're from Beijing," he said. "Have you ever met Chairman Mao?"

"No, he died when I was eight," I replied.

"He stands on the top of Tiananmen every day and you've never met him?" he asked, seemingly incredulous.

My cousins quickly led me away, saying, "Don't pay any attention to him. He's not normal."

Because my uncle was an official in Qidong, the Lius lived in a big house and had a government car to drive. Whenever my cousins wanted to take me to the beach, my uncle drove us there. If the family wanted to have people over for dinner, he sent my cousins to a local restaurant to get food; the people at the restaurant gave us as much as we wanted, and we never had to pay full price for it. My uncle was using his position to his advantage, and I realized that even in a small village and even in my own family, corrupt practices were taken for granted.

When I left my uncle's house, I took a train from Shanghai to Anhui Province to visit the famous Huangshan, a series of magnificent granite mountains. There I went swimming at night in Thousand Island Lake. The water was absolutely clear, and from where I was swimming I could see the lanterns glimmering on small fishing boats all over the lake, which made it seem infinite. The moon wasn't full that night, but its rays pierced the clear water so that I could see the outline of my body underneath. I felt a cleansing of my soul then, as if nature were purifying me.

Suddenly I understood why mountains and rivers dominate in Chinese landscape paintings, and man is just a dot on the canvas. Chinese artists paint man as if he were a worm, a bare outline with no features. For two years I had been studying the Western style of painting, in which people are always the most important subject. I had learned to sketch every part of the human anatomy, every bone and every muscle. But on that trip, the philosophy of the Chinese landscape painters became clear to me. From then on, whenever people I met wanted to take my picture, I told them to photograph me with my back to the camera, because I didn't want my face to ruin the natural beauty of the scenery.

While I was having a good time, taking the bus and the train from one place to another across the south, I forgot to worry about how I had done on the college entrance exam. Before I had left, I had told my family not to contact me about the results, because I didn't want any bad news to affect my trip.

One day, when I was staying at a hotel in Hangzhou, I received a telegram that said simply, "Accepted." I had a sinking feeling; I thought that my family was lying to me, that I had probably been rejected but they didn't want me to get the bad news so far away from home. I called home long distance, which is a very rare thing to do in China, and talked to my father for six minutes.

"How are you? How was everything with the relatives?" he kept asking me. "Are you having a good time?"

He wasn't in any hurry to tell me that I had been accepted at Beida. I became even more suspicious. Finally I couldn't stand it anymore and interrupted him.

"Did I really get in?" I yelled to him over the phone line.

"Yes, you did," he replied nonchalantly. "Why don't you come home?"

When he asked me this, I really began to worry. I bought a ticket home on a train that left in three days. I didn't even want to go to West Lake, a famous and beautiful tourist attraction in Hangzhou. Instead I bought some novels and sat in my hotel room, reading.

The day before I left, I went to a coffee shop, where I saw a young woman sitting by herself. Out of habit I walked up to her, introduced myself, and began asking her questions. She told me her name was Baijing, White Serenity, which didn't sound like her real name.

I sat down and we talked for hours. She was a second-year medical student. I told her I had just been accepted at Beida, but she didn't believe me: she thought I was older. I read her some of my poems and we talked very freely, as if we had known each other for a long time. Time went by quickly, and suddenly it was already dusk.

"Why don't we go to West Lake?" she said, after looking at her watch. "I'm supposed to leave in an hour or so, but I'll exchange my ticket for a later bus."

We walked to the lake together and sat on the benches made for couples and talked for a few more hours, looking over the lake at the pagodas. It was a breathtaking sight.

Soon it was time for Baijing to catch the late bus.

"I'm not ready to go yet," she said. "I will take the bus tomorrow."

I was excited that she wanted to be with me. We just sat and looked at each other for a long time. When she put her head on my chest, I kissed her; then we touched each other. That night was the first time that I touched a girl's body all over. Whatever feelings we had toward each other flowed so naturally that neither of us had any inhibitions.

We spent the night there by the lake, and it seemed to go very quickly. Soon the sun was coming up. We were still kissing and hugging, and the daylight gave us a sad feeling.

"I don't know your real name," I said to her.

"It's better that you not know," she whispered in my ear.

"How can I write to you?" I asked anxiously. "How can I find you again?"

She pondered my question. "Twenty years from now, on the same day, let's meet here again," she finally said.

The idea was so romantic that I agreed immediately.

A few old people were out by the lake for morning exercises. The two of us slowly got up from the grass and walked to the bus station. On the way I wrote a short poem for her. After she exchanged her ticket, I led her to a quiet corner of the chaotic bus station, and over the din of the passengers I recited the poem:

> The moonlight on West Lake holds your fleeting shadow,
> Your eyes are like the stars brought by the black night.

We are two leaves on the lake that have drifted by;
We share a thread of understanding that binds us for life.

"I'm not a poet, but I will give you this gift," she said, looking into my eyes. "I will use my whole life to bless your life."

It was time for her to board the bus, and she took her place in line with the other passengers. I stood there watching her, suddenly feeling numb. She felt so far away from me already. She found a seat by the window, and I saw her scribbling what must have been her real name and address on a piece of paper. She leaned out the window and waved for me to come over, but I suddenly wanted to leave because I was about to burst into tears, so I turned around and walked away.

Out of the corner of my eye, I could see that she was frantic. I kept saying to myself, *You can't go back, you can't go back.* I remembered a folktale Nainai had told me. During the Ming dynasty, a dragon king who was displeased with the Ming emperor sucked away all the water in Beijing and stored it in two barrels. The emperor sent two of his generals, brothers, to get it back. He told them to take their bows and arrows and shoot holes in the barrels so the water would flow back to the city. But this was a very dangerous task, because the rushing water could drown them. The emperor told them to run as fast as they could to the Beijing city gate and not to look back, or they would drown and be turned into stone. When the older brother got to the city gate, he turned around and saw that his younger brother had indeed drowned and been turned to stone — he had looked back too soon. I thought of that story and told myself not to look back.

Sadly I walked back to my hotel, but the bus seemed to follow me. It drove past me, and I saw Baijing hanging out the window, her face wet with tears. I ran to my hotel. I knew this was how the story had to end.

When my train pulled into the station in Beijing, I could see my father waiting on the platform. His face stood out in the crowd because he was beaming with pride. I collected my things and my thoughts. The rest of my family was there too, and they all greeted me like a returning war hero.

"How was your trip, college student?" my father asked, patting my back and taking my suitcase.

Qiu had come along too. "Welcome home, schoolmate," he said gleefully.

Nainai prepared a feast to celebrate both my return and my acceptance at Beida. There was chicken and duck and two kinds of fish. Everyone was so excited for me that I quickly had to stop thinking about Baijing and celebrate with them. But I didn't fully appreciate the significance of my acceptance for my parents until people from their workplaces and from the neighborhood came by the house.

As soon as he set foot in our house, the head of my father's work unit said, "Congratulations, Comrade Shen. It's not easy to have both your children admitted to the best university in the country. You must have worked very hard on your children's education."

By the end of the summer, when everyone had received notices from schools, I had found out that I was the only one from my high school class to be accepted at Beida. Dakun had not done very well on the test and had missed the cutoff for most universities by one point. I was really surprised by this, because in many ways he was a better student than I was. It was hard for me to be excited about Beida when he was disappointed.

"I can apply to the police academy," he said to me one day.

"You're not going to become a policeman, are you?" I asked, hoping he was joking.

"It would be interesting to work for the traffic division," he replied. "They're beginning to computerize, you know. I could help design a traffic regulation system."

That's more like it, I thought. I couldn't imagine Dakun as a patrolman, wearing a policeman's outfit.

Luckily, toward the end of the summer, the teachers' colleges lowered their required scores to fill some vacant seats and Dakun was accepted at Beijing Normal University. This meant he would be able to teach in Beijing schools after graduation, so he wouldn't have to go far from home to find work.

A week before I was to leave home and move into a Beida dormitory, my father said he wanted to have a party for me, with all of my high school friends. He said he would do all the cooking, which was a great relief to my mother and Nainai. So the night of the party, my parents pushed all of our tables together to make a banquet table. My father shooed Nainai away from the stove, and as the thirteen guests arrived, we greeted one another cheerfully; this was a party in honor of all of us.

Liu Yan was there, even though we had broken up a couple of months before, as were the other girls of our group of eight. Everyone was congratulating Dakun, who had been the last to be accepted by a school, and kidding him about how close he had come to becoming a traffic policeman. My friends and I sat around the large table filled with food and beer bottles, as my mother and Nainai waited on us and my father happily stir-fried one dish after another. He prepared a special chicken dish that is supposed to be slightly undercooked, but when I looked at the pieces of pink meat, I shouted to him, "Dad, this chicken isn't cooked!"

"You foolish child." Nainai pointed to me. "That's your father's specialty — it's meant to be that way."

All of my friends laughed and reached for the plate of chicken in the middle of the table.

The meal was going well, but it kept my father in front of the stove the whole time. I wanted him to say a few words to us.

"Dad, why don't you give us a toast?" I asked him impatiently.

He stopped cooking and wiped his greasy hands on a towel, then poured a sip of beer into a glass and raised it. Everyone was quiet.

"Uh, you are all good students," he said, looking down at the floor. "I wish you all success in your studies."

He took a sip from the glass, and everyone else followed suit. He had nothing more to say to us. I was so disappointed. I wanted my friends to see what a great intellectual my father was. I wanted him to tell some anecdotes about the days he had spent at Beida, about the excitement and challenge of university life. Instead, I felt that his toast had been very ordinary.

"Eat, eat everybody," he said before going back to the stove. "The food is best while it's hot."

I was just thinking about how my father had let me down when Dakun, who was sitting next to me, tapped me on the shoulder.

"You have a very special family," he said wistfully. "I don't know of anyone else whose parents would entertain us this way. Your father is personally cooking for us, and he even allows us to drink beer. You are so lucky."

Dakun had read my mind and set me straight. I sometimes took my parents for granted, but he helped me appreciate how special they were. He led all of my friends in a toast to the chef, and I could see that my father was pleased, and maybe a little embarrassed.

With beer in our bellies, we began to get boisterous. We spoke about our colleges as if we had already been going to them for years.

"At Beida, some of us have ten hours of classes each day," I said.

"At my school, some of the classes have almost a hundred students," someone else said.

"Pass the food!" Rong Dong suddenly demanded. He had been laughing loudly at every joke, and his face was red. We could see that he had had too much to drink.

"Your father is a great cook," he said while gorging himself with more rice.

Before the meal was finished, Rong Dong disappeared from the table. Dakun was the first to notice that he had been gone for some time. I followed Dakun outside, looking for our friend. We found him bent over in the alley, leaning on the wall with one hand. He had been sick.

"Rong Dong, are you all right?" Dakun said, putting his hand gently on Rong Dong's hunched back.

Rong Dong began laughing hysterically. "I'm drunk," he said.

I started to laugh too, thinking that he had been having such a great time that he had eaten and drunk too much. It wasn't until after the party was over and everyone else had gone home that Dakun and I talked about him.

"Poor Rong Dong," Dakun said. "It must have been torture for him to listen to us going on about our schools."

Rong Dong had scored slightly higher than Dakun on the entrance exam, but he had applied to only the best schools and hadn't gotten into any of them. He would have to study for another year and try again. I think we had all forgotten that he wasn't going to college, because he had been laughing and joking with us as usual. Now Dakun looked at me and saw that I didn't understand what he meant.

"He must have been so miserable around us that he tried to drown his sorrow in beer," he explained. "He was acting like a clown to hide his pain."

I was shocked that I hadn't seen what was going on with Rong Dong. I felt so sorry for him, and I was appalled by my own insensitivity.

"We should go to his house and talk with him," I suggested.

"No," Dakun said. "It's best to let him think that he fooled us all."

· 5 ·

Beijing University

I BEGAN MY FRESHMAN YEAR at Beijing University in September 1986. Even though my house was close enough to Beida for me to ride my bicycle there and back every day, I moved into a dormitory to be part of campus life, like most other Beida students from Beijing. I was assigned to Building No. 28, which is on one corner of the Beida Triangle, a central meeting place on campus. I was happy that I had gotten into this dorm, because the Triangle has always played an important role in student movements. One side consists of a row of bulletin boards, where the *dazibao* first appear. The dining hall and the bookstore are on the other two sides.

Beida students are known for their outspokenness and for the role they have played in student movements over the past century. This history goes as far back as May 4, 1919, when hundreds of thousands of university students rallied for political reform and modernization and protested European and Japanese invaders, who were carving up China for themselves. I was reminded of Beida's history of political activism each time I walked past the May Fourth Monument, a very simple sculpture of the English letters *D* and *S* (Democracy and Science), commemorating that day.

In No. 28 I shared a room with five other guys. The university grouped roommates according to their majors, and we were all biology students. The others were from small villages in Jiangxi,

Fujian, and Yunan provinces, and this was the first time they had ever set foot in a big city, so I promised to show them around Beijing and help them buy many of the things they needed for school.

The day we moved into the dormitory, I took the lower bunk of the bed that was closest to the door and started unpacking my things. Then a hulk of a man walked into our room. He was tall and built like a wrestler. Seeing the top bunk above me empty, he dropped his things. He was my fifth roommate, Fan Wenjun, whom we soon called the Giant. He had lived in California for the first fourteen years of his life, because his parents had been graduate students there when he was born. I decided he had gotten so big because he had been well nourished in America. He had absolutely no American mannerisms that we could see, though, and he told us later that he had never felt at home in California.

My first night at the dormitory I slept like a log, but I was awakened the next morning by what seemed like an earthquake. My bed was squeaking and rocking back and forth. When I opened my eyes, I discovered that this seismic activity was coming from the Giant, who was rolling over in his bed. After a couple of nights I got used to it, but it was an interesting way to begin my first day of classes at Beida.

My roommates and I were so excited to be in college that we jumped out of bed every morning. As we headed for the washroom, each with a towel on his shoulders and a washbasin, a cup, a toothbrush, and toothpaste in his hands, we sang an American song the Giant taught us:

> Johnny ate some beans that were loaded.
> Johnny went to bed; the beans exploded.
> Up his cover, up his sheet,
> Fifty-yard dash to the toilet seat.

We all liked to sing in the washroom, because our voices bounced off the cement walls and made us sound like better singers than we really were. Otherwise, it wasn't a great place. Often two or three boys were lined up behind each cold-water faucet at the long sink, waiting to fill their basins in order to wash their faces. The latrine was across the hall and was disgustingly filthy. There was one long urinal at which we had to jockey for position, and the toilets were just holes in the ground. Many of the doors to the stalls were missing, so if your friends saw you, they could begin a conversation with you right there. In our second year we started a hygiene campaign because people were missing the urinal and not flushing the toilets.

It was true that many Beida students had as many as ten hours of lectures a day, as I had bragged to my high school friends. The schedule was so tight that I learned early on to bring my tin and spoon with me to class in the morning so that I could run straight to the dining hall at noon to buy lunch. Even so, the tastier things were usually gone before I got there, and very few of the dishes had meat in them. We filled our tins with rice and whatever else was served that day and ate it as we walked back to the dormitory. Sometimes we stopped and read the bulletins at the Triangle while we ate.

In December 1984, when I was still in high school, Beida began turning off the lights in the dormitory rooms at 11 p.m. to prevent students from meeting and organizing at night. When the lights were turned out each night, all of us across campus roared and cursed, protesting the policy. People threw bottles out the windows to splatter on the pavement below. It was a good time to let out all our frustrations from the day. After about five minutes of this, we would begin singing as we took our washbasins down the dimly lit hall to get ready for bed. We sang everything from Chinese folksongs to songs by the Beatles. Sometimes I couldn't sleep, so I stood on a chair under the hall light and read (others did this too). A few industrious students lengthened the wire of the hall light so they could bring it into their rooms to read by after the lights were off. Of course, not all of the students participated in the lights-out romp. To get away from the ruckus, nonparticipants hid under their see-through mosquito netting; somehow, in our cramped quarters, we thought we had privacy there.

My roommates and I were never able to go straight to sleep, so we formed what we called a *wotanhui,* an after-hours conversation association. This usually involved complaining about our teachers and talking about girls. One night the talk of girls led us to the topic of condoms. One of my roommates was from Jiangxi Province. We thought he was a real country bumpkin, but suddenly he said, "I know all about condoms. I used to have lots of them to play with."

We were shocked. How did this guy from the countryside know about condoms?

"When did you ever play with them?" I asked.

"When I was a kid," he said. "We blew them up like balloons." He told us how his best friend's mother had been in charge of dispensing the condoms in his village, so her house had been full of boxes of them. The children in his neighborhood competed with one another to see who had the most, and not surprisingly, his best friend always won, because he could get a new one anytime the old one got a hole in it. "So you see, it's no big deal for me," my roommate said.

Some nights, while I was walking back to No. 28, I'd notice several girls lined up outside their dormitory. An old lady assigned to the girls' building locked the door at 11 p.m. to make sure no one left or came in. A half-hour later she opened the doors one last time, so at 11:29 there were often lots of girls waiting to get in. Most of them had been at a lake behind the campus where couples liked to go to talk and kiss. Sometimes even later at night we would see a girl, accompanied by a boy, knocking on the old lady's window, begging to be let in. The first floor of the building had a broken bathroom window, and it wasn't unusual to see guys pushing the girls one by one through it.

Soon after I entered Beida, I started dating Xiaoying, the shy girl I had known in high school. Over the summer we had become more than just good friends. My parents didn't like her, mainly because they thought that I was too young to have a serious relationship, so I never actually told them we were dating; but they knew. I think one of the main reasons I was drawn to Xiaoying was that I was feeling rebellious and independent then, and my parents' disapproval of her made it all the more fun.

On weekends, when my sister and I went home to have dinner with my family, I got off the bus a few stops early to see Xiaoying, who was still living at home. She was the first girl I had sex with. The night we both considered our first time making love, we met at a café after I had had dinner with my family. I didn't tell my parents where I was going, but I'm sure they knew I was going to see her. We stayed at the café, where it was quiet and only a few other couples were around, until midnight. Afterward we went to Xiaoying's room. The lights were low. She sat me down on her bed, then we started kissing and touching each other. Both of us climaxed with our clothes on, and at the time we felt we had made love.

I started to spend nights at Xiaoying's place on the weekends, although I told my parents that I was staying at Dakun's house. It was a few months before we really made love. At first Xiaoying wouldn't take off all of her clothes, because she still felt ashamed. But later she got up the courage to explore my body, and we learned together that lovemaking involves interaction between partners. We thought we were pioneers.

The experience left me feeling totally free and peaceful. It was very liberating because all my life I had heard that sex was something to be scorned and was done only to have children. In the Chinese books I had read, sex was always described as disgusting or filthy. I had never seen my parents physically show their affection for each other. In China, no one ever hugs or kisses in public. After Xiaoying and I began making love, I started wondering how two people who loved each other at night could keep from expressing that love during the day. What I had been taught didn't make sense to me.

My first experience also made me realize that sexual freedom was a part of personal liberation. Since we lived in a restrictive society, I naturally felt that having sex was somehow an anti-government activity. I already believed that before we could change society, we had to change ourselves, and for me, sex was part of that.

Whenever my roommates and I talked about sex, we discussed how repressed the Chinese were. One of the great differences between our generation and our parents' is our attitude toward sex. Though people my age are not all completely comfortable with it, we are more open about it than our parents were. However, I never actually told my roommates that I had lost my virginity. Even with all of our talk, I wasn't sure they would understand.

One day my father asked me to go and see a friend of his who was a fortune teller, a man known for the accuracy of his palm reading. Even though my parents told me they didn't believe in fortune telling, they wanted him to read my palms. So I went to him.

The fortune teller wrote down what he thought was my fate on a sheet of paper and gave it to me. "Be careful in your college years," it said. "You will be harmed by your friends and by women. If you study diligently and do not involve yourself in any outside activities, you will be all right. But if you concern yourself with matters other than schoolwork, disaster will befall you and you will undergo great changes in your life. You will be betrayed by your friends if you are not careful. If you do not keep away from the women who claim to love you, they will harm you. After five years of college, you will meet with good luck."

I read it and said to him, "No, you're wrong. I have only four years of college."

He said, "I can't explain it, but I see five years."

I didn't want to believe the fortune teller, but I was afraid not to. He told me that there was no way to change my future, but that I could do things to lessen my misfortunes. The way to avoid disaster, he said, was not to get involved in anything remotely dangerous.

I remembered what he told me for some time. Whenever I made a new friend, I wondered if he was the one who would betray me. I was so disgusted with myself for thinking this way that I finally decided to follow the advice of Beethoven, who once wrote, "I will seize fate by the throat; it shall certainly not bend and crush me completely."

I gave my parents the piece of paper, but I should have thrown it out. My sister told me that they often read it and worried about the fortune teller's predictions.

The 1980s were probably the years when the Chinese people enjoyed the most intellectual freedom they had had since the founding of the People's Republic in 1949. I became more aware of this when I entered Beida and discovered that Western influences were everywhere. Every student was required to learn English in school, and studying the language was crucial for those who wanted to go abroad. Ordinary people as well as students gathered in certain areas of public parks called "English corners" and practiced speaking English to each other, and bookstands all over Beijing sold popular English-language books, like Sidney Sheldon paperbacks. When my friends and I went out to various bars around the city, we heard new bands experimenting with rock-and-roll, and Chinese pop music was on everyone's radio at school. Alternatives to the books published by the government's official press were provided at some private bookstores, such as one called the Three Tastes, after a novel by China's leading contemporary author, Lu Xun, and another called Du Le Shu Wu, Capital Happiness Bookstore.

Western ideas began flowing freely into China after the country started trading with the West in the early 1980s. In an effort to implement his Four Modernizations program, Deng Xiaoping allowed China to open up to Western technology and science. But he and the conservative elements of the Communist Party did not expect Western culture and ideas about freedom and democracy to pour into the country as well. They thought these ideas were dangerous, and in late 1983 they mounted the Anti–Spiritual Pollution Campaign to rid China of the influences of foreign culture. Surprisingly, the campaign lasted only forty-three days. The hardliners found that it was no longer possible to launch an ideological movement; the Chinese people had suffered so much during the Cultural Revolution that they would no longer participate in a government propaganda effort.

By the time I got to Beida, in the fall of 1986, students were extremely dissatisfied with how slowly political reform was happening and how badly they had failed the year before to move the government with their protests. Just a few months into my first semester at college, what would become the largest student movement since the end of the Cultural Revolution, one involving students from more than twenty provinces, began gathering force. These protests were the first I experienced as a Beida student, and in many ways they were a crash course in modern Chinese prodemocracy movements.

Fang Lizhi, who was then the vice president of the University of Science and Technology (Keda) in the city of Hefei in Anhui Province, gave two speeches on democracy, the first in mid-November at Tongji University in Shanghai and the second on December 4 at Keda. He said that democracy inherently belonged to the people, a statement that stirred students at both schools. The speeches also led to a confrontation of words between Fang Lizhi and the government. In response to Communist Party vice chairman Wan Li's statement that the Party would eventually give democracy to the people, Fang Lizhi said that democracy is something that must be won by the people, not something that can be handed down by the authorities. When news of this reached Beida, students coined the slogan "Wan Li rapes the people's will."

After Fang Lizhi's speeches, Hefei and Shanghai students began demonstrating for more freedom. When Beida students heard about these demonstrations through letters and telephone calls, they posted the news on *dazibao* at the Triangle. Soon, in what felt like a spontaneous reaction, university students all over the country were protesting for democratic reforms.

Dazibao promoting democracy spread across the Beida campus. I didn't know what to do, or whether I should take part in the demonstrations at all. Because I was a freshman, I didn't know many people, and no one I knew was an activist. My sister, who had been involved for the past two years and already believed that demonstrations were futile, followed the movement's progress but decided not to participate. Her friends had gotten into trouble the year before, and she wanted nothing to do with it. (In the end, the decision was made for her: she had to have her appendix removed and was laid up in the campus hospital to recuperate.)

A few days after the Beida protests began, I was sitting in my dorm room when one of my classmates, Tian, ran in to tell us what had happened to him. He had gone to nearby Qinghua University to participate in a prodemocracy rally and to give a speech. A young Qinghua instructor had jumped onstage during the students' speeches and started telling them that they were wrong to protest. Tian, who had a fiery temper, punched the instructor in the face, which prompted the plainclothes policemen who had been watching the proceeding to begin arresting people. Two heavyset Qinghua students stood in front of Tian, which gave him just enough time to run away. When he reached the main gate of the university, he saw that the police were waiting there with the young instructor, so he turned his reversible jacket inside out and put on a pair of sunglasses. Luckily, they didn't recognize him, and he walked through. If Tian, a Beida student, had been arrested at Qinghua, the authorities could have labeled him an instigator, and he would have faced serious charges.

Tian became more and more animated as he told us what had happened. His adrenaline was pumping, and I could see that he felt like a real hero.

The next day the incident was reported in the *Beijing Daily*, which said, "A Beida student, unwilling to listen to the advice of a young professor, jumped out of the crowd and swung his fist wildly." The paper reported that the police were still searching for this criminal. Tian read the article and was suddenly scared. "Please don't tell anybody what I told you yesterday," he begged us.

Hearing Tian's story and watching the upperclassmen around campus organizing to join the students in Hefei and Shanghai convinced me that I wanted to be part of the movement. Beijing-area students planned to march to Tiananmen Square on January 1, and I decided I would go with them.

The afternoon before the march, many people were leaving campus to spend New Year's Day at home. My uncle came to Beida to pick up Qing from the hospital and take us both home. I wanted to stay on campus reading the *dazibao*, but I finally decided to leave because our house was close to Tiananmen Square, so it would be easier to go to the demonstration from there.

On the morning of the march, everyone in my family tried to talk me out of going. I didn't listen. My father, in desperation, sat me down and told me he had heard at work that the Beijing municipal government had installed a new video surveillance system on Changan Avenue. A friend who worked in the police department had told him that a police van was in every alley, ready to drive to the square at a moment's notice. Policemen and agents of the Public Security Bureau were posted in every building around Tiananmen Square and the surrounding streets.

"If anything happens today, it will be major," my father said. "Blood will be shed." He was trying to frighten me.

"What if I just go and watch?" I asked, trying to calm his fears.

Just then some guests arrived to visit my family for New Year's Day. Other parents would have openly opposed their children's involvement in student movements, but my parents regarded themselves as liberal thinkers and didn't want their friends to see that they were against my taking part in the march, so they said nothing in front of their guests. While they were all talking, I slipped out of the house.

It was freezing cold as I walked down Changan Avenue to Tiananmen Square with my camera, which I took because I thought this day could be historic. I hadn't gotten far from my house when I came upon crowds of students who weren't able to get into the square. Thousands of policemen had linked arms around the perimeter to prevent us from entering. I worked my way over to a large group of students from Beijing Normal University who were gathered in front of the Museum of Chinese History, on the east side of the square. They were chanting, "Long live freedom!" and "Long live democracy!" I tried to avoid the Beida students, because I knew I would not be able to keep myself from getting involved if I joined up with them. Suddenly I remembered my father's words when the Democracy Wall Movement had ended: "One needs to be concerned enough to become more educated but know enough to stay away from disaster." I wasn't sure I believed that completely, but when I saw the soldiers blocking the square, I understood what he meant. When I had been at home, I had insisted on being part of the student protest, but when I was actually standing in the street, I thought, *I really should not get too involved.*

I asked the students around me why they were marching to the square. To my surprise, many of them said they didn't know. "Everyone was told to be here on the first of January, so we're here," one of them said to me.

As I looked around the crowd, I could tell immediately who the members of the secret police were. They let us know through eye contact that they were watching us, and many of them pointed their cameras right at people's faces and took photographs in an attempt to frighten us.

A group of students in the front broke through the police barrier and rushed into the square. I don't know what happened in my mind, but I pushed ahead and went into the square too. Soon a cordon of policemen cut us off from behind, stranding several hundred of us. This was the first time I was truly frightened. Some of the students around me were being hit with billy clubs by the police, and I was sure we would all be arrested.

Now that we were in the middle of the square, I thought someone would read a statement with a list of demands, but no one spoke; instead, a group of students tried to hoist a banner high in front of the Museum of Chinese History. The policemen, in pairs, broke them up, grabbing them and throwing them into police vans. As mayhem burst out around me, I ran toward Changan Avenue, out of the square. I met some Beida students I knew, who were talking about how exciting the protest was, but I was disappointed that nothing more substantial had happened. By midafternoon we had all returned home.

This nationwide student movement gained nothing other than some small concessions from local governments, but the overall consequences were severe. The government blamed Fang Lizhi for inciting the protests, and he was relieved of his position as vice president of Keda and purged from the Communist Party. Every night we listened to radio broadcasts about Fang Lizhi's dismissal. Then, on January 25, 1987, Communist Party General Secretary Hu Yaobang was forced to resign. A reformer, he had promoted many of the economic changes the hardliners believed had led to a liberal atmosphere that encouraged student protests.

Many of us students had thought that with leaders like Hu Yaobang and outspoken Party members like Fang Lizhi, there was a chance for real change. But when these two were stripped of their positions, we became less hopeful that significant reforms could come from the government. After Hu Yaobang's resignation, I heard someone say, "Deng Xiaoping has become a dictator." In Chinese chess, there is a strategy that says, "Sacrifice the minister to protect the general." Deng Xiaoping had sacrificed Hu Yaobang, his hand-picked successor, as a gesture toward the hardliners. To remain in power, he constantly had to maintain the uneasy alliance he had forged between the reformers and the conservatives.

My father told me of other repercussions around the country. The head of the Public Security Bureau was dismissed, as were two *People's Daily* journalists, Liu Binyan and Wang Ruowang, and Keda's president, Guan Weiyan. New regulations restricting demonstrations were issued in Beijing and other cities. In Beijing, anyone who wanted to stage a march now had to apply for a permit, stating the purpose of the demonstration and all slogans to be used.

Twenty-five students were arrested in Tiananmen Square, and many more were photographed by the secret police. When the news reached Beida that twelve of our classmates were among those arrested, five thousand students gathered at the office of the university president, Ding Shisun, to demand that he negotiate with the police for their release. The Public Security Bureau agreed to release the students but did so quietly; they were driven back to the campus in a police van and dropped off at a seldom-used gate, so the police could avoid confronting demonstrators.

For several days Beida students continued posting *dazibao* to protest the arrests. The *dazibao* listed the names of those arrested and asked all students to remember them. "The university will not dare expel them now," one poster said. "But when we graduate, we must remember these students so that if the university secretly takes action against them, we will be able to react. Should that happen, we must stand together and rally around them."

The twenty-five arrested were not the only students who got into trouble. The authorities identified many students from photographs taken in the square and in the Triangle, where the *dazibao* were posted, and forced them to write self-criticisms admitting their guilt. My friend Tian was never caught for punching the Qinghua University instructor, but he had been seen posting *dazibao*. The teacher who was assigned to oversee his self-criticism was always after him, following him and standing outside No. 28 to watch his every move. Being the rebellious spirit he was, Tian often ran out and yelled, "We are all being raped!" as soon as the political instructor left.

Although I hadn't been much more than an observer at this demonstration, I was buoyed by the courage of people my own age who dared to take on the government. Others wished that Beida had been more in the vanguard of the nationwide protests, as it often had in the past. But I was glad to see that students in other parts of the country had started this movement. The Hefei and Shanghai protests clearly showed that students in other cities were as concerned about democratic reform as those of us in Beijing were.

Another major consequence of the government's actions against the protests was that many students became discouraged and lost their will to study. The slogan *Dushu wuyonglun*, Study is for naught, was heard a lot around college campuses in those days. There didn't seem to be as much of a reason to study hard if the government would not let us play a role in shaping the country's future. The failure of the movement made some of us feel that it was senseless to continue being such idealists about reforming the government, and many of us became much more selfish.

Instead of going to class, people found different things to do. Some wanted to leave the country and concentrated on passing the Test of English as a Foreign Language (TOEFL), the standardized test required of foreign students who applied to American schools. Others, known as the mahjong crowd, spent a lot of time playing the tile game and gambling. The mystics studied metaphysics and Eastern philosophy to cultivate an otherworldliness, and the lovers were interested only in dating and fooling around.

Some of us took advantage of the money craze that had overtaken the country after the government relaxed its restrictions on private enterprise. Some very venturesome types sold cars, videocameras, clothing, and gold on the black market. There was a connection for whatever a Beida student wanted to sell — even cement, steel, fertilizers, the Beijing Jeep, and foreign currency, which the most well-connected students were buying and selling. We thought of ourselves as the smartest students in the country and believed there was nothing we couldn't do. Unfortunately, we were using our intelligence to dabble in black market sales when we should have been concentrating on our studies.

For a short time I sold a cream that promised to grow hair. It was called 101 and was said to be highly effective. A jar of 101 cost 10 yuan (about $2.50) in China, but in Japan, where it was very popular, it was selling for as much as $120 a jar. If you bought a case of this cream from a Chinese wholesaler and sold it to a Japanese buyer, you made a lot of money. I sold fifty jars of it and made some quick cash, but after that I didn't do any more business. I didn't want to spend my time that way.

Instead I stayed in my dorm room, reading a lot of books and listening to Simon and Garfunkel. I wasn't satisfied with what I was learning in my classes that first year at Beida. To make up for this, I tried to recapture the feeling I had had when studying on my own for the college entrance examination. I reread, in English, the poetry of Byron and Shelley and thought it was even more beautiful in the original. And I came across a story in one of my English textbooks that helped to restore my optimism about taking part in reform movements in China. It was about a black woman living in the American South. Her name was Rosa Parks, and she refused to sit in the back of a segregated bus.

The reading went on to talk about a black preacher named Martin Luther King, Jr., who led the civil rights movement with a method of protest that intrigued me. I went to the school library one day to find out more about King, and was encouraged to read about his success with nonviolent protest. I started to believe again that we could do the same in China.

Toward the end of my freshman year the government announced that both boys and girls from the ten top universities would have to spend ten weeks in the summer undergoing military training. (In the end, we stayed only five weeks.) No one ever said why we had to go, but I had a feeling that the government wanted to punish us for the demonstrations earlier in the year and make us learn from the soldiers, who were more disciplined and obedient to the Party. But none of us really objected to the idea. It seemed like a fun way to spend the summer, and we were excited to think that when the training was over, we would be members of the reserves with the rank of captain.

Before we left, the government gave each of us a uniform, a cap, a belt, shoes, and a knapsack. I felt as if I were going on a camping trip with friends. But my father wanted me to take this more seriously. "Yuan Yuan," he said, "you should take advantage of this opportunity to see at first hand the life of a soldier. This is a chance that is hard to come by. Don't forget you were born in an army camp and your parents were once members of the People's Liberation Army."

I thought about what he said, but I had mixed feelings about the experience. What did military training have to do with the rest of my education? I believed in individualism and personal freedom, while the army stressed uniformity and obedience. I kept remembering what Einstein had written about military marches: he said that walking in locked step with groups of people made him physically ill. I wondered what my own reaction to army discipline would be, and I was skeptical that students and soldiers could live side by side.

On the train to the army base, we played cards and told a lot of dirty stories. Several Beida teachers came with us to assist the army officers and to serve as liaison people between the school and the army. Most of these teachers were at least twenty years older than we were, and they were clearly nervous about our attitudes. When they saw us laughing and joking, they must have figured out that it wasn't going to be easy to whip us into army shape.

When we reached the end of nowhere — about five hours northeast of Beijing — the train stopped in a makeshift station. The nearest town, Chengde, where the Qing dynasty emperors hunted, was two hours away. We looked around and couldn't see anything but the station. A group of army officers greeted us and made us march to the camp, which I liked, because it felt great to be outside, marching in the hot sun. Everyone sang the reserves' anthem, changing the words around to make it funny. One of the Beida teachers was designated *fuyingzhang,* vice squadron leader, which we changed to *yingfuzhang,* which means leader of prostitutes.

As soon as we set foot in the camp, everything we did had to fit a structured schedule. We lined up all the time. In the dining hall, after we were given our daily ration of food, we stood at attention until everyone was ready to sit. At the count of "One!" we pulled out our chairs. At the count of "Two!" we sat down. We had to stare straight ahead. We learned very quickly how to sit in our chairs without looking.

Fourteen of us lived in one room and made up a *ban,* platoon, the smallest unit at the camp. The officers woke us up every morning at seven, then we ran for fifteen minutes, did calisthenics, and practiced marching in formation. They had us going forward and backward, quickly and slowly, and turning our heads left and right. We were taught how to handle machine guns, but, luckily, we didn't have to train on the obstacle course. The officers also gave us lectures on military history, warfare planning, battle strategy, and military geography.

Although the program was exhausting, it was so new to us that we usually stayed up late at night talking about what we had done that day. Every night a few of us were sent out on patrol. When I relieved a classmate in the middle of the night, he would ask, "Password?" and I'd answer, "To serve the people." Then we would both laugh at how silly we sounded. We all had trouble taking this military stuff seriously.

I got on well with our platoon officer, a big twenty-eight-year-old with a booming voice from Shandong Province. We sometimes sat outside at night and talked. He told me he had fled from Shandong when he was a child because there had been a terrible famine. Being poor and not knowing what else to do, he had joined the army when he was only nineteen, but he wanted to leave it now because he had heard that people in the countryside were making good money in private enterprise.

"You are so lucky to be able to go to university," he said. "I don't want to be a student, but your future will be much better than mine."

When he found out I was studying science at Beida, he asked me a lot of questions about the stars. It seemed to be something he had always wanted to know about.

"Do you know the folktale about the moon goddess and the rabbit?" I asked him, pointing to the sky.

"Everybody knows that tale from childhood," he said.

I told him about the surface of the moon, how the moon revolves around the earth, and why it is sometimes a crescent and other times round. He was fascinated by this. It was the first time anyone had ever talked to him about astronomy.

He then told me about his life as a soldier, which was very rough. The pay was low, and soldiers weren't respected in the way they had once been in China. In my father's day, when a soldier returned to civilian life, the government always had a job ready for him. But in the 1980s many soldiers returned to their villages and couldn't find jobs, just as intellectuals hadn't been able to find work during the Cultural Revolution.

Some of us looked down on the soldiers at the camp because they were peasants, but every time I felt this way, I recalled what my father had said: "If you remember that your father came from a village of farmers, then you will see the peasants differently."

Although I liked and respected our platoon leader, many small things happened that made us question the officers' authority. One afternoon my platoon was playing soccer against another team made up of soldiers. We were ahead, two to one. One of the soldiers was getting angry that a bunch of skinny students from the city was beating his team, so in the middle of the game he grabbed one of my classmates and punched him repeatedly in the head. We all ran over and pulled them apart, and both sides cursed at each other as we left the field.

The soldier had broken my classmate's glasses and bloodied his nose. "I'm all right," this student told us, with strips of cloth stuffed into his bloody nostrils. "I don't want any trouble." He was just about to become a member of the Communist Party and he was worried that this incident might jeopardize his membership.

"You can't let that soldier beat you up and not do anything about it," I said. A dozen of us talked to the soldier's commanding officer, who knew we had a legitimate complaint. The soldier was clearly in the wrong. "He will be locked up and will perhaps be expelled from the army," we were told.

The next day at lunch our classmate was having trouble standing up straight; he was still dizzy from the head trauma he had suffered. The officer in the mess hall saw him leaning against the dining table and told him to step forward.

I exchanged glances with my platoonmates but didn't say a word. We were fuming.

"Stand up straight!" the officer demanded.

Our classmate tried but wobbled.

"How can you be so stupid!" I exploded. "One of your soldiers beat him up yesterday. How do you expect him to stand straight?"

"This is totally unreasonable," someone else said. "What kind of place is this?"

The officer was dumfounded. He never expected anyone to talk back to him, certainly not in the disrespectful tone we were using. He didn't know what to do, so he let it pass.

We found out later that the soldier who had beat up our classmate was never disciplined. We didn't raise the issue again, though. It was important to our classmate that he be accepted by the Party, and he asked us not to make any more trouble. (He wasn't joining the Party for political reasons, but because it would help him get a better job and other advantages. There is a saying in China, "*Yizhang dangpiao ding san nian,*" "One Party membership card is worth three years"; if a Party member is found guilty of a crime, he is often kicked out of the Party instead of having to serve the usual three-year prison term. This saying is a way of expressing that being a Party member can save you in many instances.)

The training period was almost over, so I did my best to behave myself. I studied for the examinations in the written courses and often went off alone to practice my marksmanship.

In the last week of our stay, Beijing's vice mayor, Chen Haosu, came to observe our training and to report back to the government on how successful the program had been. After he gave a brief speech, he wanted to talk with us informally. We saw immediately that this was a public relations stunt; Chen Haosu was the son of Marshal Chen Yi, who had been commander of the Third Field Army.

Several companies of students were told to sit in a circle in front of our barracks. The vice mayor stayed in the middle of the circle, put one knee on the ground, and tried to strike up a friendly chat with us.

"Students, I hope you are all doing well," he said. None of us answered him.

"Military training must be very interesting?" he asked, smiling a phony smile.

One of the guys in another platoon, who sang Italian operas when he was in the shower, said, "What's so interesting about it? The food is horrible. The soldiers are unreasonable. It's a waste of time."

We did everything we could to hold back our laughter. I hugged my knees and buried my face in my arms. Other people's shoulders were shaking. The vice mayor didn't know what to say. He had expected us to tell him that the weeks at the camp had built up our socialist characters, that "we had learned a great deal from our brave brothers in the army" and "we must emulate their spirit of patriotism and sacrifice to work for the good of our glorious nation." Instead the opera singer had shocked him with an honest answer.

As the vice mayor fidgeted, trying to salvage this moment, he reminded us that we were the future of China. I looked at my classmates seated around me. We had come a long way from even the last generation. We were not at all what our elders expected us to be. We were brash, willful, and dared have our own thoughts and to speak our own minds. Old slogans like "Learn from Chairman Mao, build a New China" didn't work on my generation.

My platoon leader came up to me on the last day and said appreciatively, "You saved my face." I had gotten A's in my military courses. "I had to defend you to the others, but your performance now makes me look very good," he said. He gave me his hat as a remembrance. I was the only student who got an official army hat.

We packed our bags in total silence. Our somber mood was very different from our mood the day we had arrived, full of expectations. Now we were anxious to be on our way back to Beijing. On the train we drank beer and laughed, and as I walked through the streets of Beijing at last, with all of my military equipment strapped to my back, I thought, *This is such a great city.* I ran part of the way home. I was anxious to see my family.

I had two months left of the summer before school began again, so I asked my father if he could use his contacts at the Beijing municipal government to find me an internship. He arranged for me to work in the Red Star People's Commune, the largest in Beijing. This agricultural commune, now called Nanyuan Farm, had a population of 300,000 and was a town in itself. Its factories employed only two hundred workers, but the most popular brands of ice cream and soda and other products came from them.

I started as a helper in a section of the commune that tended *milu*, a rare species of deer that is almost extinct in China. The rest of the commune was made up of a large cow farm, a chicken farm, a duck farm, and a dairy with machinery that milked and fed the cows. The commune had only one bull, who serviced several thousand cows through artificial insemination. For two days I lived on the cow farm, and there I drank milk fresh from the cow, which had a strong flavor.

After I left the deer farm, my job was to help the president of the commune, but there wasn't much to do, so I had a lot of time to talk to the commune workers. They told me that it was difficult to farm properly when the government not only set the price of grain but also determined how much fertilizer to use on a plot of land and the price of the fertilizer.

"This year I spent 2000 yuan more on fertilizers," a farmer told me. "I am required to sell the grain at 16 fen per kilo, only 2 fen more than last year. The government doesn't reimburse me for the extra money I spend on fertilizers. They say I need only eighty kilos, but I really needed a hundred kilos to have a good harvest. I had to buy the extra twenty on the open market at a much higher price. Every year I lose money."

While the farmers were operating within the government-controlled system, they also had to deal with the fluctuating prices of the free market, where they had to go to buy the extra fertilizer, which often came from corrupt officials who had bought it from the government and resold it for a profit. Most of the farmers I talked to that summer were having such a hard time they were thinking of going into other businesses. But that was just as frustrating for them, because China's experiment with free enterprise gave the people in charge many more opportunities to be corrupt. For example, if one of the farmers wanted to operate a fishery, he had to sign a contract with the government promising to pay a fixed price for the right to operate. The bureaucrats who established the prices on these contracts could charge a low licensing fee in exchange for half the profits. They also sometimes set impossibly high prices, so that the operator lost money no matter how hard he worked. Many times the government reneged on its contracts with operators, and there was nothing the operators could do.

I finished my internship in the middle of August and decided to take a trip to Inner Mongolia. I was going to go by myself, but at the last minute Rong Dong decided to accompany me. He had taken the college entrance exam again and was beginning classes at the Shanghai Chemical Engineering College in two weeks. He took me to the train station to see me off, but as the conductor announced that the train was pulling out in five minutes, I said, "Why don't you come with me?" Rong Dong took several seconds to decide, and then we were on our way.

It took about thirteen hours to get from Beijing to Hohhot, the regional capital. When we got off the train, we felt as if we had taken a trip back in time. I imagined that the city's two major landmarks, the Great Mosque and the Five-Pagoda Temple, looked the same as they had when they were built, hundreds of years ago. We tried every kind of local food — various mutton dishes and shish kebabs made with other exotic meats. I had only 80 yuan with me, some of which I had borrowed from my sister and my friends, and after three days in Hohhot we had spent 60 yuan.

Rong Dong had to go back to Beijing to leave for school in Shanghai, so we had a very emotional parting at the train station. I knew it would be another year before I saw him again. He came over and gave me a strong hug — a very unusual show of emotion, even between good friends.

After Rong Dong left, I hitchhiked from Hohhot to Baotou, stopping at a place called the Sea of Hasu, a very large lake in the middle of a plain. The beauty of the landscape made me think of Beethoven's Sixth Symphony, the *Pastoral*. I sat by the lake and wrote a lot of poetry.

> The shimmering surface of the ocean
> Reflects the dreams of fish.
> A white bird flying against the darkening sky
> Is the night's remembrance of day.
> Tall golden grass beside the ocean
> Ages in a breath of boundless wind.

On the banks of the Sea of Hasu, I met some people who were wearing rubber suits up to their waists and wading in the water cutting reeds. They spoke Chinese with heavy Mongolian accents. Piles of reeds, which the natives said they used for braiding fans and making other handicrafts, were drying in the sun. The people let me borrow a rubber suit and wade in the water with them. To return the favor, I shared with them some cigarettes I had brought from Beijing.

After a couple of hours, when a pickup truck loaded with newly sheared lamb's wool drove by, I hitched a ride and moved on. I lay in the back of the truck on a thick bed of wool and bounced along comfortably as the truck flew up and down on the uneven roads. I didn't know where it was headed, but soon we came to a stop, and border guards asked the driver for papers. Either he forgot about me or he didn't bother to tell the guards he had a passenger, because they let him drive through and I found myself crossing into the militarized zone, about 150 kilometers from the Soviet Union.

The truck let me off at a commune, where I hoped I could stay for the night. When I showed the head of the commune my Beida student ID, which said that I was a biology major, he thought I was there to study the grasslands of Mongolia. He took me to a family living in a tent on the plains so I could spend a couple of days with them.

The mother and father, who were in their forties, had four children aged between seven and ten, and the father's parents also lived with them. Once they figured out that I wasn't trying to sell them anything, as the other Chinese from town did, they welcomed me in the way that all Mongolians treat guests. I was given the best food and was told that I would sleep in the most comfortable bed — but they had only one large platform bed, so we all slept in it together.

In the morning the woman skimmed the cream off the top of a bucket of goat's milk that had been cooling in well water overnight. The cream was so thick that she lifted it off the surface like a slice of pie. Then she steamed it until the outside was solid and the inside was like gelatin. This was called milk skin, and we ate it for breakfast with a smoked tea. For lunch we had a cereal of stir-fried wheat, milk, sugar, tea leaves, and pungent dried milk curds.

During the day I read to the children and told them stories. They took me horseback riding, and I tried my hand at tending sheep on a motorbike. That night I cooked Chinese food for them. Even though they were polite and ate it, I don't think they liked it very much, except for the soy sauce I used for seasoning.

After I left the family, I found a main road and started following the electricity poles, walking about forty kilometers a day through treeless grasslands. Every now and then the high altitude made my nose bleed. I kept my watch in my backpack and tried to live in tune with the sunrise and sunset. One night I stayed in a house that was near the ruins of a temple. There was a thunderstorm that night, and the rain was so inviting that I walked out into the pitch blackness. The rain was deafening, and I couldn't see anything except when the lightning ripped the sky in two. I felt that I was at the beginning of time, that I could touch the whole universe. I walked toward the temple ruins in the distance, where there was one lone tree. I hadn't walked more than a few paces when a bolt of lightning struck the tree and split it down the middle. I ran back into the house, soaked from the rain, and went to sleep wondering if I had imagined the whole thing.

For the rest of my trip back to Beijing I kept thinking about how incredible my summer had been.

· 6 ·

Year of
the Dragon

I FIRST BECAME an activist at Beida during my sophomore year, but it happened in a strange way. I was asked to join the Beida Student Association by the newly elected chairman because word had gotten around that I was a good organizer. This was based not on any real organizing I'd done at school but on what people had heard about some of the confrontations I had had with the officers at the army camp that summer. But the Beida Student Association was an official organization overseen by the university and wasn't known for taking stands on the students' behalf. The people who chose me must have been overlooking my outspokenness and remembering that I was good at getting people together and getting things done.

The chairman asked me to be in charge of public affairs and liaison. Most of the events sponsored by the association were very dull lectures, so I wanted to liven things up. I spent most of my free time during the semester putting together a fashion show, which was also a way of making money for the association.

When I contacted the various fashion schools in Beijing and asked them to help, I discovered yet again how hard it is to get things done in China if you don't have *guanxi*, connections. To make the connections I needed, I had to entertain the people responsible for scheduling the auditorium as well as the administrators at the fashion academies, who were worried that we were infringing on their territory. I also had to promise other university groups that we would split whatever profits we made from the ticket sales with them. In the end, the fashion show was a huge success. It was one of the first student association events that made any money, and everyone who came had a great time.

Another part of my job as liaison officer was to meet groups of visiting students from other schools in China and from abroad. This gave me the opportunity to become friendly with many foreign students, because it was my responsibility to show them around and help make them feel welcome.

I thought my parents would be proud that I was now active on campus, but my father was already worrying that I was becoming too involved. When I went home for Chinese New Year, he told me that his fortune-teller friend had called him recently and was concerned about me. "Nineteen eighty-eight is the Year of the Dragon," the fortune teller had said. "Tell your son not to act, because there may be danger." When my father told me that his fears were based on this telephone call, I didn't take them seriously. I couldn't believe that my parents were listening to a fortune teller, but I don't know why I was so surprised. For centuries the Chinese have placed great faith in fortune telling, and my parents, liberal though they were, were more traditional than I realized.

On the night of June 2, a Beida graduate student was killed at a small restaurant near the campus when he tried to break up a fight between two groups of hooligans. Beida students erupted with rage when they heard he had been shot; the campus was often invaded by these troublemakers, who harassed students, and the security guards were so afraid of them that they usually looked the other way when they were around. In the past couple of months the hooligans had beaten up several students who had asked them to leave. Already feeling impotent about their own future and the future of the country, and frustrated with the deplorable living conditions on campus, most students found the hooligan problem to be the last straw.

Law students at Beida called for a demonstration, and some
two thousand students marched to the Public Security Bureau to
demand that those responsible for the murder be severely punished. Both the vice mayor of Beijing and the head of the Public
Security Bureau promised that the guilty parties would be dealt
with swiftly, and within twenty-four hours six hooligans had
been arrested. They were tried; the trigger man was sentenced
to death, and the other five were given long prison terms. These
severe sentences were clearly the result of the students' demonstration for justice, but the government's response was an easy
one, I thought. It merely placated the demonstrators in one
particular case; no real changes came about in the system. It was
a shallow victory.

Although most students were satisfied with the outcome of
this case, *dazibao* were posted all over the Beida campus criticizing the justice system. On the night of June 3, I looked out of my
dorm room and saw hundreds gathering in the Triangle. The
meeting began when a student at the front of the crowd put
down a wooden stool and clapped his hands. As if on cue,
everyone sat down quietly. Several graduate students gave
speeches, which were now about much more than hooliganism;
the speakers were using the student's murder as an occasion to
make antigovernment remarks.

I went outside to get a closer look. The students were talking
about unemployment, inflation, the problems in education —
almost everything that was wrong with the country. As they
went on, they became more and more radical. I was a little
startled when one of them, a graduate student named Xiong
Yan, said bluntly, "In the last forty years, we got rid of the
Guomindang and welcomed the Communist Party. And since
then, with all the power struggles and changes in the Party
leadership, all we really got each time was a hungrier devil in
exchange for a full-bellied one."

The next night students gathered again in the Triangle. This
time I worked my way into the crowd and sat with them. Now
the speakers were criticizing the Beida Student Association for

its ineffectiveness. "The student association is another Party organ," one person railed. "It does not represent the will of the students. We should get rid of it and form an association that will truly represent us."

As an officer in the association, I felt the speeches were directed at me. At first I thought they were too harsh, but as other students continued to talk, I began to see that they were right. We needed a student group that could do more to address our problems. I don't know what moved me at this point, but I stood up.

"My name is Shen Tong, and I am a member of the Beida Student Association. I am in charge of public affairs and liaison," I announced loudly. "The speakers are right in criticizing the student association, but we should allow it to exist. It is part of democracy that all groups have the right to be. But I agree with what the students here have said. We need to organize a group that is more independent."

By announcing my name, I had gained a measure of credibility, but it was very dangerous for me to have identified myself openly. The Public Security Bureau always sent spies to every student gathering to report who was there and what was said.

After the meeting came to an end, I walked over and introduced myself to the activists. One of them was a graduate engineering student named Feng Congde, and another, Liu Gang, had connections with dissidents and intellectuals off campus. That night, June 4, eleven of us founded the Committee of Action, which we called a human rights organization. I was the only novice; the others were all graduate students, many of them key figures of the Wednesday Forum, an unofficial group that met every week on a grassy knoll surrounding the Miguel Cervantes statue to hear guest speakers talk about political and economic reform. Winston Lord, then the U.S. ambassador to China, and Fang Lizhi were among the speakers at these gatherings. The forums were organized by students, but the rumor on campus was that they were backed by a number of famous young dissidents.

We filled out a name chart and signed our names, indicating our willingness to stand behind the committee's work publicly. I could tell that some of the committee members were having second thoughts about this, so I pointed out that no matter how careful we were, everything we did would be found out anyway. "We may as well let everyone know exactly what we are doing," I said before we left the Triangle. "Otherwise, we will be no different from the government."

I thought our most important work would be keeping our fellow students informed of what we were doing and what we planned to do. One of the committee members managed to get us the use of an office at the philosophy department's branch of the Communist Youth League, and soon we were using their photocopying machines to publish a leaflet announcing the formation of our group. We scheduled a rally in Tiananmen Square for June 8 and drafted a list of demands of the government: a free press, human rights for all, freedom of thought, pay raises for teachers and intellectuals, educational reform, and open debate on the legality of the ban on demonstrations that had been put in place after the 1986 movement. I was so excited to be part of a group that was actually doing something worthwhile that I didn't mind taking on a lot of the legwork, so I was the one who ran off copies of our leaflets, distributed them to every dorm room at Beida, contacted the press, and checked the weather prediction for the day of the rally.

At one of our meetings I suggested that we should always air our demands through proper legal channels, because the government would be more likely to consider them and would have less reason to say we were an illegal group. To do this, the committee decided to contact various members of the County People's Congress and ask them to present our agenda at their next meeting. We also hoped they would forward our demands to the National People's Congress.

We tried to call Li Shuxian, Fang Lizhi's wife, who was a member of the County People's Congress, but we never got through. Every time we tried to place the call, we got a busy signal before we had even finished dialing, so we suspected that her phone had been tampered with. After a few times we stopped trying, particularly because I was beginning to have second thoughts about contacting her. Fang Lizhi had been expelled by the Party and branded a dissident in 1987; associating with him might hurt us more than help us.

Almost immediately after we formed the Committee of Action, we could tell that we were all being watched. Whenever we met, black cars with tinted windows, probably from the Public Security Bureau, were parked nearby. We began walking from place to place during every meeting to try to shake them.

One of my friends, an official of the Communist Youth League on campus, told me that I was being reported on daily by students in the youth league who worked for the Public Security Bureau. (He told me this because we had been friends since the Beida Student Association shared the profits from the fashion show with his group.) He said that spies were sent to the Triangle to watch what happened and report what the activists said. "I know you're the one they say is always wearing a khaki-colored jacket," he told me.

I didn't see my roommates much during those few days, because I returned to my room very late at night and left early in the morning. Whenever I wasn't in class, I was at the committee headquarters, running off leaflets and making contacts with the newspapers.

On June 7, the day before the rally was scheduled, I went to see my sister at her dormitory. Over and over again she told me that I was being childish and naive and that I didn't realize how dangerous the Committee of Action was. Many of my classmates also said I was stupid to become so involved. Qing's roommates laughingly claimed that they would be bringing little drums and horns to the demonstration, but I was exhausted and didn't think this was funny.

The first sign that the authorities planned to crack down on us appeared when I went to our office that afternoon and found several strangers in the room. I asked them where the other committee members were, but they didn't answer.

"Where are the leaflets we ran off?" I asked.

"There are no leaflets here," one of them said. "This is the office of the philosophy department branch of the Communist Youth League. No underground activities take place here. You should not come here any longer."

"I'm just getting my things," I said. I collected my books and left. Later another committee member told me that the man I had spoken with at the office was the teacher who had originally let us use the space. He had been pressured by the authorities to kick us out. The Communist Youth League's central office had also sent representatives to every dorm room to question students about our activities.

I had asked Dakun to walk beside me at the rally, and in the early evening he came to Beida to be with me. Soon after he arrived, the campus loudspeakers began broadcasting a warning: "There is a small clique of people who are manipulating the enthusiasm of the students who support reform and the Communist Party. They are creating chaos. They are seeking to destroy socialism." The government had made this same announcement in Tiananmen Square in 1976, at the Democracy Wall in 1979, and after the student movement in 1986. Whenever it used the phrase "a small clique of counterrevolutionaries," there was serious trouble for those involved. There was no mistaking who the small clique was this time — it was the eleven of us on the Committee of Action. And I had made it clear from all the running around I had done that I was an active member. Suddenly I felt a shiver go through my body.

The Communist Party has always taken the kind of organizing we were doing very seriously. We were a grassroots group with a clearly stated agenda, and we also had the ability to publish what we thought was wrong with the government. The authorities had had no trouble figuring out what we were up to, because we had made such a point of doing everything in the open. In this situation, they didn't care that we were in favor of freedom of thought and human rights; they labeled our activities antisocialist and therefore counterrevolutionary. The Party has always crushed groups like ours in their infancy.

The announcement over the loudspeaker had exactly the effect that was intended, because I began to get a bad feeling about what might happen and asked Dakun to leave.

"I'm not going," he said. "I'm staying here with you tonight."

I knew it was too late for me to get out of trouble. I felt like a character in a poem I had memorized as a child, which described the feelings of an assassin who was sent to kill the first Qin emperor and who realized when he was departing on his mission that there was no turning back for him. There was no turning back for me now.

The committee was meeting one last time that night at the Cervantes statue. On my way there, I walked through the Triangle and saw a number of Communist Youth League spies hanging around. Halfway to the meeting place on the other side of campus, I met up with Xiong Yan and two others. They all seemed very anxious.

"Don't go there," Xiong Yan said. "The few people who got there early are being tailed by plainclothes policemen. It's no use — many of the committee members are not going to show up at all."

I was angry because our plans were ruined. The public announcement that night had frightened even the leadership. The four of us stood in the Triangle and decided that we had only one thing left to do. "We should disband our committee and try to distance it from the demonstration tomorrow," I said.

Xiong Yan and some of the others were so afraid at this point that they didn't even want to hold a meeting to draft a statement that we were disbanding, and some members had quit and were never heard from again. Later that night, the rest of us got together one last time in a room in No. 38 dormitory, which was five minutes' walk from the Triangle. As I headed there, I was followed at a little distance by a black car. I tried to relax and walk normally, pretending that nothing was happening, but it was hard.

Two students stood outside the room to warn us in case the authorities came in and caught us. We were all very tense and jumpy. I asked one of the committee members whose calligraphy was good to write a *dazibao* announcing our intentions.

"We must say first that we are not against the Communist Party and socialism," I dictated as he wrote. "Second, the committee was formed to help channel the students' reactions to an unfortunate incident into some constructive changes in our society. Third, the Committee of Action is disbanding because the movement has developed beyond our original intentions. If we continue, our committee's work will be misunderstood. We hereby announce that the committee is disbanded and the scheduled demonstration has been canceled."

We knew that this demonstration was not being held for a strong enough reason. It had started with the death of a graduate student, and no one in the government was sympathetic to us, because they felt they had already dealt with the incident. If we went ahead with our plans, the members of the Committee of Action would probably be punished. What charges we faced would depend on how the authorities decided to view us. They could say that the eleven of us had instigated the whole thing and were entirely responsible for what they thought of as subversive acts, or they could say that we had been the pawns of some more prominent dissidents. In an effort to deny that students were really dissatisfied with the state of the country, the government often said that we were manipulated, either by dissidents or by foreigners. If the officials said that we had been used by others, they might let us off easier. But if they labeled us counterrevolutionaries, it could mean ten years in prison.

At the end of the meeting we decided not to have any more contact with one another, to avoid even the most common, everyday exchanges. We didn't want to give the government any reason to think that we were still together and had simply gone underground. It was already past midnight when one of the committee members took the finished *dazibao* to the Triangle. On my way out of No. 38, I saw my friend from the Communist Youth League and some of his colleagues waiting for me outside the door. They quickly surrounded me. "Don't talk, just walk," my friend whispered as they escorted me back to my dorm. He had come to protect me in case the authorities decided to arrest me that night.

I finally convinced Dakun not to stay at Beida any longer, and he left. I was too tense to sleep in my dorm, so I went home to be with my family. When I walked into the courtyard, I saw that the lights were still on. My parents were sitting at the dinner table, and from the way they were talking, it seemed that they were preparing for me to go to prison. They didn't scold me. In fact, they were both very calm.

"I know that we criticize you all the time, and we did tell you not to join these movements," my father said solemnly. "But your mother and I have given this a lot of thought. When you are in prison, we will come to see you no matter how much trouble that may bring us. You will always be our son."

Those words meant a lot, so much that I didn't know how to reply. But hearing my parents talk about my going to prison frightened me even more. People in China sometimes go to prison for fifteen years just for attending rallies and watching from the sidelines. The government believes that even that much involvement makes you a troublemaker. The officials don't give you a chance to explain why you were there. And if you join in calling out slogans — like Wei Jingsheng's call for a Fifth Modernization during the Democracy Wall Movement — you can spend the rest of your life in jail.

I slept for only a few hours and in the morning rushed back to school to go to class. I went to all of my classes that day and didn't go anywhere near Tiananmen Square. Everyone knew the rally was supposed to take place, but only a few scattered groups of students went to the square. I was trying so hard to appear uninvolved that when some students came to my dorm room and asked me what was going on, I told them I didn't know anything. In fact, I made a point of not knowing anything. Still, I knew that each Committee of Action member would be questioned, so I was waiting nervously.

My friend Tian had warned me that I would probably have to write a self-criticism, maybe even multiple drafts, like the ones he had been forced to write in 1987. He also told me to play dumb and not incriminate myself in any way. Tian was still being watched by the government, and as a way of getting the authorities off his back, he had been applying to American universities. That spring he had been accepted by one of them, and he planned to leave the country in a few weeks, after the semester was over. He urged me to do the same.

Tian's advice turned out to be very helpful. A few days after June 8, as I was studying for my final examinations, a teacher came looking for me at my dorm. A man in his forties, he was responsible for all the students in the biology department and was the same teacher who had overseen Tian's self-criticism. In my head I quickly ran through all the responses I had rehearsed.

I stood up and greeted him politely, but he got straight to the point. "Why don't you tell me what you've been up to the last few days?" he said, without any emotion.

It was time to protect myself. "I was fooled into getting involved," I lied. "I heard the activists making patriotic speeches in the Triangle, and that got me interested. The only reason I participated was to find out exactly what a student movement was. But when I found out that we were being used by radicals, it was my idea to disband."

It didn't go over well. "Don't think we don't know what you've been up to," the teacher said. "We have been getting information about you from another biology student."

It was a shock to find out that someone close to me really was a spy. I suspected it was someone who lived in No. 28, though I never found out for sure. At this point I figured there wasn't much use in lying, because the authorities knew all about my activities. In fact, the teacher told me certain things that only someone at our committee meetings would know. Suddenly my father's fortune-teller friend and his warning to be careful about the friends I chose flashed through my head.

"I want you to write a self-criticism," said the teacher.

"Yes, I will," I answered, "but can't I finish my final exams first?"

"You will not take any finals until you have properly explained your actions," he said, and left my room.

I dashed off a short essay, still trying to give the impression that I was innocent. "I was trying to understand what some members of the student body were up to, since I was head of the Beida Student Association public affairs and liaison department," I wrote. This clearly was not satisfactory to the teacher, who gave me a hard time about it.

"What is this?" he asked me, waving the single page at me. "You have to write this again. You must account for your actions every minute of every day. Write down what foreign counter-revolutionary groups you were in contact with. Was it China Spring?" This is a political organization made up of Chinese scholars living in the United States. "Tell me what the background of the political action committee is. Who are the black hands behind your group? What do the wooden stool and the hand clap at the beginning of your meetings mean? Where did you get that signal?"

He clearly meant business, so I tried a different tack. "You're right," I said. "My attitude is not correct. I didn't realize how important this assignment is. But you have to help me, because I've never written a self-criticism. After I finish a draft, let me know what's wrong with it and help me revise it. This way I will learn from the experience. I will work on another draft."

"Now you have the right attitude," he agreed. "Try it again."

My second report was twelve pages long, but still listed only the things I knew they knew already, except for some berating of myself for being ignorant and childish. "I was a fool for mistaking a political movement for a student gathering," I wrote. "I may have unwittingly allowed myself to be used by the black hands behind the scene, and I regret it very much."

I was stalling as long as possible in the hope that this would blow over quickly. I didn't sign the final draft of my self-criticism, which I thought of as a small way of denying what I had written. It was purely symbolic, because the drafts were in my handwriting and had my name printed at the top.

Right after finals, I was due to leave Beijing for a botany internship in a mountainous region in central China. The day I left, I mailed the last draft to the teacher and sent my application forms, which Tian had given me, to three American universities. It was probably too late for me to be admitted for the fall, but I took a chance anyway.

When I came back from the summer internship, the teacher never spoke to me about my self-criticism, but I was expelled from the Beida Student Association. The government was no longer pressuring me, but everyone I knew took the chance to say that I'd been a fool. A friend who was a big businessman on campus said, "Don't bother with politics. You're no revolutionary," referring to the time I had sold 101, the hair cream.

I also got into a big fight with my father, who was relieved that I wasn't going to jail but took this opportunity to criticize me for what I had done. "It's the Year of the Dragon, the Year of the Dragon," he kept saying. "You were told not to get involved."

At first I thought he was joking about the fortune teller, but then I saw that he was serious.

"You are so stubborn. You don't think before you act," he said angrily. "You don't listen to your sister and her friends. They told you not to get involved."

"I didn't like their attitude," I replied defiantly.

"They were telling you that for your own good," he explained patiently.

My mother was the only one who said anything in my defense. "If the students don't stand up, who will?" she said. "Yes, they're foolish, but who else besides the students is going to speak up?"

I was very angry with my father for giving me a hard time about something that had already happened. I had done what I thought was right, and all he could think was that the Year of the Dragon was an unlucky year. I remembered that when my sister had started college, in 1984, the year Beida first instituted the lights-out policy as a reaction to student protests, my father had disagreed with the school's actions and had said, "Students who don't take part in protests are not truly good students." This remark had made an impression on me because it was out of character, given his cautious nature.

"You once said that those who don't participate in student movements are not truly good students," I shot back.

My father didn't answer me. He just walked away.

I had trouble sleeping that night, because I couldn't understand his reaction, and when I pushed him to tell me why he felt the way he did, he couldn't explain himself. I kept thinking about this for days, tossing it around in my head, trying to figure out the mixed signals. Finally, I was so bothered that I asked my sister what I should do.

"What is so hard for you to understand?" she said.

"He doesn't make any sense to me," I said. "One minute he's agreeing with all of the things I'm trying to do, and the next minute he's angry at me."

"It's not that he doesn't agree with you, that there aren't things that need to be changed," she replied. "He just doesn't want to see his only son in jail."

For the rest of the summer I thought a lot about my father and about what my sister had said. When nothing much was happening in the student movement, it was easier for me to convince myself not to get involved again. I had to realize, as my father had, that those who are active in political protests in China are putting their future in danger.

When my junior year began, I was determined to stay out of trouble. As I expected, none of the American schools I had applied to accepted me, because my applications arrived too late and I hadn't taken the TOEFL exam. I began memorizing the Chinese-English dictionary to prepare for the test and spending much of my time in the library. Going to the United States didn't excite me much, but it was probably the smart thing to do. I moved into Tian's old room on the second floor of No. 28, which was small, but I had only one roommate instead of five. The room also had an electric cord plugged into the hall light so we could read even after lights out.

In my new, quiet surroundings, I realized that I didn't know enough about the demands on the Committee of Action's list and that my actions had been based on emotions. I needed to learn more about things like democracy, human rights, censorship, and educational reform so that I could figure out what they meant to me. I went through countless books then, some of them about American history and the makeup of other democratic societies, and I began discussing what I read with my new roommate, Sheng Pei, and two others on my floor, Qing Nian and Hong. Together we discovered how valuable it was to share our ideas on everything from the philosophy of science to Zen Buddhism. Hong was as interested in poetry as I was, and we often exchanged collections of Chinese poems as well as those by Kahlil Gibran. During my first two years of college I had been overlooking a wonderful resource — my classmates. All of us had come to Beida expecting it to be a place where we would meet great people and learn from them. But the great people I had been waiting to meet were my fellow students.

I rarely went to class that semester and instead read my schoolbooks, studied English, and had hours of conversations with friends. One person I spent a lot of time with was an exchange student from Portugal named Victor who was studying Chinese philosophy. We met through a tutoring program; Victor helped me with my English, and I helped him with Chinese. One day, after I had told him about the girl I'd met at West Lake and hoped to see again in twenty years, he said, "I told your story to a friend of mine from Brazil, and she was very moved. She wants to meet you very much."

I had just broken up with Xiaoying and was studying hard for the TOEFL exam, so I didn't want to meet anyone new. But after

Victor pushed me a couple of times, I finally went to see his friend one day after class. When I got to her room, she was being interviewed by a reporter writing a story about foreigners living and studying in China. I was immediately struck by her curly blond hair and by her height.

"I'm Shen Tong. You wanted to see me?" I said, feeling a little embarrassed by the situation.

"Ah yes. I'm Andrea," she said. "I would like very much to talk to you."

It was love at first sight. I didn't do anything for two weeks but be with Andrea. She was different from anyone I had ever met. It was quite odd at first to hear a Westerner speak such perfect Chinese, but in many ways Andrea *was* Chinese, because she had been born and raised in Beijing. Her sensibility for a culture other than her own was very attractive to me. We also had many things in common: we both liked music, and she read and loved the same poetry I did.

Andrea's parents were Brazilian journalists, and she had gone to high school in Brazil. She was studying economics at Beida, and most of her friends were also from other countries, because foreign students lived in separate dorms from the Chinese students. I liked her friends, but through them I learned some very disquieting things about what foreigners think about the Chinese. Some of them looked down on us and criticized us for having bad manners, like the nasty habit some people have of spitting in public places. I had never really thought of myself as being part of an ethnic group or having any nationality at all, but the more time I spent with Andrea's friends, the more Chinese I felt. They were right in some of their criticisms, but they had no reason to lump all Chinese together. I became a little defensive, thinking to myself, *I am Chinese and I must acknowledge it.* When I was around foreigners, China seemed very real to me, and my awareness of what it meant to be Chinese was strengthened.

I also found that many Chinese just accepted the fact that foreigners were a privileged class in China. Whenever I took a taxi with Andrea, the driver treated us better if we paid in foreign currency. Some Chinese went out of their way to be nice to me in order to please Andrea, and others were rude to me because they thought I was latching on to a foreigner for my own advantage.

As Andrea and I grew closer, I told her how I had gotten into trouble for my activities on the Committee of Action the semester before. She saw that I was still very interested in politics, so she bought me issues of the Hong Kong political magazines, which I, as a Chinese, had no way of buying. These magazines reported many things that the Chinese government tried to keep from us, and I brought them to the discussions I had with my dormmates. The information we got from their articles helped us read between the lines of the official Chinese news reports.

By the middle of the semester, the discussions in my dorm room had become such an important part of our life at Beida that when our schoolwork started preventing them from happening spontaneously, we decided to formalize them. One night each week, seven of us went out to dinner at a restaurant off campus and held our talks over Mongolian hot-pot and beer. We argued and exchanged ideas about everything from Karl Popper to Heisenberg's uncertainty principle. After a few weeks of this, we agreed to hold more regular meetings on Wednesday evenings, in the tradition of the Wednesday Forum, and to take minutes of our discussions. We also decided to keep the group small and focus on academic matters, in an effort to stay out of political trouble. Our motto was "Use rational means to approach all things."

"The group needs a symbolic name," I said. Everyone was quiet while we all tried to think of one. "How about the Olympic Institute?" I suggested.

No one liked this name until I told them why I had thought of it. "This was the name of Einstein's group," I said. "The three members of the original Olympic Institute were a physicist, a mathematician, and a philosopher, which shows that their interests were as varied as ours are. And Olympus is a mountain in the Greek myths. We should take a name connected with the

Greek gods, because they have human weaknesses. They are not perfect, so people will see that we don't think of ourselves as perfect either."

My explanation convinced them, and we excitedly got started with the new Olympic Institute. After I asked a number of Beida's young professors to be our advisers, we held our first meeting in my dorm room. It lasted five hours. Two graduate students studying scientific philosophy were the guest speakers, and after they talked about what they were concentrating on, they allowed us to ask them questions.

Over the next few weeks our meetings varied: when we didn't have a speaker scheduled, we passed around the Hong Kong magazines, like *Zheng Ming* and *The Nineties*, and discussed current politics. There was some disagreement in the group about contacting the more famous dissidents, like Fang Lizhi and Li Shuxian, but we finally decided that because we were all science majors, such people could speak to us on scientific topics. If the discussion following the lectures moved on to more political subjects, that would be all right.

When educational reform came up at one of these meetings, we all started learning about different educational systems. I talked to Andrea and her friends about education in Brazil, the United States, and other countries. Somewhere in the Olympic Institute discussions, we concluded that by the time most Chinese students were nearing the date of the college entrance exam, they weren't prepared for it at all. We kicked around the idea of starting an alternative private school that would help students tie up all of the subjects taught in high school in a way that would lead them to think for themselves.

My former roommate the Giant, who was an American citizen and was planning to return to the United States to continue his graduate studies, came up to me and said privately, "If we can start this alternative school, I won't go back to America. I'll stay here and see it through with you. I have $6000 of savings that my parents put away for me in the United States. We can use that as our seed money." I was really touched.

Now that I was giving so much time to the Olympic Institute, I was only halfheartedly preparing for the TOEFL exam. In my heart, I didn't want to leave China, and I told my friends that I wasn't going to go to the United States because there was so much I wanted to do at home.

One night when we were walking back from the dining hall, my roommate, Sheng Pei, and I saw a poster about a discussion of a new political theory that was being held in one of the large classrooms. There were only a few people in the room when we got there, so we waited outside, assuming that others were on the way. Then someone came out and asked if we were there for the discussion group. He was one of the organizers, and he asked us to come in, so we joined the six people already there and began talking.

One of the others, Yang Tao, was a nineteen-year-old freshman who immediately impressed me as a clear thinker. "China does not need a movement for national salvation," he said. "We aren't fighting external enemies like the Japanese anymore. Our leaders are always promoting national salvation movements that aren't based on any clear ideology, the best example being the Cultural Revolution. What China needs now is personal liberation. What our generation needs to do is to push for individual freedom."

Yang Tao sounded very confident when he spoke, and I agreed with everything he said. But as soon as he finished speaking, he stuck out his tongue like a lizard, showing that he was a little embarrassed about talking in public. He seemed like a combination of a twelve-year-old boy and a fifty-year-old man. I liked him right away.

When it was my turn to speak, I said, "Mao was the most obvious example that modern China still has an emperor. Now we have Deng Xiaoping as an emperor. In between, how did such an untalented politician as Hua Guofeng get the Party's support? It's clear now that he was only a temporary caretaker until another emperor emerged. His only achievements in the time he was Party secretary were building the Mao mausoleum and publishing a fifth book of Mao's selected writings."

The group broke up after lights out, and Sheng Pei and I walked back to the dorm with Yang Tao, who told us that he was part of a weekly discussion group and invited us to come.

"What discussion group is that?" I asked him.

"We call ourselves the Democracy Salon," he said.

"Then you must know Wang Dan," I said excitedly. "I read about him in the newspaper and I've tried to look for him." The Beida school newspaper had published an article the previous semester about an unofficial campus group called the Democracy Salon and its organizer, a first-year history student named Wang Dan. I had wanted to meet him ever since I read it.

"By the way, what's your name?" Yang Tao asked.

"I'm Shen Tong. I'm a third-year biology student."

"Oh, I know who you are. You were on the Committee of Action," he said.

When we got to No. 28, we invited Yang Tao up to our room and talked for several more hours. It turned out that he was Wang Dan's right-hand man in the Democracy Salon. Their group's advisers included people such as the noted political scientist Yan Jiaqi and several of the same young professors we were interested in reaching. My roommate and I told Yang Tao all about the Olympic Institute.

"Wang Dan is incredibly smart," he said. "He has great connections with activists off campus. If you'd like, I could arrange for our two groups to meet."

"I'd like that very much," I said, glad that we had gone to the meeting that night.

I showed him the latest copy of *Zheng Ming* magazine that Andrea had gotten for me. I would be in trouble if Yang Tao reported that I had an illegal publication, but I knew that I could trust him. Those of us who were interested in being active in democracy movements, even at this low level, almost felt that we were part of a brotherhood. Sharing the Hong Kong magazines was a gesture of trust and the way we established a bond.

When Yang Tao looked at the issue date, he was very impressed. "We have a few issues from last year, but not the latest," he said. Before he left, he told us to meet him the next day in Wang Dan's room in No. 30. I went to bed excited.

The next day I walked into Wang Dan's dorm room with three other Olympic Institute members, and Yang Tao came over to greet us. A couple of students were sitting on the bunk beds, and a lanky young man wearing glasses was standing in the corner. Yang Tao pointed to him and said, "Shen Tong, that's Wang Dan."

"I hear you have the latest issues of *Zheng Ming* and *The Nineties*. Let's see them," he said abruptly.

He spoke very little and seemed to be holding himself back, but I figured a lot of people on campus must try to talk to him and that probably made him impatient. I gave him the magazines. Not knowing how else to begin a conversation, I said, "How did the Democracy Salon get started?"

"We're leftovers from the Wednesday Forum," he replied, not looking at anyone in particular. "When that was disbanded we started up again, using another name."

Wang Dan was really a second-year student, but he had changed his major and had to repeat the first year. Maybe he was shy or had a lot on his mind, but he didn't say much after that. While the others in his group were talking with us, he stayed quietly to the side.

Someone suggested merging our two groups, but I was opposed. "I think it's better to keep separate," I said. "If we were to become involved in any kind of student movement and the government cracked down, perhaps one of our groups would be able to stay alive even if the other were disbanded."

Wang Dan seemed to think for a moment, then suddenly spoke up. "I agree," he said. "We should have a tacit agreement with your Olympic Institute to cooperate on all events, but we shouldn't use the same slogans or participate in the same way. Each group must maintain its own integrity." Then he added ominously, "Things will happen this year."

"I know," I said. "The world is already focusing on China's

record on human rights because of the Lhasa incident last December." I had read about the Chinese Communists' brutal treatment of Tibetan protesters in one of the Hong Kong magazines. "And of course we are coming up to the seventieth anniversary of the May Fourth Movement."

Wang Dan became more engaged as we talked about the possibilities of student movements. "The National People's Congress will convene this spring," he said. "July fourteenth is the two hundredth anniversary of the French Revolution. October first is the fortieth anniversary of Liberation."

"Many of the old Party cadres will want a big celebration, because they'll never live to see the next major anniversary," I said. As everyone laughed at this, I continued, "But if they want to celebrate, things will happen."

Wang Dan nodded. "This is a very important year."

Even though the Olympic Institute was primarily a scientific, not political, group, we agreed to support the activities of the Democracy Salon. If they posted a *dazibao*, we would write one echoing it. When we made this agreement, we were clear about what it could mean: national movements had been started by one or two *dazibao* posted at the Beida Triangle. The Democracy Salon would also share with us all their resources, especially Wang Dan's off-campus contacts, and we would help them through our contacts with other student groups on campus.

This meeting was a turning point for the Olympic Institute. Many of our members were opposed to the alliance with Wang Dan's group, because it was taking us into dangerous territory. The Olympic Institute had been founded as an academic, scientific discussion group, and we were trying to steer clear of politics. But unconsciously I gravitated toward people like Wang Dan, and under my direction, so did the Olympic Institute.

Shortly after that meeting, I contacted Li Shuxian, a physics professor at Beida and the wife of the dissident astrophysicist Fang Lizhi, and she agreed to speak to our weekly gathering. She brought with her an article Fang Lizhi had written called "China's Hopes and Disappointments." On the same day in early March that she came to our meeting, that article was posted in the Triangle by Wang Dan's group, which made me realize how closely associated Li Shuxian was with the Democracy Salon.

Our meeting with her was an informal talk about a number of things, but the highlight was listening to her tell the misadventure of how she and Fang Lizhi had tried to attend a reception on February 26 hosted by the visiting American president, George Bush. They had been invited by the American embassy and were on their way to the dinner when the police stopped their car, told them they were going the wrong way, and made them get out and walk. They waited for a bus, but none of the buses stopped for them, so they finally made their way to a hotel, where they held a press conference to tell the foreign journalists their story.

Many university students considered Li Shuxian and Fang Lizhi to be champions of human rights, and Li Shuxian's story of how they had handled themselves when harassed by the police was worth more to us than a thousand lectures on those rights. All of the Olympic Institute members who attended this meeting were stirred by her talk, but many were now even more concerned that our group was becoming too political. I felt as if I were being pulled in two directions internally. I was intensely interested in reform activities, but I wanted to maintain the idea that the Olympic Institute was an academic organization.

To calm the others' fears, as well as my own, we turned our attention to a research project on the state of education in China, as a foundation for our private school. We also wanted a clearer picture of what the prospects were for our careers after graduation. We began by going through newspapers, government annuals, publications of the education ministry — everything we could get our hands on. Seven of us devoted every moment we had to the project. If we weren't in class, we were in the libraries at school and all over Beijing. What we discovered was that China's problems with scientific research were caused by problems in our social system. We were shocked by how poorly teachers were paid: most teachers made less than the average factory worker, and teachers' salaries were the same as they had been at the time of Liberation, forty years ago. We were able to find a number of articles that said that countries like Japan, which is known for its superior high-tech industries, have traditionally put a lot of resources into education.

Most of us wanted to go on to graduate studies, so we tried to find out how difficult it would be to get a spot at a research institute and what kind of life we would have if we did. The way the government allocated funds for scientific research seemed completely out of line to us. Most of the money went to high-profile projects like rocket research and nuclear fission; projects that would better meet the needs of the country, such as those in transportation, were neglected. We also discovered that athletes received more government support than research scientists; the authorities gave enormous amounts of money to athletes so that their successes in international competition could be used as propaganda tools. Consequently, the chances of moving ahead in a career as a researcher were very slim. No matter how hard many graduate students worked, their results belonged to the professors. That is true in other countries as well, but in China there are few guarantees that a hardworking researcher who gets good results will advance.

We were helped in some of our investigation by Chang Jin, an education major who lived on the fourth floor of No. 28 and who was a core member of Beida's student committee on education, which gave him access to official documents. During our research period, he often came to my room and talked to us about educational reform.

When we saw what we had compiled, I suggested that we write a paper and publish it under the pen name Olympia. In our report we discussed nine major problems and made seven suggestions, one of which was to establish a system of law to govern how researchers are paid and treated, their working conditions, and patent rights. I hand-wrote the report through eight drafts. By the fifth and sixth drafts, two of our members had withdrawn from the Olympic Institute because it was clear that our paper was about much more than scientific research or educational reform; it was a critique of the political system. One of those who left said to me, "My father told me that the political situation this year may be volatile. I don't think the Olympic Institute should get involved in anything remotely political or controversial." No one had said anything about politics during our study, but the problems of scientific research were so closely tied to the failure of China's social and political system that it was hard to keep politics out.

I was pleased that the project had become more than it had set out to be. It was just what I had wanted — an indirect and subtle way to get back into the political debate. It was also a way of trying to address a few of China's problems in detail from our perspective as students, rather than focusing on the whole range of the country's difficulties.

The final report, which was five thousand words long, was called "Problems and Suggestions for China's Current Basic Scientific Research." We held a meeting to discuss what to do next. I wanted to get the paper published and suggested that we contact newspapers. One of the members said we should introduce it as a bill in the National People's Congress, which had traditionally been a rubber stamp but in recent years had become more challenging to the Party line. But none of us knew how to get the paper before the congress. For students who had been clamoring for democratic reform, we were extremely ignorant about how the governing bodies worked.

We found out that only members could bring a bill to the body's attention, so after class I asked my professors if I could address my classmates and then announced, "If anyone knows someone who is a member of the National People's Congress, please come see me. I'm trying to get a bill introduced."

I finally tracked down one of the members, an elderly professor at Beida. When I went to his house, he was touched by my initiative and accepted our paper, but he didn't seem to understand much about what was in it. He corrected our grammar, edited our language, and read a condensed two-page version before the meeting of the congress. The article got a strong response. Although it couldn't technically be a bill, several other congressmen signed it, then passed it on to the state council and the National Science Association. We had succeeded in one measure.

We then divided up the newspapers in Beijing and, on our bicycles, went to ask the editors to publish our paper. After a number of places turned us down, the *Guangming Daily* agreed to publish highlights, along with a short interview with me about the Olympic Institute and the purpose of the report. In the interview, I didn't criticize the system too harshly, because I didn't want to jeopardize getting in the paper. I said we were all science students concerned about the future of research, and I concluded by stating, "I think college students should increase their participation in society." This may seem like a throwaway line, but Chinese readers are used to looking for hidden meanings in newspaper articles, so they knew I was saying that students should become catalysts for social change.

I also wanted our report to be in the Beida school newspaper, but the top editors had already gotten into trouble for their profile of Wang Dan and the Democracy Salon. Therefore I talked to the editor of the fourth page, which was not the usual place for such reports, and he published the entire thing. I don't think he had considered its contents very carefully.

Shortly afterward, at the end of March, Wang Dan introduced me to a man in his mid-thirties who was from Anhui Province. This man had graduated from Qinghua University and had been an activist during the Democracy Wall Movement. After the government arrested the leaders of that protest, he and others like him had fled Beijing and settled in other cities, but he had continued working for democratic reform by secretly organizing workers and journalists in Anhui. There he had set up a democracy salon that had more than three hundred members, and now he and four others were traveling all over the country to establish contacts with political activists among workers, journalists, and students.

For the next three days, some of the five were constantly in my room, talking. They went without sleep and stopped only for a quick bite to eat. Sometimes, when my friends in the Olympic Institute thought the conversation wasn't too political, they sat in. I kept the door closed so that others couldn't hear what we were discussing, but my dormmates gave me dirty looks whenever I walked down the hall to the latrine.

The man from Anhui laid out what he saw as the whole picture of the country and gave reasons why he thought it was time for the students to mount a massive movement. He made several major points:

1. The intellectuals, who were already exerting pressure on the government for more rapid reform, could come together and form an opposition party.
2. China's economy was very unstable, having experienced seven major policy changes in two years. The conservatives and the reformers within the Party were fighting, and the news from Hong Kong was that General Secretary Zhao Ziyang was preparing to attack the conservative elements led by Premier Li Peng.
3. The Chinese military had changed in recent years because of the changing economic conditions in the countryside. With the introduction of limited free markets, peasants had more opportunity, so new recruits were joining out of a sense of duty rather than as an escape from the deplorable living conditions in the countryside. Now that they could take advantage of increased free enterprise, most planned to return to civilian life after a few years of service. These recruits were less likely to follow orders blindly than the traditional recruits had been.

    Also, China had reduced its military by one fourth in 1985, and the middle- and lower-ranked officers who remained were educated and would probably sympathize with a student reform movement. High-ranking officers — about four hundred members of the Old Guard — had mixed feelings about Deng Xiaoping and Yang Shangkun, vice chairman of the Military Commission. During China's war with Vietnam, Deng had promoted many middle-level officers who were loyal to him, to the disadvantage of the Old Guard. Yang had very little military experience and used his rank to install his brother and son-in-law in positions of power, which many officers resented. If a student movement were to arise, the military would not necessarily follow Yang's orders.

4. Students were dissatisfied with their chances of getting good jobs and with the corrupt atmosphere in every level of society. They would need very little encouragement to rise up in protest.

5. When Li Peng had issued a directive stopping all construction projects in an effort to bring the economy back under tight central control, almost two million workers had lost their jobs. These workers and their families, who had come from rural areas to take these jobs, were now causing great economic and social pressures on the cities. If unemployed and homeless people got behind the students and intellectuals, they could be a powerful force.

6. The year 1989 was full of significant dates, among them March 29, the tenth anniversary of Wei Jingsheng's arrest as a Democracy Wall leader. "The participants in the Democracy Wall Movement are now scattered all over the country. They have not given up," the man from Anhui said. "They are all waiting for a chance to stand up again. We have to create an opportunity. Every movement before now — in 1979, 1986 — reached a certain level. In 1989 we have to surpass that level in order to achieve real gains."

The last major point he discussed was how to design a new government. "Who do we put forward to take over from Deng Xiaoping if we succeed in getting rid of him?" He mentioned Hu

Yaobang and Zhao Ziyang, both protégés of Deng Xiaoping with reputations as reformers. We all agreed that Hu Yaobang was probably the better of the two.

I wasn't at all prepared to talk about a new government. My friends and I had been talking about social reforms, but we believed they would have to happen over years, or even decades. This man from Anhui was already designing a government he believed would come together soon. I was actually frightened by how radical he was. I admired his courage and frankness, but I wasn't ready to follow his lead. I thought discussing the role of China's intellectuals and the country's long-term political development was more valuable.

When the man saw our blank faces, he asked us to put him in touch with some of Beijing's dissidents. I arranged for him to meet with Li Shuxian, but she was not very enthusiastic about his ideas either. The five visitors were extremely disappointed in us. They had come to Beida hoping to initiate a movement; they wanted to start a hunger strike on April 5, and they invited Wang Dan and me to organize a support group, but both of us declined. We agreed with them about many things, but not their method or timing.

After they left Beida, they met with students at Qinghua University. We heard that they were being followed by Public Security Bureau agents after the man from Anhui gave an interview to a *New York Times* reporter at his hotel. When I saw him again at Beida, I told him to be careful. Several nights later he rushed into my room, his face ashen. "Can I stay here for one night?" he asked.

He said that he had been returning to the Qinghua University dorm where he was staying when he had heard a Public Security Bureau agent asking for him. "He moved out already," the Qinghua student whose room he used had said. The man had hurriedly left, but as he approached the gate of the school, he saw more agents. He had climbed over the wall and run to Beida.

My first instinct was to protect him, because I could clearly see that he was in trouble, but he was a radical organizer and if we were found hiding him, we would be in serious trouble ourselves. After a long talk, my roommate and I decided that it was just too dangerous for him to stay with us. One of the Olympic Institute members offered to take him on a bicycle to the train station.

"I'll be hiding in Tianjin," he said before he left. "I will contact Wang Dan once a week to let you all know that I am safe. If you don't hear from me, it means I've been arrested. Record everything that I did." I write about him now to remember him, because after he left in April we never heard from him again.

The Communist Party is deathly afraid of someone like him, who understands the political situation perfectly and has the courage to travel around the country organizing. The man from Anhui had a powerful effect on Wang Dan and me. By telling us about his travels around China and visits with peasants, factory workers, miners, and soldiers, he gave us a sense of the whole country.

At the time, I didn't think I could ever be as active as he was. I didn't have even a fraction of his commitment to the cause of democratic reform. My weakness and cowardice came through that night when I refused to take him in. I was inspired by his activism, but I also knew my own limitations. I had within me then the same internal battle my father had fought his entire life. This time, I was afraid for myself. I was still telling myself not to get involved — a reflex I had learned through a fear instilled by the government.

· P A R T I I ·

MOVEMENT

· 7 ·

Hu Yaobang
Is Dead

I KNEW MY FATHER had something on his mind when I called him one day shortly after the man from Anhui left. I tried to tell him that we'd gotten our paper published, but he didn't want to talk about that. "I hope you will concentrate on school now," he said. "I don't think you should do any more extracurricular projects." I waited a few seconds more, and he finally told me what was bothering him. "My fortune-teller friend is concerned about you. You passed through the Year of the Dragon without too much harm, but you should be doubly careful now. This is the Year of the Snake. When one escapes calamity in the Year of the Dragon, the snake can turn into the dragon and bring much more evil. I've told you I don't really believe in this, but you should be careful." I didn't know whether to laugh or cry at this superstition. I didn't say a word, just listened. "The fortune teller said you should lie low this year and nothing will happen to you. But if you don't, your life will change forever."

I went back to my dorm room wondering whether my father took this fortune teller seriously or was using him to keep me out of trouble. I couldn't help thinking about it. I knew I was being slowly drawn into becoming politically active again, and because I had spent so much time writing the research paper and getting it published, I was terribly behind in my classwork. Whether or not I believed the fortune teller, I thought, I should concentrate on school and stay out of politics.

April 15, Saturday

In the afternoon I was walking back to my dorm from the library when I saw lots of people reading *dazibao* in the Triangle. I worked my way over to the bulletin boards and saw black-and-white portraits of Hu Yaobang, who the *dazibao* said had died. Hu Yaobang had become something of a hero since he had been made the scapegoat of the 1986 student movement and ousted as general secretary, and many of us had hoped that he would be brought back someday to lead China on the road to reform. I ran into No. 29 to call my father at work.

"Dad, Hu Yaobang died," I said as soon as he answered.

"What are you talking about? That can't be true," he said. Though my father worked for the Beijing municipal government, the news hadn't reached him yet. "Don't worry about these rumors, just work on your studies," he counseled before hanging up.

On my way back to the Triangle, I began to doubt the news myself, thinking it must be a joke concocted by the graduate students in the Chinese language department who had written the *dazibao*. But by now many Hong Kong journalists had come to the Triangle, and they confirmed that Hu Yaobang had died that morning at 7:45. They showed us drafts of their reports on his death, which had already appeared in the Hong Kong papers. I went back to my dorm, sat on my bed, and thought, *Hu Yaobang is dead.* I lay down, feeling very tired. I hadn't slept much in weeks, since I had spent every waking moment working on our education report and talking to the visitors from Anhui.

I closed my eyes and remembered what my father had said about Hu Yaobang. In 1956, when my father was a freshman at Beida, Hu had come to the school to encourage students to criticize the Party. But as soon as they spoke up, the government launched its Anti-Rightist Campaign. "I don't trust him," my father had said. I thought old Hu was rather timid compared to the arrogant Deng Xiaoping, but like many other students, I placed a lot of my hope in him, because he had always been one of the more open-minded and honest of the Party leaders.

As the news traveled, the Olympic Institute members gathered in my room. "Old Hu is dead," I said. "Should we do something?" No one had any ideas. "Why don't we just make a banner and hang it?" I suggested. One of the guys had just come back from the computer room and had sheets of computer paper, so Sheng Pei, a good calligrapher, wrote in very large characters: "Yaobang is gone. We mourn." We hung the long computer paper out of our second-floor window so it faced the Triangle.

More and more *dazibao* went up, and the Triangle soon became crowded with people who had come to read the posters. Everyone in the Beida community immediately recognized Hu Yaobang's death as much more than the passing of a Party official. There seemed to be an outpouring of emotion over what he had come to represent. To honor him at the time of his death was a way of challenging the current Party hierarchy. I didn't think much would happen, though — just this flurry of *dazibao* and then things would calm down. The other members of the Olympic Institute and I went out and read all of the *dazibao*, which gave us something to discuss at our weekly meeting. That was the extent of our participation that day.

This happened on a Saturday, and my sister had invited me to a party her friends were having that night. I was meeting Andrea at the Friendship Hotel before we went to the party together, and as I walked up to her, I saw that she was surrounded by several Chinese students who seemed to be interviewing her.

"You should talk to him," she said, pointing to me.

The students, who were from the journalism department of People's University, wanted to know what was happening at Beida, so they had asked her, thinking that a foreign student would speak more frankly than a Chinese one. I was careful about what I said.

"Hu Yaobang's death has the potential to start a student movement," I stated. "How are things at People's University?"

"It's getting exciting," one of them answered. "There are *dazibao* everywhere. Someone drew a picture of Li Peng as a pig, and it's on public display."

When we got to the party, no one was talking about Hu Yaobang's death, which surprised me. One of the people there, a big businessman on campus, walked up to me and said, "So, Shen Tong, what have you been up to lately?"

"I've been getting a paper on scientific research published. But you wouldn't know anything about it — you barely finished grammar school," I joked.

"I hope you're not getting involved in whatever happens this time," he said seriously. "Your sister tells me that you're applying to go abroad. If you screw up your chance to leave the country, you'll regret it for the rest of your life."

I couldn't tell him or anyone in my family that I didn't want to leave China. No one, except my closest friends in the Olympic Institute, would understand. Almost every university student wanted to leave the country; even Qing, who had just graduated from Beida, was applying to American graduate schools. If I told them I wanted to stay in China, they would think I was insane.

April 17, Monday

More and more *dazibao* began appearing in the Triangle. No longer just memorials to Hu Yaobang, they included inflammatory declarations like "Those who should die don't die."

Sheng Pei came into our room and said, "Wang Dan is fund-raising on campus."

"What's he raising money for?" I asked.

"He wants to buy a floral wreath for Hu Yaobang," he said.

"That's a good idea. Has anyone gone to Tiananmen Square?"

Sheng Pei didn't know, but two of the Olympic Institute members, who had ridden their bicycles to the square, told us that a lot of students were gathering there and some were staying overnight. There were wreaths everywhere, and someone had placed a large portrait of Hu Yaobang on the top step of the Monument to the People's Heroes. Many groups were on the streets of Beijing with cardboard boxes, asking for donations to buy flowers. At Beida, some of the students wanted an area on campus set up as a memorial to Hu. I heard that the government, in an effort to make us think it believed that mourning Hu's death was natural and even good, had ordered each work unit to organize its activities so that they didn't get out of hand. This was a signal that the authorities were watching what was happening very carefully.

Wang Dan led a group of Beida students to the National People's Congress that afternoon with seven demands: restore Hu Yaobang's reputation; end the Anti–Bourgeois Liberalism Campaign; guarantee a free press, free speech, and the right to peaceful demonstrations; increase the budget for education; and end official corruption. A movement had begun.

In keeping with our agreement, I thought the Olympic Institute should support Wang Dan and contact intellectuals and dissidents so they could help this student movement turn out to be more than a few days of unorganized protests. "Why don't we call Li Shuxian?" I said.

But some of the other members were against it. "I don't think we should do that now," one said. "Fang Lizhi has become Deng Xiaoping's personal enemy. If we contact him or his wife, the government will have an excuse to label us an illegal group. The whole reason for not merging with Wang Dan was so that we could survive a crackdown even if the Democracy Salon doesn't."

I thought about this, then dropped the idea.

April 18, Tuesday

The next day several schools, including Beida, organized marches to Tiananmen Square. About a thousand students were holding a spontaneous sit-in outside Xinhuamen, the entrance to the Zhongnanhai compound, where the top-ranking Party officials lived. I didn't go to the square because I still wasn't sure how involved I should get. But in the afternoon, when students began coming back and talking excitedly about what was happening there, I couldn't sit still any longer.

That night I gathered the members of the Olympic Institute and told them, "It's time for us to act. If we don't do anything now, we'll miss this chance to take part in these calls for reform. We must give the conservatives a hard time. Who represents the conservatives better than Premier Li Peng? Let's draft leaflets denouncing him."

The others agreed that we should take part in the movement but were nervous about writing leaflets, because circulating them was considered a counterrevolutionary act. "We can find a way to do it without letting anyone know who wrote them," I said.

I wrote eight characters on the leaflet: *Yaobang yiyan: Ado wuguo*, Yaobang's last words: Ado ruins the nation. Ado, a character in the story *Romance of the Three Kingdoms*, was the very stupid son of Liu Bei and inherited his father's throne. Our allusion to him referred to Li Peng, because he was the highest-ranking official and owed his success directly to family connections (Li Peng is Zhou Enlai's foster son).

That night Qing Nian and Ji An, two other Olympic Institute members, and I wrote out three hundred leaflets by hand. Ji An was clearly nervous. "I'm just helping you, I'm not involved in this," he said. "No one else needs to know that I was here writing leaflets with you, all right?"

When we finished, around midnight, Qing Nian and I rode our bicycles to Xinhuamen to distribute our work. The streets were unusually busy for that hour, as many people were coming back from the square. As soon as we turned onto Changan Avenue, we saw more police than were normally there. They were posted on every corner, and they became more obvious the closer we got to the square.

Qing Nian and I left our bicycles on Changan Avenue and walked to Xinhuamen, agreeing that if anything happened, we would just run and not worry about our bicycles. We split up the leaflets and stuck them in our jackets. A crowd of students was seated directly in front of Xinhuamen, and a crowd of onlookers was standing behind them. Qing Nian and I edged our way into the standing crowd, feeling a bit afraid because many of the people around us were clearly plainclothes police. We needed to find a way to distribute the leaflets without being noticed, and I decided it was best just to throw all of them at once instead of handing out one or two at a time.

I turned around and saw Qing Nian's pale face. He didn't have the nerve to go through with it. "Give them to me," I said to him. "I'll do it." I took all of his leaflets from him. Then, standing behind two people who were straining to see what was going on in front, I took the whole stack of three hundred leaflets, and after practicing the gesture several times so no one would notice it, I threw them into the crowd. People's hands went up in the air and grabbed the sheets of paper as they fluttered to the ground. They were fighting one another to get a look at them, and they were staring right at me.

My body tensed, and I felt a cold shiver and then a hot flush. If a plainclothes policeman was around, he would report me immediately. The government would consider what I had done a calculated move, and therefore counterrevolutionary. As Qing Nian and I tried to get away, I heard some people in the crowd asking, "Who's Ado?"

April 19 and 20, Wednesday and Thursday

At our regular Olympic Institute meeting on Wednesday night, I didn't tell anyone what happened when Qing Nian and I distributed the leaflets. I didn't want them to scold me for putting the two of us in danger, nor did I want them to know about it in case the authorities were looking for us. It was hard for us to have our usual meeting with so much going on, so we broke up early.

Sheng Pei and I were reading when we heard what sounded like hundreds of people outside our window. The Triangle looked exactly as it had in 1988. When several student activists began addressing the crowd, I said, "Let's go listen."

"Our country has many problems that need reform," the speaker was saying. "We have to start the change. Let's begin by overthrowing the official student association and establishing one that really represents us." I didn't recognize this person, who was saying the same things we had said the year before. He was a dull speaker, so Sheng Pei and I started to go back upstairs. Then I saw Wang Dan and Yang Tao. Feng Congde and Xiong Yan, who had been on the Committee of Action, were also standing in the center of the crowd.

I ran back into the dorm to wake up the other members of the Olympic Institute. The first one I grabbed was my old roommate the Giant. "If they're starting an organization, we should be in it," I said. "We can't miss this chance." We rounded up the others and went back outside.

Wang Dan, Yang Tao, and several others were now facing the crowd, announcing their names and their majors.

"What's going on?" I asked the students around me.

"They just said that anyone who has the courage to get up, give his name, his major, and what class he's in is automatically a member of the Beida Solidarity Student Union Preparatory Committee."

One by one, Wang Dan, Yang Tao, Xiong Yan, Feng Congde, Chang Jin, Ding Xiaoping, and Ti Bo went forward and spoke. I was all the way in the back with the other Olympic Institute members, anxiously wanting to get up there too. I began squeezing my way through the crowd, but I noticed that none of my friends were following me. They were not sure we should be part of the Preparatory Committee.

I was five or six meters from the speakers when Feng Congde said the meeting was moving to the area in front of the library because the Triangle was getting too crowded. As people started to leave, I finally got to the front.

"Feng Congde, remember me?" I said. I hadn't seen him since the Committee of Action disbanded. "I think the Preparatory Committee should have its own meeting now instead of continuing this large gathering." He was so busy looking for various people in the crowd that he didn't hear me.

Xiong Yan saw me and walked over. "Shen Tong, you're here,"

he said with a smile. "You've got to become part of this committee."

Feng Congde, Xiong Yan, and I walked together to the library. Feng was carrying a wooden stool, and when he found a spot he liked, he put the stool down. I was standing beside him when some people came up and took our photograph, and that's when I thought, *Oh no, I'm in it again.*

The seven people who had addressed the crowd before and given their names took turns speaking again. I wanted to be part of the committee, so I spoke up too.

"Beida is a school with an honorable tradition, a tradition of leading democratic movements," I said, loudly enough for everyone to hear. "But recently Beida has fallen behind other universities. Hu Yaobang's death is the perfect moment. We should seize the chance to recapture our tradition of democracy and science, but we must proceed with reason and planning."

Some students from Qinghua University interrupted me with the news that policemen had surrounded the students in front of Xinhuamen. Three hundred Qinghua students were on their way to give the students at Xinhuamen their support, and they wanted us to go with them. But Wang Dan and Feng Congde were immediately opposed to going, and I agreed. The most important thing now was for the Preparatory Committee to devise a strategy for the movement instead of marching here and there without a plan.

Along with four other Olympic Institute members, I talked to the Qinghua representatives. "I'm sorry, we can't leave Beida right now," I said. "We're trying to establish a leadership committee, and we're not ready to do anything until we are sure of our own organization."

Some of the Beida students in the crowd started shouting, "We want to go to Xinhuamen! We have to support the other students!" Many started forming a line behind the Qinghua students.

"See if you can take their leader aside and talk to him while I try to persuade the Beida people to stay," I told my friends. I stood on the wooden stool and started shouting. "In the last few years, we've had rampant official corruption and lawlessness in our society. Isn't it time that we changed our country?"

"Yes!" the crowd shouted.

"Do you suppose the officials who benefit from corruption, and all others who take advantage of lawlessness, will be the ones to lead us to a better society?"

"No!"

"So the responsibility falls on us, the students," I said, scanning the crowd. I had their attention; no one was leaving. "Hu Yaobang is dead, and we have begun a student movement. Are we trying to create turmoil in society, as the government always accuses us of doing?"

"No!"

"But whenever we march, we stop traffic and create disorder in the streets. Should we change the way we protest?" I asked.

"We should!"

"If we're going to hold orderly rallies, we need organization. I don't mean political organization," I added quickly, hoping that the government spies would not use my words to say that I was from a counterrevolutionary group. "We need organization to preserve order. That is the most important task right now, isn't it?"

"Yes!"

"Then let's not go to Xinhuamen now. Let's stay here and get organized."

"That's right!"

"Look at the Soviet Union. There economic reform is accompanied by political reform," I said. "No one knows what Gorbachev's fate will be — even he's not sure — but he has taken a great step toward democratic reform that our leader has not been able to."

By now the members of the Preparatory Committee were coming forward to finish their speeches. Afterward, as all the students were leaving the library area, we walked to the Cervantes statue for the first meeting of the Preparatory Committee, although Feng Congde and Xiong Yan went to Xinhuamen to see if the Qinghua students were right about what was happening there.

Just after the meeting started, Ding Xiaoping said, "We agreed that the committee would be made up only of those who stood up and announced themselves in the Triangle. Those who did not should leave now."

I was taken aback by this. "I didn't get up to speak in the Triangle because I didn't have a chance to get to the front," I said. "But you saw that I spoke to the crowd in front of the library. Many of you know me. I've worked with student movements before. Why are you asking me to leave?"

Ding Xiaoping said, "You'll have other chances to get involved. Leave now and let us have our meeting."

I couldn't believe I wasn't welcome, but I left. Chang Jin and Yang Tao came after me. "Don't get upset," Yang Tao said.

I turned to Chang Jin, who had helped the Olympic Institute with the research paper. "Why don't you represent the Olympic Institute on the committee and let us know what they decide?" I suggested.

It was 2 a.m. when I got back to my dorm. Several people wearing dark raincoats were putting up *dazibao* in the Triangle, but as I walked toward them, they scurried over to a black car and sped away. I walked up to the bulletin board to read their *dazibao*. It said that Wang Dan had been secretly working with Li Shuxian and had spent all the money he had raised to buy flowers for Hu Yaobang on cigarettes and fancy dinners with friends. "Whenever there are police around," the *dazibao* said, "Wang Dan and his cohorts are always the first to run. I don't understand why Wang Dan tells us one thing and does another." The writer had tried to make the *dazibao* look as though it had been written by a student, but I knew it was the work of the Public Security Bureau.

Some other students reading it wanted to tear it down, but as they grabbed the top of it, I stopped them. "Don't," I said. "This is the best proof we have that people are out to get Wang Dan and hurt the movement. I'll write another *dazibao* detailing what I saw a few minutes ago." I ran back to my room and wrote a *dazibao* titled "Isn't it strange?" which I posted right next to the phony one. Soon after I put up my *dazibao*, though, someone tore down the one defaming Wang Dan.

At that point I saw Feng Congde and Xiong Yan coming back from Xinhuamen. Xiong Yan said that the situation there was tense; the police had surrounded the students and divided them into three groups, so that those farthest from the compound had been frightened into leaving and those nearest couldn't go anywhere. "We've got to take a group of people to support them," he said.

I told them about the committee meeting and how I hadn't been welcome. On our way back to the dorm, Xiong Yan said, "You have to come to the committee meeting in the morning, even if they don't want you to. Don't argue with them, because we all have to work together. Whatever they say, just ignore it. Swallow your pride for now, because we need your help." I said I would talk to them in the morning.

I tried to sleep, but after only an hour a deafening noise woke me up. The Triangle was filled with people chanting slogans. Their shouting was so loud I thought they would crack the building. Bleary-eyed, I stuck my head out the window and yelled questions at some people below, who told me that at 2:30 in the morning the police, without warning, had beaten the students in front of Xinhuamen with leather belts and billy clubs. Police cars had also run over their bicycles so they couldn't leave. When the students at Beida heard this, they were incensed and came out to vent their anger.

Chang Jin came to my room and said that nothing had happened at the Preparatory Committee meeting and that the members were gathering again in the morning. I went to this meeting, and this time no one said I should leave. I thought it was strange that Wang Dan wasn't there.

"We must do something about what happened at Xinhuamen," Yang Tao said. "Let's send a delegation of two hundred to Tiananmen Square to protest." Ti Bo was selected head of the *jiuchadui*, a brigade of marshals to keep order at rallies, because he was a very big guy. I told him that I would begin fund-raising so we could buy megaphones, cloth for armbands and banners, and other supplies. Then I took my desk from my room and moved it out into the Triangle, where I could quickly raise money because hundreds of people, including workers, journalists, and teachers, were coming to read the *dazibao*.

At noon Yang Tao came over to me. "What's going on?" I asked.

"Wang Dan and I have left the Preparatory Committee," he said.

"Why?" I asked. I knew that the committee could not be a significant force in the movement without the two leaders of the Democracy Salon.

"There are enormous pressures on us," he explained.

I suspected that this had been Wang Dan's decision, because Yang Tao was not happy about it.

"Did you see my article next to where the *dazibao* about Wang Dan was posted?" I asked. He said that he had. "What was that all about?"

"Wang Dan has nothing to do with the money we collect," Yang Tao said. "He's never even seen a cent that we collected, so how could he have spent it?"

Yang Tao was obviously upset that he was no longer part of the Preparatory Committee, so I asked him if he could get a group of thirty people together to help buy equipment and act as marshals for the march to the square. "I'll see what I can do," he agreed.

It was probably wise for the members of the Democracy Salon to lower their profile for a while. But at the time I thought that Wang Dan should not have left the leadership.

Qing Nian and Sheng Pei came back from class and watched me from a distance for a long time before walking away. I knew they were surprised to see me involved again. A while later, the two of them showed up with a pail of lunch for me, their way of showing their support for my decision. Ti Bo and I made a banner out of red cloth that read, *Heping qingyuan,* Peaceful petition. This was the movement's first mention of nonviolence.

The members of the Preparatory Committee came down at around 1 p.m. to start lining up the marchers. After suggesting that they go to Qinghua and pick up some more people, I closed up the fund-raising table and went back to my dorm. Just before two o'clock, my friends from the Olympic Institute stopped in my room on their way to class. "Don't go," the Giant said simply. I assured them that I would stay on campus. The word was that about four thousand police, armed with rifles, were poised just outside Beijing on Third Ring Road, in case they had to deal with any trouble.

After my friends left, the whole dorm was completely empty; everyone was either in class or lining up to go to the square. I looked out my window and could hardly believe my eyes. There must have been two thousand students, and about two hundred more acting as marshals. Sitting at my desk, I thought about what I had heard about the armed police. The students began walking toward the gate of the school, and I had an awful feeling that they were an army going to be slaughtered. I was already late for my two o'clock class, but I couldn't get myself to move. How could I, knowing that the police were ready to march against the students? I couldn't sit there and do nothing. In the split second when the marchers disappeared from my sight, I decided that I had to join them. Looking around my messy room, I grabbed a pair of shoes, then put them on as I ran down the stairs.

I raced to the front of the group to find Ti Bo, and told him about the armed police. "I'm going with you," I said.

"That's great," he replied, patting me hard on the back.

We went to Qinghua University first, but the school gates had been locked and a truck with a loudspeaker was broadcasting a message: "Students of Beida, the Qinghua students are not participating in your march. Go back to your school and to class. Do not come to our campus and create chaos." We walked to another gate. All of a sudden, the skies opened up. In the pouring rain we tried every gate, but they were all locked or just being closed by school security. The broadcast van followed us from one gate to another, repeating the warning.

The rain was coming down very hard, and many of the marchers were running for shelter. I thought our group was falling apart, but then I saw many familiar faces in the crowd, including the two graduate students who had been the first speakers at our Olympic Institute meeting. They smiled and waved at me and yelled out my name. Seeing them lifted my spirits, and suddenly I got up the courage to grab the megaphone from Ti Bo and address the crowd: "If the Qinghua students can't go, we'll go ourselves." Then I led the Beida contingent toward Tiananmen Square. As we marched on, someone told us that some students from Beijing Normal University were waiting for us a few kilometers ahead. Most of our banners were soaking wet, but we still held up the Beida flag and emblem.

On the way, we passed the University of Political Science and Law, and the students there applauded and cheered us, then invited us to their auditorium for bread and hot water to warm ourselves. "We're not participating today," one of their leaders said, "but we support you." After we dried off a little, Zhang Zhiyong, another committee member, suddenly said to the marchers, "Let's not go to the square today. The rain is coming down hard. Let's just go back." Many of the students, their spirits dampened by the rain, seemed ready to agree. They weren't as eager to walk the fifteen kilometers to Tiananmen as they had been earlier.

Ti Bo panicked. "Shen Tong, go and tell him not to cancel the march," he said, grabbing me by the arm. "Go speak to him."

I took the microphone and jumped onstage, anxious to persuade everyone to continue. "Listen, everybody, we're already on our way," I said. "This morning several hundred students had their heads bashed in by the police. So what's a little rain?" I suddenly felt very emotional. I gripped the microphone with both hands and took a deep breath, trying to steady myself. "Thousands of other students are waiting for Beida. We've got to get there."

That was the last time anybody spoke about going back.

As we passed Beijing Normal University, we saw that its gates were locked too. Lots of students were hanging out of their dorm windows banging on tin plates as a show of support, so we chanted, "Come on out!"

Five people had been designated to lead the slogan chanting, but as we got closer to the crowded areas, where people were going home from work now that the rain had stopped for a while and where the police were obvious, some of the slogan leaders were losing their nerve as well as their voices. I took the megaphone from one of them and led the chants: *Dadao guandao*, Defeat official graft; *Fandui fubai*, No more corruption; *Aiguo wuzui*, Patriotism is not a crime; *Renmin wansui*, Long live the people. I walked up and down alongside the marchers, encouraging them by calling out some of Mao's sayings from the Cultural Revolution. Referring to the Red Guards, he had said, "Those who put down student movements have a bleak future" and "If the students don't act, who will?" — slogans that seemed perfect for us now.

I was surprised to see Yang Tao and glad that he had come along, even though the Democracy Salon was distancing itself from the march. People on the public buses and in the streets were looking at us with admiration, not annoyance that we were disrupting traffic. Climbing up on the railings that separated the pedestrian walkway from the street, I could see the faces of many Beijing residents smiling warmly at us.

I knew that once we reached Changan Avenue, I should stop being one of the leaders of the marchers. The government had video surveillance equipment all along the avenue, and I would be very visible if I continued to lead the chanting. As we approached Xidan, just around the corner from my house, I was still telling myself, *You've got to stop now, you've got to stop now,* but as we turned the corner, I realized that I couldn't stop.

"Long live the people!" I shouted, even louder and more confidently than before.

Just at this point one of my neighbors, the sixth brother, saw me as he got off a bus from work. "Isn't that Yuan Yuan?" I heard him say as he ran over.

"Please don't tell my parents" was all I said to him; then I kept going. I didn't want my family to find out what I was doing.

When we walked into Tiananmen Square, we saw that tens of thousands of students were already there. They went crazy when they saw us: "It's Beida, it's Beida! They're here!" My heart was full of hope and excitement. We made our way toward the Monument to the People's Heroes in the center, and everyone crowded around. I stood on one of the top steps of the monument, with the marshals who were keeping order on the surrounding steps. Umbrellas and rain ponchos of various colors were everywhere. We were wet and tired, but no one seemed to care. There was great expectation in the air.

Things were fairly chaotic because people in the front blocked the view of those in the back, and it was hard for everyone to stay still with umbrellas in the way. I was looking around for Chang Jin and the others, expecting them to come up on the steps, when a very striking young man walked up to me and introduced himself.

"I'm Wuer Kaixi, from Beijing Normal. Let's get some speakers together," he said. "We've got to get some order here."

"Everyone sit down," I directed with a megaphone. From front to back, rows and rows of people slowly sat down. "We're all soaked already," I said. "It will be easier for everybody to see if we fold up our umbrellas." To my surprise, everyone did so.

Very quickly, Wuer Kaixi and I began finding people to speak to the waiting crowd. The first was Chen Minyuan, a noted professor and poet who had edited and published a collection of poetry from the 1976 Tiananmen Square movement. He said that the scene before him reminded him of the outpouring he had witnessed after Zhou Enlai's death.

"I come here first as a citizen, then as your teacher, as your friend, and as an old warrior in the struggle for democracy," he said, using the megaphone. "I want to be the first of your professors to come here and say that I support you." The cheers and applause were deafening. For him to stand up for us in public like this was very gratifying, since the endorsement of such a respected teacher made our movement more legitimate.

The next speaker was Wuer Kaixi, who was very emotional. "This morning they beat people up," he said, waving his fist in the air. "Just look at my forehead. I was hit by the police." He pushed his hair away from his forehead to show us the wound. "Hu Yaobang is dead, he hasn't even been laid to rest, and they've already done this to us." He didn't say anything new, but people were moved by his boldness, and I was impressed by the way he worked the crowd and the response he got.

One after another, student leaders took the megaphone to speak. I sat down on the steps, feeling exhausted. The rain was falling again, and I watched the water drip from my hair, half listening to the speeches, half daydreaming. Looking out over the crowd, I saw that the ink on the banners had washed out. Then I looked up at Hu Yaobang's portrait on the top of the monument. It was soaked too. I suddenly thought of my family. *What troubles will I bring to my parents this time? They must be worried about me. I might be going to America this year. I wonder if Andrea would go with me.* I was still in a daze when someone handed the megaphone to me. I hadn't planned to speak, so I had to think fast.

"We have completely achieved our goal today," I said. "Being here is a victory in itself. We walked past five universities over a long distance and reached Tiananmen Square. What we wanted to do was to use nonviolent means to protest the beating of patriotic students in front of Xinhuamen this morning, and to ask the government to reevaluate Hu Yaobang's ouster from the Party. We have not disrupted society, we have not halted traffic. We have done this in a very orderly way."

After I spoke, I noticed a circle of people gathered just beyond the edge of the crowd. Something was going on. I asked the other students on the monument steps what was happening, and they told me that Zhang Zhiyong and some leaders from other schools were discussing how to set up a united Beijing students' association. "They're getting into heated arguments," someone said. "Go see if you can tell them that this is not the time or the place."

Everyone was wet and exhausted, and I thought it was time for us to leave the square. I went over to where the leaders were meeting and heard them arguing.

"Zhang Zhiyong, why don't you calm down now? I have an idea," I said. "Everyone just listen for a second. I'll ask the marshals to form two lines. The Beida students will get up and walk out of the square, flanked by the marshals. This is not a good time to get into a serious discussion. Everyone is tired."

But the representatives from Nankai University in Tianjin insisted on forming a united association right then. I suggested that it would be better to meet again on April 22, the day of Hu Yaobang's memorial service.

I had a lot of money with me from the fund-raising that morning, so I gave some of it to the marshals so they could rent buses to take the students back to Beida. Some people had gotten sick from being in the rain, so I gave them money to take taxis back. Then, because I was losing my voice, I told Ti Bo and Chang Jin that I was going home. I was lucky to live so close to Tiananmen Square.

It was around nine when I got there. I had left my dorm in such a hurry that I hadn't put on socks, and my feet had blisters from soaking in my shoes. My clothes were drenched. My father took one look at me and I at him, and I could see that he was angry, hurt, worried, frustrated, all rolled into one. I was sure he would say something, but he didn't.

After Nainai fussed over me, getting me dry clothes and a towel and hot water to soak my feet, my father finally said, "I

can't believe you walked for eight hours in the rain." I understood what he meant to say, even though those weren't the right
words.

"Don't worry, Dad, I think I've done enough for this movement already, and that's all I'm going to do," I replied. I was very
tired, and I did believe that I wasn't going to get any more
involved. "If anything bad happens because of today, I'll have to
accept it," I added. "But you don't have to worry about me from
now on."

After Nainai fixed me something to eat and the swelling on
my feet went down, I felt so much better that I started to tell my
parents all about what had happened. My father was half angry
and half excited as he listened. I showed him the megaphone I
had carried. "There were tens of thousands of people in the
square," I said. "I talked through the loudspeaker, and everyone
listened to me." I was afraid to tell him more, because I didn't
want to get him more upset.

April 21, Friday

The next morning I got up early and went back to school. I
must have caught a cold the day before, because I was feeling
sick. I lay down on my bed as soon as I got to my room.

"Where have you been?" Sheng Pei asked me when he came
in.

"I went home. Why?"

"Andrea came around last night looking for you," he said.
"When you didn't come back to the dorm, we were afraid the
police had picked you up."

Ti Bo and Chang Jin walked in and told me that they hadn't
been able to rent buses, so most of the students had almost
crawled back to school. "Beida students are really tough," Ti Bo
said. "We walked back a step at a time. It was not easy. And those
idiots who stayed out in that weather to hold a meeting — they
didn't accomplish a thing."

I told them exactly what I had told my father the night before.
"I'm not going to be out in front at any more rallies. You all know

that I've participated in the past, and you saw what we did yesterday. But none of us are that important as individuals. I'll help out the best I can, but I'm not interested in being part of the leadership."

"You should know that Wang Dan and the Democracy Salon are back in the Preparatory Committee," Chang Jin said.

I couldn't understand this. These students had disappeared during the rally, and now they were back in. What were they doing? But I kept these thoughts to myself.

"I think now is the time for the Preparatory Committee to think about bringing the movement to a peaceful close after April twenty-second," I said. "We've already created a newly charged atmosphere at the schools. We should work toward long-term organization so that the rallies will not have been for nothing." But this suggestion didn't go over too well. The march the day before had been so successful that most students found it difficult to think about ending the movement.

After Chang Jin and Ti Bo left, a very big man with a square and earnest face came into my room. He introduced himself as Lao Wang, a Beijing factory worker. I judged him to be in his thirties. He said he had followed the students back to Beida from Tiananmen Square the night before and stayed on campus talking with people.

"I've been going to the square every day since Hu Yaobang died," he said in a low but loud voice. "Everyone said to wait for the Beida students, and you people finally came yesterday. I saw you speak at the monument. I support you wholeheartedly."

He offered me an unfiltered cigarette, and I asked him to sit down. "If the workers could get together and join your movement," he continued, "it would help enormously."

"Why don't you leave me your address so we can keep in touch?" I suggested.

He agreed, and not only gave me his address but said he would come and see me again in a few days.

That afternoon the Preparatory Committee met in Chang Jin's room on the fourth floor, which it turned into its headquarters. I didn't attend, because I thought it was better for me to withdraw from any participation. My father's calm tone the night before had actually made me relatively content with this decision. *I should study hard and go to America next year,* I kept telling myself, even though I didn't really want to do that.

The committee's first action was to declare a class boycott to protest the beatings at Xinhuamen and the government's reporting of that incident: the authorities had said, completely falsely, that students had beaten the police and shouted counterrevolutionary slogans. But the committee's members spent most of the afternoon planning what to do the next day at Hu Yaobang's memorial service. We had heard that the police intended to cordon off Tiananmen Square beginning at five o'clock in the morning, so students from various schools had gotten together and decided to occupy the square before that. Most of my dormmates in No. 28 started gathering in the Triangle at around 11 that night, preparing to march to the square en masse.

Although I agreed that holding rallies was a great way to vent our frustrations and show our emotions, I wasn't convinced then that such demonstrations could accomplish anything real. So while almost 200,000 people gathered for the memorial service, I stayed in my dorm room, trying to study. But what was happening in the square that night was never far from my mind, and I followed it through periodic reports from people who came back to the dorm.

April 22, Saturday

In the morning the sound of a loud radio woke me up. Two students had set up a broadcasting station in the middle of the Triangle, using a homemade machine and two little speakers, and they were reading reports about what was happening in the square.

"When the students marched to Tiananmen Square last night, all along the road, Beijing citizens came out to support them," the broadcaster said. "People gave out cases of soda and juice, bread and eggs. The square was full of people sitting in for the night. At dawn, police started to appear. The students demanded that the authorities guarantee their safety, let them enter the Great Hall of the People to pay their last respects to Hu Yaobang, and acknowledge that armed police had beaten students on the morning of April 20. The government agreed only to the first request, that students in the square would be safe."

The report went on to say that the students had waited patiently as the official memorial service for Hu Yaobang took place in the Great Hall of the People. After preparing a petition listing seven demands to present to the Party officials gathered at the service, they had sent three representatives to the Great Hall, but no one had come out to receive them. The representatives had knelt on the steps of the hall, imploring Li Peng to come out and accept the demands.

That afternoon, as my friends made their way back from the square, they told me angrily that the representatives had knelt for forty minutes, but no one had ever come out of the Great Hall. The officials had left through a back door. One of my old roommates said through clenched teeth, "If I had a cannon, I would have blown up the Great Hall of the People." Hungry and tired from sitting all night at the square, he was nearly hysterical.

Almost everyone who had been there was as angry as he was. The students had given a reasonable and patriotic request to the government, but the Party officials had completely ignored them. I noticed that many students who had never cared about politics and protest before were now raising their fists in the air. That day was one of the turning points of the movement.

The two students broadcasting in the Triangle were studying radio at Beida, so I told them that they could use my room as a radio station. We put the speakers in my window, facing the Triangle. The homemade machine broadcast over FM on the 101 band, though the signal was only strong enough to be heard on campus radios. But the speakers served as a public address system that could be heard around the Triangle.

Now that we had a broadcast station in place, I started putting together a news center, which I thought was the perfect way to help the movement without being too visible. I persuaded Sheng Pei and the other people on my floor to turn our room and the adjacent rooms into a suite of offices in a corner of the hallway. One of the rooms was a reception area for visitors from other schools and for journalists; another room we designated as our meeting room. After some of my dormmates found two mimeograph machines, we set up a publishing center in a third room, and the Giant's room on the first floor, which was my old room, was where we stored all of our printed materials.

Once we were set up, lots of students volunteered to work for the news center. We had people writing radio scripts, reporters gathering news, editors rewriting copy, announcers, and two people who spent the entire day working the mimeograph machines, churning out news releases. We posted a guard on the second floor to keep out teachers. By that afternoon we were producing six different leaflets, ranging from articles to news. One of them, a chart of twenty-seven high-ranking Party officials — including Deng Xiaoping, Zhao Ziyang, and Yang Shangkun — and their children, many of whom held important government positions because of nepotism, was soon all over other campuses as well as Beida. Another leaflet reported the beatings at Xinhuamen. We collected the leaflets we printed into a press packet to give to anyone who came to the news center, a practice we continued for weeks.

That first night we kept the broadcast station going until dawn. The next day the professors who lived in a faculty building nearby came to see us, red-eyed. "We support what you are doing," they said, "but please let us have some sleep." After that our broadcasts began at ten in the morning and ended at midnight.

Although we had set up the whole operation in one day, it was surprisingly professional. Our broadcasts could be heard by all who came to the Triangle, and, unexpectedly, people started to drop by and donate money. On our first full day of operation, the staff of one of the government-funded magazines gave us 1000 yuan, which the employees had secretly collected. That

night we received our first donation from the United States —
$276 given by fifty-three Chinese students at Kent State, who
had sent the money to friends at Beida and asked them to give it
to an appropriate student group. Our total for the day was about
4000 yuan.

We assigned a reporter to cover developments at the Beida
Preparatory Committee each day, and we formed a team of
students to go to the different schools around Beijing and ask
each one to send a representative to us with daily reports. It
wasn't long before we were getting information from forty-three
schools in Beijing, Tianjin, and Shanghai.

As word spread about the news center, we began hearing
about unrest elsewhere in the country. For instance, two students from Xian, the capital of Shaanxi Province, came to tell us
of an incident there on April 22. They sat in our offices crying
uncontrollably as we tried to get the details out of them. It
seemed that students in Xian had planned a peaceful demonstration on the day of Hu Yaobang's memorial service, but some
of the participants had been unemployed workers who had
looted stores. The police rushed the demonstrators, killing many
innocent people, and in response the demonstrators burned
police vehicles. The Public Security Bureau people dragged
many of them into the yard of the city government offices and
beat them to death or threw them against a wall. We listened to
this story in disbelief, but the students seemed so sincere that we
broadcast what they told us and published it in leaflets. We did
send two people to Xian to find out more, but they were unable
to verify what had happened. In that respect we were not professional and objective.

We protected the news center like a little kingdom. Guards
were posted to keep out people who weren't there on official
business. Our accountants recorded the donations, which were
now pouring in, and kept track of our expenses. I sent a couple
of volunteers out to buy some paper, and they came back with
cartons, all of it free; the Beijing salespeople had found out that
the paper was for the students and had sent the volunteers to

the paper factory, where the workers had given them the paper as a way of supporting the movement. We also got many other supplies for free. It was wonderful that people beyond Beida's campus were openly helping us.

Various people came up to me and gave me money for the news center — so many, and in such small amounts, that the accountants couldn't keep up with it all. At first I took taxis everywhere and took the news center people out to dinner, but after a few days I realized that spending the money so freely was wrong. At a meeting of the staff, which had grown to about twenty people, I told everyone to be very careful in reporting what we spent. We established a rule that whenever we spent any money, even if it was to buy sodas, it had to be reported to the accountants, with receipts.

Many journalists and others started coming to us for information and to interview us about what was happening in the student movement. It was hard not to notice the news center, because as soon as you walked onto campus you could hear our broadcasts from the Triangle.

April 24, Monday

The Preparatory Committee thought it was time to elect its members formally, because its present leaders had not been selected democratically. Some people at the news center suggested that I might be elected if I went to the meeting, but I was happy directing the work at the center, so I didn't go. The meeting held that afternoon was uneventful, even though two thirds of the Beida students — an unprecedented number — were there, and no election took place.

Meanwhile, two days after the news center opened, we reported that twenty-one universities in Beijing, including Beida, had gotten together and formed the Federation of All Beijing College Student Unions so that the student movement could speak with a unified voice. The chairman was Zhou Yongjun, a student at the University of Political Science and Law whom I had met on April 20. Wang Dan was a member of the standing committee. The federation's first official action was to declare that an unlimited class boycott protesting the police beatings at Xinhuamen would begin on thirty-five campuses in Beijing.

Two students from People's University who were members of the new federation soon walked into the news center with an unexpected request: they wanted us to be the federation's spokesmen, because they were impressed with our apparatus. I designated one person to go to all their meetings and deal with the press for them, which would also keep us on top of their work.

As this was happening, one of the Olympic Institute members suggested that the news center could also publish a newspaper. I was very much against it at first. "There's enough work to do with the broadcast station and the leaflet printing, and now working for the federation," I said. "If we start a newspaper, we'll be taking our resources away from that."

"Don't you realize how important a newspaper is?" he asked.

"A newspaper is not like a leaflet," I argued. "You have to publish it regularly, with enough news to fill several pages, with editorials . . ."

"We'll do all the work," he said. "Don't worry about us."

He convinced me that it was important to have our own paper, and the Olympic Institute members seemed so committed to getting it done that I couldn't continue to be opposed to it. I was glad that they were getting involved in the news center and that our group was taking a role in the movement, even if it was behind the scenes.

April 25, Tuesday

Feng Congde and Chang Jin came by the news center and asked me to go to a meeting at noon, once again to elect the Beida Preparatory Committee. The general meeting the day before had been so chaotic that this time each of the twenty-nine departments at Beida was sending two student representatives to attend. "You should be there to represent the news center," Feng Congde said.

One of the other students at the center and I sat in the last row of the large classroom where the meeting was held. A number of professors and graduate students were running things, and Wang Dan stood at the front of the room telling everyone what the procedures were. The ten people who had already been nominated would address the student representatives, after which everyone would vote for the five people they wanted to fill the five committee spots. The top vote getters who had received at least half the votes would make up the new Preparatory Committee.

After listening to the candidates, I wanted to say something, but I hesitated to speak up. Just before the students were to cast their votes, though, I stood up.

"I'm not running for the committee, but I want to take this chance to tell you what we're doing over at the news center," I said. I explained our operation and asked everyone present to bring us news when they had it. "I haven't heard any of the candidates mention how we are going to preserve ourselves when this movement is finally over, so that our work can continue over the long term. All of you have seen student movements come and go and know that a crackdown can come at any time. The leaders this time have to consider the aftermath. We have to make sure that students and their organizations survive when the movement is over. We've all seen the power we have collectively, and we've all seen our commitment to the cause. But at the height of our movement, the leaders must consider what to do at our lowest moment. Only in this way can we have continuity and build on each experience."

When I finished, everyone applauded in agreement with what I had said. Then someone nominated me to be a candidate.

"Shen Tong, do you want to be a candidate?" Wang Dan shouted to the back of the room.

"No," I said. "I'm not in the running."

One of the student representatives said to Wang Dan, "You said a candidate can be nominated by someone else."

"Yes, but the person has to agree to be nominated," Wang Dan replied.

Several people turned around. "Shen Tong, do you agree?" a few people near me asked.

I was still shaking my head when my friend from the news center nudged my elbow and said, "Don't be stupid. How can you say no at this point?"

"But I'm working at the news center," I protested.

"I'm sure everyone there is behind you too," he said.

I reluctantly agreed. While the results were being called out, I was excited and nervous. Wang Dan stole glances at me when his vote count was ahead of mine, and I looked at him when my votes exceeded his. We were in a kind of unspoken competition. In the end, we each got thirty-seven votes.

The top two vote getters were graduate students; Feng Cong-de came in third, and Wang Dan and I became the fourth and fifth members of the Preparatory Committee. The results were posted in the Triangle on a large *dazibao*, and the news traveled quickly around campus.

The committee met for the first time that afternoon and decided that our number-one priority was to bring about a direct dialogue with the government. I suggested that we send our request through the school administration, because of the students' miserable failure when they had tried to submit a petition to Li Peng in front of the Great Hall of the People. We also agreed to meet every day to plan strategy. Feng Congde's wife, Chai Ling, was the secretary of the committee, taking down the minutes of our meetings and notifying us of the next one.

When I returned to the news center, everyone was talking about an editorial that was supposed to appear in the next day's *People's Daily*. As we were trying to get more information, the official government radio station started broadcasting the text of the editorial, so we all stopped and listened, and one of the staff members tape-recorded it. In all-too-familiar language, it said that "a handful of individuals with ulterior motives have used the grief of students to create turmoil." It accused students of setting up illegal organizations and printing counterrevolutionary leaflets to "instigate dissension, create national disorder, and sabotage the stable unity in politics," and it called the movement a "plotted conspiracy and upheaval to negate the leadership of the Chinese Communist Party and the socialist system."

Throughout the day, the news center rebroadcast the editorial, which made the already tense atmosphere on campus even worse. We were running around like crazy, and I was in the middle of putting together a leaflet about the editorial when someone ran in and said, "Shen Tong, there's a long distance phone call from the United States for someone from the Preparatory Committee."

"Are you kidding?" I said. "Who would call here from the United States?"

Ten minutes later he came back and said, "The person on the phone won't hang up until he speaks to someone on the committee."

I thought it had to be a crank call, but I answered it anyway. The voice on the phone kept asking me who I was, and wouldn't tell me anything until he was satisfied that I wasn't an agent of the Public Security Bureau. He then told me that he had gotten electronic messages from China about the student movement and that he knew that No. 28 was the center of Beida's activities. He represented a group of Chinese students at the University of Massachusetts at Amherst, and he said that they were starting a fund-raising drive to help us.

When I met Andrea that evening, she had already seen the poster announcing the election results. "I saw your name and I had such a fright," she said. "I wasn't sure if it was really you. I thought you said you weren't going to join the leadership."

"I'm less worried about that than about what we on the committee can actually do," I said. "I don't know how the five of us can handle such a large movement."

Later, when I returned to the news center, I got a call from the student assigned to the federation. The group had met for hours, but the only thing they had decided was that a major rally would be held two days later, on April 27.

"I'm their spokesman, but I don't have much to say to the reporters on the federation's behalf," my friend complained when I asked him how things were working out.

"There's so much to do here that if you think you're wasting your time, just come back," I said.

We had been continuously broadcasting the *People's Daily* editorial all day long, and the news center was jammed with people we didn't know, who were coming in to tell us about various developments we had no way of checking. One person told me that the government had begun moving troops to Beijing. I didn't know whether to believe him or not, but late that night, when I finally went to bed, I had time to wonder briefly whether I had made the right decision in joining the Preparatory Committee.

· 8 ·

The Spirit of
May Fourth

April 26, Wednesday

The *People's Daily* editorial signaled a change in the government's position on student demonstrations: mourning activities
for Hu Yaobang were now officially over, and any student who
continued demonstrating would regret the consequences. All
day long the government broadcast warnings on the radio and
on television, saying that the rally scheduled for the next day
was illegal. By telling the students to call it off, these warnings
actually helped get the word out. Rumors that the rally was
going to be a showdown between the students and the police
were spreading like wildfire at Beida, and on other university
campuses.

In the morning I went with one of the graduate students on
the Beida Preparatory Committee to meet with school officials
about setting up a dialogue with the government. Three administrators — Beida's dean of discipline, the campus vice chairman of the Communist Party, and the head of the Beida chapter
of the Communist Youth League — were waiting for us. Walking
into the dean's office, I was a little nervous, because I expected
an argument. The other student representative and I were both
surprised when the officials readily agreed to forward our request and said that they hoped a dialogue could take place.

"However, the students should go back to class and not take
this too far," the campus Party chairman said.

I knew he was trying to get us to cancel the next day's rally. "Don't put too much hope in persuading us," I replied. "This is a grassroots movement. Our job is to represent the other students. If the government doesn't do anything positive, then you can't expect our position to change."

The head of the Communist Youth League said, "As the people in charge of Beida, we know we won't be able to control the students if we don't do our best to make your meeting with the government happen. But if you continue to boycott classes, it will be difficult for us to work with you. We also don't want you to hold a demonstration. The only way we can speak on the students' behalf to the government is if you guarantee that nothing will happen tomorrow."

"I don't think it's possible to call off the rally," I said. "But we'll do our best to make sure it's orderly. We might be able to persuade some of the students to stay on campus and not go to Tiananmen Square."

We didn't give in to the administrators' request during the meeting, but on the way back to No. 28 it occurred to us that we may have overlooked an opportunity. If, in exchange for not going to the rally, we could get a dialogue with the government, we should consider it. The other committee members agreed, so we took the decision to a meeting of the student representatives that evening. Just before I started to present the committee's case, I looked around and saw that Wang Dan wasn't there. He had agreed with us about not going to the demonstration when we had met earlier, even though he was part of the federation, which had called it.

"The school thinks that if we don't appear at the rally tomorrow, we can use that as leverage to ask the government for a dialogue," I said. "If the government doesn't deliver, we can hold another demonstration at a later date. So you see, we're not really giving up anything."

The students didn't seem to agree with this; they were determined to go to the square. They didn't want to buckle under to the threats made in the *People's Daily* editorial and the government broadcasts, and they were also angry about being called instigators.

I tried again to persuade them. "I'm not afraid of being criticized. I'm asking you all to take one step back so we can take a larger step forward."

After much arguing, we reached a compromise: Beida students would take part in the rally, but we would walk from campus to Third Ring Road, only a third of the way to Tiananmen Square. We would then turn back, before we had to face the authorities.

Just as we were voting on the compromise, Wang Dan walked in. "I just met with the members of the federation," he announced. "The rally is on."

Those words got everyone excited again and ready to march all the way to the square. It took a bit of doing, but we convinced everyone, including Wang Dan, to stay with the compromise.

As we walked back to No. 28, the school public address system was blaring the same warning the government had broadcast all day: further demonstrations were illegal, and those taking part faced severe punishment. There was no mistaking the government's position now — we were criminals. The warning over the loudspeakers was chilling. In the past few days the Triangle had been festive, but now it was deserted, and the news center had stopped broadcasting for the night. When I entered the dorm, everyone was busy getting ready for the rally, but all this activity couldn't hide the tension and fear beneath the surface. We were sure that this was the last night of our student movement.

When I got to my room, none of the news center people were there, but my sister, her new boyfriend, Andrea, and Li Jin, a friend I'd made in the Beida Student Association, were waiting for me. Just after I arrived, the Giant walked in. I sat on a chair and they surrounded me, talking all at once.

"Don't go to the rally tomorrow," Qing said. "I can't believe I have to keep telling you this."

"It's not too late to change your mind," her boyfriend said.

"Stay at the news center," the Giant urged. "There's plenty to do to keep busy."

I told them that I had tried to persuade the others not to go to the rally, but the best I'd been able to do was reach a compromise.

"Then why do you still want to be in the middle of it?" my sister asked. "They don't listen to you."

"That's part of what happens," I explained. "I say what I think we should do, but once the students have decided to march, it's my duty to be there with them."

Qing saw that I had made up my mind. Like my father, she didn't want to see me get hurt. "If you're so committed, I guess we will all support you," she said. "But don't be a fool. If the police start to beat up people, run. We don't need another hero. When the crackdown comes, what does it matter if there's one more wounded or one less? At that point, think about your own safety. You've got a life ahead of you."

When they saw that there was nothing more they could say to me, they got up to leave. As I walked my sister and her boyfriend out to the Triangle, I suddenly remembered that it was Qing's birthday. I had completely forgotten. Her boyfriend pressed two 10-yuan bills into my hand and said, "Take care of yourself."

As I reentered the dorm and walked down the hallway, I saw clusters of orange light coming from a few of the rooms: my dormmates had built little fires to burn the physical evidence of our democracy movement. If the government found our papers, they would persecute everyone whose name they discovered. The staff members of the broadcast station, the publishing center, and the Preparatory Committee were destroying all of the letters sent by students outside Beijing, notes of support from workers, copies of official documents given to us by well-connected people, minutes of meetings, leaflets, and radio scripts.

No. 28 was silent. Some students were preparing to die, shaving their heads and writing their wills. On my desk I found some of these wills, written by people who wanted us to publish them. "Dear Mother and Father," one of them said, "I am part of this student movement because I love my country. I am not a counterrevolutionary. I am not a lawless agitator. Please understand my actions. Thank you for the money you sent so I could buy food and clothing. I will not be needing it anymore. Rest assured that your son will not bring shame upon you. I will not die in disgrace." Seeing these students' shaved heads and their pale faces in the glow of the dim firelight, I shivered at their courage.

Before I went to bed, I walked up to the Preparatory Committee office on the fourth floor and discovered that almost everyone was there. "I know we agreed to march part of the way," I said, "but tomorrow all that could easily change in an instant. We've got to stick to our original plan, for the safety of the students and for the chance of a dialogue with the government."

For a while we sat in the office, not saying much to each other. Some people came around asking for leaflets to distribute at the rally. Our mimeograph machines had been running nonstop and had produced more than 40,000 leaflets. Then three students walked in. I immediately recognized Wuer Kaixi, whom I'd met the week before in the square.

"Shen Tong, I've been looking for you," he said. "I'm Wuer Kaixi, from Beijing Normal."

"Yes, I remember you," I replied.

"We've established our own Preparatory Committee," he said. "I need to talk to you about something."

We walked downstairs to my room.

"The dean of my school and the campus Communist Party leader came to see me today," he explained. "They told me that if I and the other student leaders could persuade the students from Beijing Normal not to take part in the rally tomorrow, we wouldn't be punished for the organizing we've done so far. They also said they would try to get the government to talk to us. Don't you agree that we should try to keep our two schools from marching tomorrow? I'm going over to Qinghua to ask them too."

"The administrators at Beida said the same thing to us this morning. I agree with you that we shouldn't march tomorrow,"

I said. "But we had a meeting tonight, and as a compromise we decided that Beida would walk part of the way to Tiananmen Square and no farther, to show the government that we will cooperate but we can't be intimidated."

"You know that if Beida and Beijing Normal don't march, then the other schools won't either," he said.

"Maybe, but it's too late for Beida to change its plans," I replied.

Wuer Kaixi left for Qinghua after I convinced him there was nothing I could do. Over the course of the night, while we waited nervously until it was time for the march to begin, I talked with a number of other people about what we were doing. No one could sleep, and talking seemed to relieve the tension. Also, for the past week we had all been running around like headless men, getting one thing or another organized, but none of us had had a chance to stop and think about what we were trying to accomplish.

Soon after Wuer Kaixi left my room, Feng Congde stopped by. He and Chai Ling lived in off-campus housing for married students, but like everyone in No. 28, he thought that this was the last night of this movement, and he didn't want to go home. We talked about our work on the Preparatory Committee as if the movement were already over.

"Look at how hard it was for everyone to agree," he said. "Our committee had so many differences of opinion, how could we have done a good job of getting everyone together?"

He left when a young professor from the Institute of Social Sciences, Lao He, came to see me. In the past Lao He and I had had a number of really good conversations about political theory, but tonight he was worried about the danger we all faced by going to the rally the next day.

"We should be prepared to react immediately to whatever steps the government takes," he said. "If it takes drastic measures, our actions in return should be even more dramatic. We have to fight fire with fire."

"I don't agree," I said. "We can't always react to what the

government chooses to do. If we believe in nonviolence, we have to act that way in all circumstances. We can't give up on nonviolence the first time we see that it's not easy."

He thought for a while about what I had said. "Maybe the leadership wouldn't disagree so much if each person took the time to think things through, as you seem to have done."

"It doesn't really matter what I or any leader thinks," I replied. "I've found out already that sometimes it's more effective to be charismatic than to have a clear head. The Preparatory Committee was right about not going to the rally tomorrow, but there was nothing I could say to get the students to go along. I was not a very good leader tonight."

After Lao He left, I tried to sleep. Some time after that, around 5 a.m., I was woken up by loud knocking on my door. It was one of the Preparatory Committee members, who had a worried look on his face. He simply handed me a slip of paper and left.

"In order to preserve our strength and leverage for a long-term struggle," the paper said, "the Federation of All Beijing College Student Unions has decided to cancel the rally on April 27." It was signed by Zhou Yongjun, chairman of the federation.

"What the hell is going on?" I said. "It's too late to be making these last-minute decisions."

I was so tired that I fell back on my bed and tried to go to sleep again. But this announcement was too puzzling, so I got up to find out what was really happening. When I found Feng Congde and some of the other committee members, none of them knew how this decision had been made. We all suspected that Zhou Yongjun had made it by himself, because no other signatures were on the message, and we didn't think the federation could have had a meeting in the past couple of hours. In the end we agreed to proceed as planned.

April 27, Thursday

Just before eight o'clock, a couple of hundred students began lining up in front of No. 28. I was surprised at how few there were; perhaps people were staying away because of the government's warning, or they had heard that the rally had been canceled. But about ten minutes before we were scheduled to leave, thousands of marchers showed up all at once, and the line stretched from No. 28 all the way to the main gate. More than eight thousand Beida students were ready to march. As I walked by the other Olympic Institute members, lined up with students from the biology department, I shook hands with each of them. "If you run into any trouble out in front, come back here and we'll hide you," Qing Nian said.

Feng Congde, Wang Dan, and I walked at the head of the line, but the two other committee members marched with their departments. As we left the campus, I couldn't believe what I saw ahead of us. Throngs of journalists, photographers, camera crews, and curious onlookers were just outside the main gate. We could hardly get out, it was so crowded.

As we marched, we picked up students from some other universities along the way. First came the students from Qinghua University, followed by those from the Agriculture College, making us a long column of marchers. Everyone had disregarded the announcement canceling the rally. I was holding a megaphone, marching beside some students who were hoisting the flag of China, Beida's school flag, and several large banners. Chai Ling and others were handing out the leaflets we had printed.

It wasn't long before we ran into our first wall of policemen, who were standing three deep with their arms linked. Wang Dan and I stopped the marchers and went to talk with the head of the police, who was a very old man.

"You know you can't stop us," I said. "You're only three deep, and there are thousands of us. Why don't you let us pass? We're only going to Third Ring Road and then turning back. If you don't let us pass, we're going to rush your line, and after that none of us will be able to control the students."

He didn't say a word to us, just ordered his men to move aside. Wang Dan and I looked at each other and smiled, surprised that it had been so easy.

When we got to People's University, I told the student leaders there that we were only walking a little farther before turning back and asked if they still wanted to follow us.

"You can't do that," one of them said. "If Beida leaves halfway, what will happen to the rest of us?"

"I'm sorry," I said, still committed to our original plan. "That's what the student representatives decided last night and that's what we have to do."

But when we started marching again, Wang Dan said, "I know we planned to stop at Third Ring Road, but all the students want to go on to the square. How are we going to stop them?" Feng Congde didn't say anything, but I sensed that he agreed with Wang Dan. Everyone behind us was eager to keep marching, and I was the only one holding to our compromise agreement. There were more police ahead of us, so we had to consider everybody's safety. But if the students were determined to go on, I couldn't stop them. And so, just that quickly, we abandoned our plan and kept going toward Tiananmen Square.

The next time we ran into a wall of policemen, at the Friendship Hotel and the National Library, they seemed to move aside almost as if our numbers made them realize there was no way to prevent us from going ahead. We had to break through six more barriers of policemen before we reached the square.

We had sent some marshals ahead to find out what was happening in other parts of the city, and on their return they told us that every university in Beijing had taken to the streets. We could see for ourselves that this was a big day. More than a million people had come out to support us. They too had heard the government's warning, and had left their offices and their homes as a way of protecting us. Some climbed trees to get a better look, and others lined the streets and applauded us, calling out, "We love the students!" and "We support you!" as we walked by. To my surprise, Lao Wang, the worker who had visited me and given me his address, was leading these chants. The 40,000 leaflets we had printed were gobbled up immediately by the enormous crowds.

The *laobaixing,* ordinary people, gave us the courage and determination we desperately needed to go on, because as we got closer to Tiananmen Square, soldiers carrying rifles were everywhere. The 38th Army had been dispatched to the streets around the square, and a truck with regiments of PLA troops was on every corner. We started singing the army songs we had learned at camp two summers before to show that we were friendly. We also shouted, "The people love the People's Liberation Army, and the army loves the people!"

As we walked, the runners told us that the chief editor of the *People's Daily* had resigned to protest the editorial criticizing the students, and that Qin Benli, editor-in-chief of the *World Economic Herald* in Shanghai, who had published articles supporting the students, had been dismissed that day for violating Party discipline. When we heard this, we shouted slogans supporting these men and demanding their reinstatement.

Just before we got to the intersection of Xidan and Changan Avenue, we were forced to stop behind the group from Beijing Normal University. There was a huge wall of police ahead of them, waiting to keep us from getting to the square. This group was not giving way as easily as the others had, but Wuer Kaixi, leading the Beijing Normal students, managed to rush through, allowing us to force our way through behind them. As we surged past the police, who had been pushed to the side, we came face to face with them — but we were no longer afraid.

When we got to the Gate of Heavenly Peace, it was already afternoon. The square was overflowing with students. About twelve of us, including the members of the Preparatory Committee, Chai Ling, and others at the head of the line, held hands and raised them in victory as we walked along the north side of Tiananmen Square. One hundred and fifty thousand students from more than forty universities had defied the government and were reveling in the square — it was a fantastic sight. Tiananmen Square is an enormous space, and seeing it filled with people was amazing.

In the late afternoon the Beida students started to scatter.

When people went to take the subway back to campus, they discovered that the subway workers had opened a gate just for us and were allowing us to ride for free. We had been expecting the worst, which hadn't happened, but I was still worried that a crackdown would come. I rode back to Beida with one of my old roommates. "If anyone grabs me," I told him, "you should run away and tell what happened. We can't help each other if we're both arrested."

Everyone at Beida was celebrating, and some young faculty members had posted banners welcoming us back in triumph. The night before, many students had been prepared to die, but now they believed that the citizens of Beijing had saved our lives. Banners thanking the *laobaixing*, the Beijing citizens, appeared all over campus.

That night I called home.

"Yuan Yuan, what's the matter with you?" my father said. "You won't even see your old man? I wanted to talk to you, and you told your friends to keep me away."

"What are you talking about, Dad?"

"One of your classmates made me stay in the hall and wouldn't let me into your room. He said you weren't there, and he even tried to lecture me. He said, 'Shen Tong is a good kid; you don't have to worry.' It made me so mad!"

I told my father I didn't know anything about this, which was true. "I'll come home Saturday and we can talk then," I said.

I asked around the news center and learned that one of my classmates, who had been guarding our suite, had kept my father away. He thought my father had come to take me home, because several parents had yanked their kids out of school to keep them from taking part in the march. One of the student leaders had gotten three telegrams saying his father was gravely ill, a story his family concocted to get him to leave school.

April 28, Friday

We held a press conference the day after the march — the first formal one since the movement began at Beida. We were expecting a few reporters from the Chinese and Hong Kong press, but more than fifty media organizations from different countries filled the three-hundred-seat lecture hall. There were videocameras, lights, everything. So many students wanted to get in to watch that we had to post guards to keep the room from being overcrowded. I, as the head of the news center, and my roommate were designated spokesmen. We talked about the beatings on April 20 and answered the reporters' questions about the rally the day before. The five of us on the Beida Preparatory Committee were introduced to the press, and I handed out the first issue of the *News Herald,* our newspaper.

My friends had done a great job with this. While I had been busy with the committee, they had put together eight pages of news about the April 27 demonstration, reports from students around the country, and an open letter signed by more than one hundred intellectuals and professors, asking the government not to use force against the students. We gave out eighty copies to the reporters, some of whom told us afterward how surprised they had been at our professional handling of the press briefing. Their one criticism was that we hadn't provided a translator for the journalists who didn't speak Chinese.

Immediately inquiries about the *News Herald* poured in; we were even contacted by a group of Chinese students in New York who wanted to raise funds specifically for that. Some reporters from the Hong Kong papers began giving us copies of their dispatches, which we could use in our newspaper. The news center instantly became busier, so I asked Yang Tao to take over the broadcast station. We moved the equipment out of my room to another one down the hall, where he could devote all his time to making the programming more professional. He began inviting intellectuals and dissidents like Ren Wanling to speak, and he also held panel discussions. In addition, he interviewed many well-known professors and read the interviews over the air.

Later in the afternoon the federation met to reorganize its leadership and to plan the next step in pressing the government for reform. We had proven on April 27 that this time the government could not easily turn us back, but the federation had to be ready to take us forward. The members met at Beijing Normal University, and Wuer Kaixi suggested that he replace Zhou Yongjun as the chairman of the federation. Everyone agreed to this, because they admired what he had done during the march and because, as I heard it, he said that he would fight to the end and never resign. Wang Dan and Feng Congde were both elected to the standing committee. Wuer Kaixi called again for an open dialogue between the students and the government and reissued the seven demands the students had made on April 17. He also pointed out that the federation leaders were in danger of arrest because the authorities had accused them of planning to overthrow the government.

April 29, Saturday

Someone at the federation told us that Wang Dan and Wuer Kaixi were holding their own press conference in the evening at the Shangri-La Hotel. Wuer Kaixi had captured the media's attention first by almost singlehandedly rushing through the police barricade at the rally, making way for the students to follow him into Tiananmen Square, and then by becoming the head of the federation. Wang Dan had also become very visible through his activity as Beida's representative in the federation.

When I went to the hotel to see what they had to say, I found dozens of reporters and cameramen, many students, and a crowd of curious onlookers waiting in the parking lot. The press conference started an hour late because the hotel management wouldn't let us into the conference rooms, but eventually Wuer Kaixi and Wang Dan came outside, and in front of the lights and cameras they began by saying that they were speaking not on behalf of their schools or the federation but to dispel the rumors that had been spread about them. Wuer Kaixi explained that he was not Tibetan, as some people believed, but a member of the Uigur minority, and that stories about his father being a high-level government official were untrue. Wang Dan asserted that he hadn't taken a penny of the donations given to the student movement. But they also talked about some of the federation meetings, including information that had been discussed in closed sessions. Afterward some students criticized them for holding this press conference and for talking openly about what student leaders had said privately, but I thought they handled themselves well in front of the reporters, and the way they expressed their personal views reminded me of the Western politicians I had seen on television.

After the press conference I went home to see my father, as I had promised I would. I hadn't seen him since I had led the Beida group in the march, and I expected him to be furious about that. But instead, when I walked in the door, he calmly sat me down at the dining table.

"Officials in the municipal government came to talk to me already," he said. "They are offering you two ways out of this mess. One is to leave the Preparatory Committee. The second is to remain on the committee but report what happens to the government."

I remained silent.

"I'm only telling you what they told me. The decision is yours. I only hope that you take some time out to consider your future seriously."

After hearing what my father had to say, I didn't feel like staying for dinner. He walked me to the bus stop to go back to school, and while we were waiting, he saw that my watch was broken. "Here," he said, "use mine." He took his watch off and gave it to me. I wanted to return the kindness by saying something to make him feel better, but I had no intention of taking either of the government's options. I was too involved now to stop, and I was disgusted by the government's suggestion. Before I got on the bus, I gave my father my usual answer: "Don't worry, Dad."

On the way back to school, someone sitting near me was listening to a radio broadcast of a dialogue between Yuan Mu, a government spokesman, and some students. Everyone on the bus was paying careful attention to what was being said. I was excited at first that a dialogue was in progress, but the more I listened, the stranger it seemed. I didn't know how this could have happened.

One of the students, who didn't sound like any of the federation leaders I knew, politely asked if reporters in China were free to write about anything they saw. Yuan Mu replied that there was no censorship at all in China. He said that the editors of the newspapers decided what went into their publications, but they had a responsibility to the public not to print rumors. Another student, whose voice I didn't recognize either, asked what the government was doing to clean up official corruption. Yuan Mu gave a lengthy explanation of the auditing process, which was a way of not answering the question.

I was confused about what was going on, because I didn't hear anyone mention the seven demands the federation had put forward, and the students weren't asking tough questions. I got off the bus at Beida and ran to the Preparatory Committee room to find out who had gone to this meeting with Yuan Mu. None of the other committee members knew. They had called people at the federation, who didn't have any information but who did say that no one had seen Wuer Kaixi and Wang Dan since the press conference. They thought the two of them were hiding out, because they had heard that the government was secretly arresting student leaders. There was also a rumor that Wuer Kaixi had shaved his head and written his will.

April 30, Sunday

By midmorning *dazibao* denouncing the previous night's dialogue were plastered all over the Triangle. The government had put together its own student delegation, made up primarily of students from the officially sanctioned school associations, in order to fool people into believing that it had begun genuine talks with the protesters. For the most part, the students who had taken part in this "dialogue" were very complacent and uncritical of the government. Only one had asked challenging questions, but he hadn't gotten very far. Four Beida students had participated; one of them, Guo Haifeng, worked for the Preparatory Committee, and some of the *dazibao* criticized him for taking part in the government's charade.

I was very surprised when Guo Haifeng, his face very tense, came to talk to me that morning. "Everyone is giving me a hard time for going to the dialogue," he said nervously. "My intentions were good. I knew the official student representatives were going, and I thought we should have a voice too."

"But having you there gave people the impression that the government was really working with students," I explained to him. "If the group had been made up only of official student representatives, it would have been clear that the dialogue was fake. Everybody heard about this meeting. The people of Beijing couldn't tell that this was not a genuine dialogue." He was upset, but the damage was already done. "Just forget it," I said. Guo Haifeng left my room and later wrote a *dazibao* saying that I had sanctioned his participation. I was shocked by this, but I didn't write a rebuttal.

The fake dialogue made us even more determined to pressure the government to talk with genuine student leaders. Feng Congde, who was now interim chairman of the federation because Wuer Kaixi was in hiding, began devoting his time to setting up a real meeting. But this was almost impossible, because the government had repeatedly called the federation an illegal group. Between meetings of the federation and the work of the Beida Preparatory Committee, Feng Congde became so busy that he started to live in my room instead of going home at night.

May 1, Monday

As more foreign journalists came to Beijing, they discovered that the news center was a good place to find spokesmen for the movement. Those of us involved had grown accustomed to having reporters asking us questions and camera crews jamming into our tiny suite. I had already been interviewed by reporters from Hong Kong, the BBC, and the *Asian Wall Street Journal*. This time ABC News came to talk to me, after an outdoor news conference, and interviewed me about student reactions to the fake dialogue.

"It reignited the students," I told them. "The federation is pressing the government for negotiations, but Yuan Mu says that we are unreasonable. If the government doesn't agree to discussions, the students will probably demonstrate on the anniversary of the May Fourth Movement, and it could be an even bigger rally than the one on April twenty-seventh."

After the interview I rushed off to a dinner I had planned with my friends the Giant and Qing Nian. I hadn't spent much time with them in the past couple of days, and we went back to the Mongolian hot-pot restaurant where we had held our first meetings. In the middle of the meal the Giant said, "I've got to tell you something, Shen Tong. Some of the Olympic Institute members think you're becoming a showman, and other people have also been criticizing you."

"What are they saying?" I asked.

"Yesterday we were talking to Chai Ling and she called you a traitor," he replied.

"Me? A traitor?" I couldn't believe she would say that.

"*Traitor* is not the word she meant," the Giant explained. "She was saying that you didn't want the students to march all the way to Tiananmen Square on the twenty-seventh, and you cut a deal with school officials."

"How could she have said that?" I asked. "I walked with her the whole way to the square that day. She even told people around me jokingly, 'A guy like Shen Tong, if he's arrested by the Communist Party, it'll take three bullets to kill him.' "

"I don't know why she was saying this," the Giant said. "Just be careful."

Qing Nian was afraid that I was neglecting the Olympic Institute and that the movement had made me forget that our original plan had been to set up the institute as a long-term project.

This photo was taken 100 days after I was born. I am being held by my grandmother, Nainai.

Above: With my father when I was three years old. The words on the building say, "Revolution depends on Mao Zedong thought." *Right:* Playing in the Forbidden City. I am pretending to be a soldier, saluting.

I was very proud of the PLA uniform my mother made for me. This photo was taken on Changan Avenue, the Avenue of Eternal Peace.

In the Summer Palace with my mother, father, and sister, Qing. I am wearing a PLA air force cap.

My best friend, Dakun, and I, after running in a national park.

This photo of my family was taken when I was in high school. Qing is holding our cat, Panda.

I dressed as a Taiwanese for the 1984 National Day Parade for China.

Studying for my college entrance exam—the Big Test, as we called it. I put the word "Smile" on the wall to remind myself to relax. Below that I wrote "Think More."

This photo was taken in Huangshan, a beautiful mountain range in Anhui Province, while I was traveling in the summer before I began Beijing University.

Dakun and I after we began our university studies.

Above: With my friend Rong Dong at a gathering.

Right: The Giant, one of my roommates during my freshman year at Beida, with me at the first gate of the Great Wall, near the sea.

Above: No. 28 dormitory, where I lived at Beida.

Left: Andrea and I on campus.

Entering Tiananmen Square on May 4. The man in profile at the left of the picture above is Wang Dan; I am carrying a megaphone.

Handing out copies of the *News Herald* to reporters after a press conference

When I came out of the government liaison office after asking for a reply to our petition for a dialogue, I was surrounded by journalists wanting to know what had happened.

With Xiang Xiaoji, after another trip to the liaison office.

With my family on the night before I left China
to come to the United States.

"Qing Nian, my first loyalty will always be with the Olympic Institute," I assured him. "I'm doing my best to concentrate on the news center and not get involved in the politics within the student leadership. I know the movement is only short-term. When it's all over, we'll still be able to work on long-term problems through the Olympic Institute. We can turn our attention back to educational development."

By the end of dinner we seemed to have renewed our friendship. We even laughed about old times. It was great to be able to talk like this with my friends during this crazy time.

May 2, Tuesday

A young girl came to the news center and asked to speak with someone in charge.

"What is it?" I said to her.

"My parents believe in what the students are doing. They want to help. We have a Chinese-language typewriter they want to donate," she replied meekly.

The *News Herald* staff rushed up to her, barely able to contain their excitement. We had been secretly using a Chinese-language computer in the school computer room, but it was hard to get access to it. "Where is it? Do you have it with you?" they asked, surrounding the girl.

"It's at home," she said. "I rode my bicycle here to tell you this. My parents are afraid to bring it themselves. Could someone come to my house and get it?"

I grabbed two other guys and we followed her out to get the typewriter. For a few seconds I wondered whether this was dangerous: we had to go to the suburbs of Beijing and wait in the street because the girl didn't want us to enter her house. We made it back to Beida safely, though, and were bringing the typewriter up to the second floor of No. 28 when Chang Jin stopped me in the stairwell.

"I'm sorry about what happened," he said.

"What are you talking about?"

"We just held another election for the Preparatory Committee," he explained. "I'm afraid you weren't reelected."

I couldn't believe that this vote had taken place. We had talked about disbanding the committee and electing a new one, but I hadn't known it was going to happen that day. Still, in a way I was relieved by the outcome. It had been so difficult over the past couple of days to get all the members together that I had become frustrated by how unproductive we were.

"That's all right," I told Chang Jin. "I was probably going to leave the committee anyway. So who are the new members?"

"Well, it's Yang Tao, Xiong Yan, Feng Congde, me, and Wang Dan."

Chang Jin told me the whole story of what had happened, and as it unfolded, I became upset. While I was off getting the typewriter, Chai Ling had called a meeting of the twelve-person steering committee that had been established at the beginning of the movement to oversee the Preparatory Committee. They had decided to disband the old committee and select a new panel of five. Wang Dan and I had each gotten six votes, and after a run-off he had won. Before the run-off vote was taken, someone said, "We'll vote again to decide whether Shen Tong or Wang Dan will be the fifth member. Shen Tong is not here. Wang Dan, as you know, has been involved in the democracy movement for a long time." Someone had asked why I wasn't at the meeting and Chai Ling had said, "I posted a note on his door, but he didn't come." Chai Ling knew I had gone to get the typewriter, so I don't know why she did this. But things were so chaotic during this time that many of us acted on impulse and said things we believed were for the overall good of the movement, even if some people got hurt.

I went straight to the committee office to talk to Feng Congde. As soon as he saw me he said, "Shen Tong, don't worry."

"I'm not worried. I was going to leave the committee anyway and concentrate on the news center," I replied. "But I don't think the makeup of the new committee will work. I'm concerned about Xiong Yan, for example." I reminded Feng Congde that

Xiong Yan had been afraid to go to the final meeting of the Committee of Action in 1988.

"But Yang Tao is now the chairman of the committee, and we both agree that he's an excellent leader," Feng Congde said. "He has already said that the committee formed today will exist solely to put together a demonstration on May fourth. They'll actually be in charge for only three days."

"You're right, he is a very good leader," I agreed. "But I don't see how he can head the committee and also run the broadcast station. That's too much for him to be effective at anything."

Seeing that I was becoming increasingly agitated about all of this, Feng Congde said, "The government has rejected the federation's request for a dialogue, and we'll probably never get a real meeting with any officials if we continue using the federation's name. Wang Chaohua and I think we should form an independent dialogue group. That's something you could do." Wang Chaohua, a graduate student in her thirties, was the federation's liaison among the different schools. She and I had become friends in the past week or so.

"That sounds great to me," I replied. "You know I've always thought that one of our main goals should be discussions with the government."

"Why don't you become one of Beida's dialogue representatives? Our other three are Yang Tao, Wang Dan, and Xiong Yan, but I doubt that they'll have much time to organize this. We need you on the delegation. Come with me tonight to the federation meeting."

"All right. And thanks," I said to Feng Congde. I was still concerned that the leadership committees were always made up of the same people, but I thought that a dialogue delegation could really accomplish something.

A little later, when I was working in the committee office, my father came in. He said he had looked all over campus for me. "Could we talk in a quiet place?" he asked.

We walked to the May Fourth Monument, behind No. 28. We

sat under the sculpture, and I told him that I had just been voted off the Preparatory Committee, which I thought would please him and convince him that he wouldn't have to worry about me anymore. But he had something else on his mind.

"This would be a good time for you to apply to leave the country," he said. "You have your acceptance from Brandeis University. You already have all the papers you need to get a visa and a passport." My IAP66, which is the first step in applying for a visa, had arrived a few days earlier. "Your mother and I haven't really given you a hard time about your involvement this time, but you've done enough. Now that I hear you're no longer on the committee, I feel even more strongly that you have a golden opportunity to make an exit. No one will say that you were a quitter."

Many of my friends were watching us from a distance and whispering to each other, probably thinking that my father had come to take me home. Some of the news center people were waiting impatiently for me, because there was a lot of work to be done.

After a long pause, my father continued. "I am not against the student movement. You have all done the right thing. In 1957, before the Anti-Rightist Campaign, I was also involved in a student movement. We even stormed the office of the Far Eastern languages department to have a showdown with the administrator. I acted as a guard while my friends went to look for him. My job was to make sure he didn't escape. So I understand this more than you probably realize.

"I won't go on about me," he continued, smiling as he remembered his college days. "You know your mother and me. You know what kind of environment you were brought up in. We gave you as much freedom as possible. But look at how much trouble you've brought on yourself by getting involved in these demonstrations. This time you were one of the top leaders at Beida, and in all of Beijing. You've made your contribution. You've given more than enough. You don't need to feel that you have to take on all the responsibility. Other leaders have emerged. You can't take on this whole thing yourself."

"Dad," I said, "I'm not doing this just for the country or for the movement. I'm also doing this for myself. I want to be involved."

I don't think that he understood what I was saying, and from his reaction I could tell that he didn't believe that a need to be in the thick of things was a valid reason to put myself in danger. At the time I didn't appreciate my father's visit or his words, because I was so wrapped up in the changes in the leadership committees. When he got up to leave, I gave my pat answer again: "Don't worry, I'll apply for the visa and passport as soon as I can."

That night I went with Feng Congde to the federation meeting at Beijing Normal. More than a hundred Beijing schools sent representatives to this meeting, where the first order of business was planning a May 4 rally. Soon a huge argument broke out over how things should be organized. It seemed to go on and on; the members were getting nowhere, and I was tired of sitting and listening to them. I interrupted to announce that by the next day, each school should select one to three representatives for an afternoon meeting to form an independent dialogue delegation, from which a core group would be selected to meet with the government.

The federation meeting was so disorganized and people were expressing so many different opinions that it was impossible to figure out where it was heading. After staying a little longer, I went home.

May 3, Wednesday

The turnout for the dialogue delegation meeting was disappointing. Only ten schools sent representatives, and I had to serve as the head of Beida's dialogue team because no one else was able to come. I asked everyone to gather in one of the Beijing Normal classrooms and started by having them say what they thought we should do.

"I have an idea about organizing our talks with the government, if we get the opportunity," said a graduate law student from the University of Political Science and Law, Xiang Xiaoji. He was the one student who had distinguished himself during the April 29 dialogue orchestrated by the government. "We should explore three major areas," he went on. "The current student movement, the progress of political reform, and the thirty-fifth clause of the constitution, which guarantees the people's right to assemble, to hold rallies, and to publish freely."

Everyone was so impressed with what Xiang Xiaoji said that by voice vote he was made the chairman of the official Dialogue Delegation. I was elected general secretary, but both of us said that we preferred to be called simply co-organizers. I suggested that those working on our delegation should not also work on the May 4 rally, so that we would be ready to move quickly to contact the government on the heels of the demonstration.

That afternoon I was getting ready to run errands for the news center when a group of Beijing journalists stopped by my dorm. They wanted to join our march the next day. "It's almost impossible for us to organize, because our supervisors are watching us very carefully," one of them said. "Could the news center make banners for us and meet us before the rally? We'll get everyone together as best as we can." I thought it was great that they wanted to take part, so I asked some of the other students to start making the banners. On white sheets and large white placards, they wrote such slogans as "News must tell the truth," "Freedom of the press," and "We want to tell the truth."

After the journalists left, Lao Wang, the worker whom I had talked with before, came to see me. He seemed worried.

"What's wrong?" I asked.

"My work unit has been pressuring me," he replied. "My supervisor told me that if I continue going to rallies, I might lose my job — or worse."

"How did he know that you've been supporting the students?"

"Someone at the factory saw a picture of me leading the demonstrations in a foreign news magazine," Lao Wang said. "I don't know what to do. Is there some way the students can help me?"

I knew there was nothing we could do to help him with his work unit. "Why don't you let us know what they do to you at the factory?" I suggested. "Maybe we can use you as an example and publicize it so it won't go unnoticed."

Lao Wang nodded his head. "I guess there's not much else the students can do," he said before leaving. He never came to see me again.

Everyone knew why the next day was important: it was the seventieth anniversary of the May Fourth Movement, the first student-led political movement in modern Chinese history. We all worked with special zeal so that our rally could stand up to the historical significance of the day. Amazingly, our mimeograph machines churned out 100,000 leaflets, and in the evening several key student leaders and intellectuals — Wang Chaohua, Feng Congde, Wuer Kaixi (who had resurfaced after a few days in hiding), Zhou Yongjun, Lao He, and Liu Xiaobo, a Beijing Normal lecturer who had returned from the United States to join the movement — gathered in the news center to draft a declaration that would be read in the square. The final draft, completed at around 3 a.m., called for democracy on college campuses and eventually in all of China. Wuer Kaixi and I said we would take care of sending vans equipped with loudspeakers to the square so that everyone could hear the declaration when it was read the next day.

May 4, Thursday

Early in the morning two other students and I rolled up the banners they had made for the journalists, tucked them under our arms, and rode our bicycles to our meeting with the reporters. We passed the New China News Agency building and saw that policemen were already lined up outside the entrance to prevent the journalists from joining in the demonstration. But a great many reporters had managed to get outside and were ready to march with us. We met them a little farther along, and as I watched them unroll the banners, I could see that they were excited to be participating. I was excited too, because we were secretly helping them stand up to the authorities. They hoisted the banners, and we three students followed them on our bicycles in the direction of the square. On the way, more than eight hundred journalists from different Beijing publications, including representatives from the *People's Daily*, the China News Service, the *Worker's Daily*, and others, fell in line behind them and defiantly shouted demands for freedom of the press.

As we got closer to Tiananmen Square in the late morning, the two other students and I saw the Beida group marching ahead of us on Changan Avenue and sped up, leaving the journalists. I told the other two to follow me to my house, where we could drop off our bicycles.

As soon as we turned into the alley, I heard people yelling, "Yuan Yuan's here!" My neighbors had heard that I was one of the student leaders at Beida and had come out to welcome me. My sister ran from the courtyard, shouting excitedly, "I want to go too, I'm going with you!" She wasn't afraid of participating in this rally, because this one was different from the April 27 demonstration. Many Beijing residents were already in the streets that morning. I didn't see any police or army troops, and we were not afraid of a crackdown. It seemed a lot like a national holiday. The people of Beijing knew that May 4 was a historic day, and they cheered us and handed out food and drink as marchers passed by.

I was happy to have Qing with me. The four of us walked to the corner of Xidan and Changan Avenue, where we stood to watch some of the other schools pass. Soon we saw the Beida contingent, which made me proud because the marchers seemed more orderly than those from all the other schools. In front of them were some students holding a large placard that read *"Yuan Mu qiu yu,"* "Yuan Mu is a fool."

I walked up to Wang Dan, who was at the head, leading the slogan chanting, as someone yelled out my name. I was handed a megaphone, and Wang Dan and I took turns calling out the slogans. He had a distinctive style of doing this, and he was really good at it. The students were accustomed to hearing his hoarse voice amplified over the megaphone and followed him enthusiastically. I was a little hesitant at first, because I wasn't as good as he was, but by the time we were near Tiananmen Square I had gained some confidence and was just as loud and strong. I felt that Wang Dan and I worked well together as slogan callers. Neither of us looked at the other, but we sensed each other's presence and knew when to lead and when to let the other take over. However, as we neared the square, my sister ran up to caution me. "Stop shouting slogans," she said. "That's enough — stop shouting slogans."

Just after noon the different schools began converging in the square. We didn't know where to go or where to stand; many of the school groups had already scattered, and Beida's students also started getting separated. Tiananmen Square and Changan Avenue were packed, not only with students but with *laobaixing*, who carried their own banners with slogans: "Never forget the spirit of May Fourth" and "Down with graft, fight official corruption." People were climbing the Monument to the People's Heroes and standing on the stairs of the buildings, and everyone was making so much noise that it was hard to hear anything.

We were so worried about keeping order that none of us heard the May Fourth declaration, which was read while I was talking to Feng Congde about what to do. While we were getting our group reorganized, we saw that the people gathered around the monument were already beginning to leave.

"What's going on?" I asked someone coming from that direction.

"They read the declaration. The rally is over," he said. He also told us that Zhou Yongjun, the former chairman of the federation's standing committee, had announced that the class boycott would end today.

"How can it be over when we didn't even hear the declaration?" I asked. The student shrugged and kept going.

Feng Congde led what was left of the Beida group out of the square, and I headed down Changan Avenue to my house. We later learned that mass student demonstrations had taken place all across the country — in Shanghai, Nanjing, Hangzhou, Guangzhou, Changsha, Wuhan, Xian, Fuzhou, and Chongqing. There were also protests by Chinese students abroad. While all this was going on, General Secretary Zhao Ziyang was speaking about the student unrest to the annual meeting of the Asia Development Bank. What was interesting about his speech was that he didn't use the harsh language of the *People's Daily* editorial when he referred to the demonstrators, and he left open the possibility of dialogue.

When I stopped at home to pick up my bicycle, my father was furious with me. "I thought we agreed that you were going to leave the leadership," he fumed. "At work we were all watching the videotapes that the Public Security Bureau made on Chang-an Avenue, and I saw you there, right in front, shouting slogans!"

After he said that, he calmed down. I could see that he was angry and happy at the same time. It had been a great day for students and the democratic movement, and like other Beijing residents, he supported us wholeheartedly. But he still didn't like my being so visible during the rally. As I was leaving, I heard him say to my mother, "My friends at work were all asking me why my son is so fearless."

"And what did you say?" my mother asked.

I was out in our courtyard, grabbing my bicycle to go back to school, but I stopped abruptly to listen.

"I told them it must be because we — the people of our generation — have been cowards for too long."

· 9 ·

Dialogue
Delegation

May 5, Friday

If the student movement was about pressing the Chinese government for reforms, then the responsibility for putting our demands before government leaders fell squarely on the Dialogue Delegation. We held our first formal meeting in a conference room at the University of Political Science and Law. An open meeting, it was attended by about thirty students from various schools. Anyone who had been democratically elected was automatically a member, though we had asked each school to keep its representatives to between three to five. We gathered around a rectangular wooden table, with Xiang Xiaoji and me at one end so we could moderate the meeting. The room wasn't really big enough for all of us, so a lot of people sat and stood along the walls. We were determined to avoid the political fights that often went on in the federation leadership, and that seemed very possible because all of us believed strongly in the delegation's single purpose: to get the government and the students together for an open dialogue. The meeting began in a good spirit.

The only privilege Xiang Xiaoji and I had as co-organizers was to recognize people who wanted to speak. If one of us wanted to say something, he too had to be recognized. Our meetings were very orderly, and because of that we developed a good reputation among the professors and intellectuals. Instead of focusing right away on which of us would actually go to the dialogue meetings, we wanted to be sure we had a clear agenda for the government officials. To be successful and effective, we had to be prepared, so we agreed to follow Xiang Xiaoji's suggestion for dividing the substance of the dialogue into three parts: first, the current student movement; second, the advancement of real reform; third, the clause of the Chinese constitution that guarantees the right to speak and assemble. We broke up into three groups, each of which would take one of the three parts, but before the groups began their discussions we agreed to meet every day. I suggested that we study the speeches of high-ranking Party officials, something that was on my mind because the night before, when I returned to Beida, one of the intellectuals who was advising the Dialogue Delegation had talked to me about Zhao Ziyang's speech to the Asia Development Bank. This adviser said that we should be looking for signals in such speeches, because there was clearly an internal struggle going on between Li Peng and Zhao Ziyang. If we could decipher these messages, I stressed to the group, we would be better able to know what was happening at the highest level of the government and could base our actions on that.

Beijing's campuses were chaotic after the federation's announcement that the class boycott was over. Students at Beida and Beijing Normal continued it, but those at other schools reluctantly went back to class. Although Yang Tao had said that the Preparatory Committee would disband after the May 4 rally, it was still in place (and remained so until the movement's end). It posted a *dazibao* in the Triangle urging all Beida students to go back to class and telling them that returning was not a surrender, but as soon as the *dazibao* was posted, it was torn down. The overwhelming sentiment on campus was that ending the class boycott effectively meant ending the movement. Students came to the broadcast station, which we had moved back into my room after Yang Tao became head of the Preparatory Committee, to voice their opposition over the airwaves. One of the most effective speeches was made by a student who came from the city of Wuhan. "Beida is the leader of this movement," he said, his voice booming over the loudspeakers. "And as leaders, you've got to continue the boycott."

My main concern about ending it was that such an action might take away the leverage the Dialogue Delegation needed. *What if we all go back to class and the government chooses to ignore our demand for discussions?* I thought. I kept my feelings to myself, however, now that I was no longer on the Preparatory Committee.

Later that night the Preparatory Committee announced that each department at Beida would take a vote about the boycott at noon the next day. The results would be tabulated and announced at 4 p.m., which would give the Beida students enough time to contact the other major schools and agree on a strategy.

May 6, Saturday

At the second Dialogue Delegation meeting we drafted the text of a petition to the government, asking for an immediate discussion that would be broadcast live nationwide. In the afternoon Xiang Xiaoji, two other delegates, and I took the petition to the public liaison offices of the Chinese Communist Party Central Committee, the National People's Congress Standing Committee, and the State Council, which were located in the same building complex. All three liaison officers had agreed beforehand to meet us, and they were waiting for us together. This was our first experience with government agencies, and their coordination gave us a sense of how little separation of powers there was among them.

Taking a taxi to the building, we were amused to see that we were being followed by several other taxis full of reporters. When we got out to walk into the liaison office, a number of the journalists trailed us. I don't know what they expected to see; on this trip we were just delivering the petition.

To get into the office we had to go to a back door in an alley lined with dilapidated houses. Some other people, also with grievances, were waiting in line to see the liaison officers. The four of us walked in, but the reporters had to wait outside. Once in the office, we were met by three deputies rather than the liaison officers, and they took the petition. We asked for a reply in two days, on Monday, May 8.

When we arrived back at school, the loudspeakers were broadcasting the results of the vote on the class boycott. The students had cast their votes by marking a form that was given to each dormitory room. Over 60 percent had said that they wanted to continue the strike, versus 20 percent who wanted to end it and another 20 percent with no opinion. The ballot had also asked the students whether they supported the Beida Student Association or the Preparatory Committee, and more than 98 percent of the student body had recognized the Preparatory Committee as the legitimate leadership. As a result of this vote, the committee continued the boycott and urged Beida students to hold discussions on the spirit of the May Fourth Movement and democratic reform in China. Beijing Normal joined us and asked other schools to do the same.

May 7, Sunday

After the May 4 rally there was a general feeling of inertia and letdown among the students. We had been successful in gathering in the square a number of times and we knew we had gotten the government's attention by doing so, but now we were just waiting for the officials to respond to our request for a dialogue.

Bright and early on Sunday morning, Wang Dan, in an effort to keep people involved, began reading transcripts of his conversations with leading dissidents, such as the journalist Dai Qin, over our loudspeakers. When enough students had gathered in the Triangle, he went down and led them in talks about various democratic movements and other subjects that he and the members of the Democracy Salon had discussed. These talks did a lot to keep everyone focused on the issues and to maintain enthusiasm at a high level at a time when not much was happening, and after this they became a daily occurrence in the Triangle, giving students something productive to do now that they weren't going to class. One day when I spoke to a gathering of students about the Dialogue Delegation's role in the movement and our objectives, I said that I believed we should hold formal elections at Beida for the delegates instead of just accepting whoever was interested, as we had done.

An encouraging signal came with the May 7 publication of the *People's Daily*, which quoted Zhao Ziyang as saying that the government should consider a dialogue with the students. The newspaper also reported our request for direct talks with the authorities.

In the afternoon Xiang Xiaoji and I walked over to Beijing Normal for a meeting of the federation. Wuer Kaixi, who had resumed his position as head of that group, changed the meeting place to his dorm room at the last minute, so we all headed over there. His room was similar to the one I had had as a freshman at Beida. He had several roommates, but they left when Xiang Xiaoji and I arrived. The other federation members, including Feng Congde and Wang Chaohua, joined us, and we sat on the bunk beds or on wooden stools around a small desk that had been pulled out into the middle of the room. It was really cramped with ten of us squeezed in.

We exchanged greetings, and Xiang Xiaoji began telling the others what we were doing. "Shen Tong and I are co-organizers of the Dialogue Delegation," he said.

"Yes, we know that," someone replied.

"The Dialogue Delegation is not a political organization," Xiang Xiaoji explained. "We want to remain separate from the federation, both on the surface and in practice. We don't want to be seen as a partisan group. It will be easier to deal with the government if we remain intermediaries."

I disagreed slightly. "It is true that we should give the impression that we are totally separate from the federation," I said, "but actually we must cooperate with each other. You are the number-one umbrella organization of the movement. But the Dialogue

Delegation was formed as a bridge between the government and the students when the government labeled you an illegal group and refused to talk with you. It's crucial that we work together closely, even if secretly, so we can present the students' demands."

"We agree," a federation member said. "In fact, we have some internal documents we will share with you which will help you in your talks with the government."

"You could also help us by using your connections to get more schools to send representatives to the delegation," I added.

When Xiang Xiaoji and I got up to leave, the federation members patted us on the back and asked us to keep them informed of our progress.

May 8, Monday

Knowing that the government wanted the class boycott ended, the Beida Preparatory Committee posted a *dazibao* stating five conditions that the authorities should meet before the students would return to class: an apology from the *People's Daily* for its April 26 editorial and a fairer assessment of the student movement; recognition by the government of the democratically elected student organizations; disclosure by the State Council of official corruption cases and the establishment of a department to investigate and punish the guilty; the reinstatement of Qin Benli as editor-in-chief of the *World Economic Herald;* and repeal of the ten requirements that had been imposed by the Beijing municipal government for a permit to demonstrate.

I was very surprised to read yet another list of demands. I agreed with them, of course, but in making them the Preparatory Committee was creating problems for the Dialogue Delegation — another indication of how the leaders of the student movement had the same goals most of the time but were unable to organize enough to speak with a united voice. There were so many of us, so many groups, often going off in different directions, that the government couldn't possibly have been sure what we were asking for and who was asking for it. I thought that all our demands should be aired through the Dialogue Delegation. We had submitted a request for talks based on one set of demands, and now another group was already raising something new.

That afternoon Xiang Xiaoji, two other delegates, and I went back to the liaison office of the Party Central Committee for our reply. We took a taxi again, and again we were followed by a crowd of reporters. The taxi driver was especially nice to us and promised to wait outside until the meeting was over.

This time the head of the liaison office for the Central Committee, Zheng Youmei, a man in his late fifties or early sixties, greeted us. "We don't have a reply for you," he said. "But the government feels that dialogue is good, and we are working toward that."

He made a lot of general comments, giving us the impression that the government was stalling for time but hadn't ruled out the possibility of meeting with us. This was another sign, we felt, in addition to what we had learned from Zhao Ziyang's speech, that there was an internal struggle in the Party. Zheng Youmei told us that he would call as soon as he had word from above.

"What happened? What did the government say?" All the reporters rushed up to us as soon as we stepped outside the liaison office.

"They have no formal reply," I answered, trying to fend them off. "We're going back to discuss what to do next."

Waiting for me on my desk when I returned to the dorm that night were several messages from my father. He wanted to see me; he had something he wanted to discuss.

May 9, Tuesday

A government official on campus who knew about my involvement in the Committee for Action approached me and said he would help us get a dialogue "through the back door" — unofficially. He told me that he might be able to get Yan Mingfu, the head of the Secretariat of the Chinese Communist Party Central Committee and the minister of the United Front Department, to meet with a small group from the Dialogue Delegation. He said, however, that Yan Mingfu was in the hospital with a fever, so any meeting would have to wait until he was stronger.

"You students should remember to speak with one voice," he advised. "I will continue to negotiate with the government if you do your best to make sure that the Dialogue Delegation is organized."

At the delegation meeting that day I told Xiang Xiaoji the news. We decided to keep this development to ourselves, because we thought that if word got out, it might kill any possibility for a secret meeting.

Later that afternoon, when I was riding my bicycle on the Beida campus, I passed Andrea. I hadn't seen her or talked to her since I had started working on the delegation, and I was worried that she would be angry with me.

"I've been really busy. I'm sorry," I said. "Where are you going?"

"My parents are having a dinner for me," she said. "I left something for you in your room." Then she rode away on her bicycle.

The people working at the news center looked at me with sly smiles on their faces when I walked in.

"What's the matter with you all?" I said.

"Someone left some goods in your room," one of them said, using a word that smugglers use to refer to illegal booty.

They all followed me into the room. An envelope lay on my bed. I picked it up and waved it at everyone.

"Is that it?" they said. Then they left, a little disappointed.

I opened the envelope, which contained a photograph of Andrea and me and a note sealed with a kiss. The note said, "My birthday is your birthday too because we are one." I had completely forgotten that May 9 was Andrea's birthday.

A little later my father and Qing came to my room. It seemed I was forgetting a lot these days: I had never answered my father's message from the day before. They reminded me to apply for my passport and visa. I was still unsure about leaving

China, especially with all that was happening, but my family was very worried, and thought that leaving the country was my only way out of the political mess they believed I was in.

May 10, Wednesday

On my way to the Dialogue Delegation meeting in the morning, I followed Qing Nian and about a thousand other students on bicycles out of Beida's main gate. They were headed for Tiananmen Square, where a bicycle rally was being held to support Beijing's journalists, who were meeting that morning with Hu Qili, a member of the CCP Politburo Standing Committee in charge of the press. Some of the students wore green headbands with slogans such as "Free Press" and "Equal Dialogue" written on them. Many were banging on round wooden drums to mock the State Council spokesman, Yuan Mu, whose name sounds like the words for *round wood;* "Beat *yuan mu*" was a pun for beating up on the government spokesman. All the bicyclists were in a festive mood, laughing and joking as if they were going on a school outing.

"Isn't it great that people are actually attending rallies with smiles on their faces?" Qing Nian said. "Just two weeks ago we thought we would die at the hands of the police. I've never seen anything like it. This movement has become so different from all the others in the past."

As we rode on, I thought about what he said and felt hopeful. Since the movement had begun, many students had joined as active participants, and they seemed to come up with new ways to voice our demands and express our feelings.

I smiled at Qing Nian and said, "It'll be interesting to see what happens next."

When we got to the front gate of the University of Political Science and Law, Qing Nian and I parted. "Have fun at the square," I said, before going off to my meeting.

By now, many more Beijing schools had sent representatives to the Dialogue Delegation, and there were over seventy delegates, many of them graduate students studying law or economics. (Luckily, everyone didn't come to every meeting in the small conference room.) Xiong Yan and I were the only two Beida students who regularly attended the meetings, and I was an undergraduate, which I thought made Beida's presence weak. A couple of days earlier I had tried to hold another election in the Triangle to get more people on the team, but no one had come forward. I needed help with research on the issues we wanted to raise with the government, so I asked an undergraduate law student named Jun to work with me. He wrote a *dazibao* saying that the *People's Daily* had no legal right to label the students instigators, and this well-argued essay became one of the most widely circulated documents during the movement.

In the afternoon, after the meeting, I dropped off the applications and documents for my passport at the Public Security Bureau. I was the last person to submit his paperwork that day. I then stopped by my father's office to tell him I'd done this and to say that he shouldn't worry anymore. To my surprise, he walked me out to Changan Avenue and talked to me about my involvement in the movement.

"A dialogue with the government is the right thing to work for," he said. "It's important that the officials know what the movement is about."

Before we said goodbye, he told me to do a good job on the Dialogue Delegation. I hadn't expected this support.

That night the government official who was arranging the back-door meeting came to see me again. "I hope the students are prepared for a dialogue," he said. "There is a good chance that a meeting will take place soon. Yan Mingfu has expressed an interest."

I was glad that we might have a chance to talk to Yan Mingfu, but I couldn't figure out why we were holding a dialogue with the United Front Department, the function of which was to forge alliances with the elements of society that were considered natural adversaries of the Party — capitalists, ethnic minorities, and intellectuals. But were we natural adversaries of the Party? The truth was, we were meeting with Yan Mingfu because he was the only one interested enough in solving the impasse to contact us. Most other high-ranking Party members, like Premier Li Peng, didn't care about a real dialogue.

Still, I was excited at the news, because this was the first positive sign from the government. I was also nervous. "We're about to take such a big step; I don't think I'm ready for it," I told the official. "I'm not yet using all of the resources we have here at Beida to contribute to the discussions."

"Don't worry — I will put together a group of young professors who can help you," he replied. "I'll let you know when I've set up a meeting."

May 11, Thursday

I was given a campus building number by the government official and told to go there the next morning. The address turned out to be the apartment of a Beida professor. When I walked into the room, nine Beida professors, all in their thirties, were waiting there for me. These men, from the departments of economics, international relations, politics, literature, history, mathematics, and computer science, were important figures in China's economic and democratic reform movement, and most of them served as unofficial advisers to several high-ranking government officials. I was excited and grateful that they had agreed to help me, and a little embarrassed by the special attention they were giving me. We sat in a circle, each with a cup of tea. The professors gave me a number of pointers for conducting the dialogue, and they also let me ask them as many questions as I could think of in the four hours we were together.

"Focus on long-term goals," one of them said. "Don't just make short-term demands."

"You have to realize the potential of this dialogue," another said. "If it is broadcast on television, it will be a great way to educate the people of China as to what the prodemocracy movement is about and what is really going on in this country. Many people don't know the extent of our problems."

"The most important thing to remember is not to let your

opponent lead the discussion," a third added. "Stay on the course you have charted and be sure to say everything you want to say."

Before I left, the professors told me they would give me research papers they had written on educational and economic reform, which I could take to the Dialogue Delegation meetings to help us prepare. I went back to my room feeling energized.

Yang Tao was waiting for me at the news center to tell me that he was holding a press conference that afternoon. As head of the Preparatory Committee, he thought it was time to update the reporters. He wanted me to go along, so we went to a lecture hall that the news center had designated as the meeting place and found reporters from more than fifty publications jammed in.

Yang Tao fielded questions very confidently. Since the movement had begun, many of us had gained a large measure of self-confidence and were no longer afraid of speaking in front of crowds. The reporters asked about the progress of our negotiations for a dialogue and how long the class boycott would last, but we didn't really have answers for them. We were waiting for the government to respond to our demands, and we couldn't predict anything.

One question came up repeatedly during the two hours of the press conference: "What is it that you students really want?" I took the microphone from Yang Tao and answered the question based on the talk I had had with the group of professors.

"We see the movement in three stages," I said. "The first is to gain attention so that the people of China understand our concerns. The second is to make our campuses democratic castles and strengthen our own commitment to democratic reform, while giving students in other cities and those in other sectors of society — workers, peasants, and journalists — the time to gain their own political awareness. And third, after this has been achieved, we will probably hold a nationwide prodemocracy movement in the fall, to educate people as to what democratic reform is all about."

After the press conference I began to hand out the latest copy of the *News Herald,* but before I had a chance, reporters and students in the room swarmed around me and grabbed the papers out of my arms. It was almost impossible to keep the journalists from ripping them to pieces. I was amazed at how popular our newspaper had become.

May 12, Friday

The Triangle was buzzing with people arguing the pros and cons of a *dazibao* that had been posted the night before. "It is time for us to hold a mass hunger strike," the large characters said. This wasn't the first time I had heard the idea of a hunger strike, but until this point no one had made a public declaration like this. The authors of the poster listed two conditions for ending such a strike. The first was that the government should officially declare the movement a patriotic action. The second was that it should conduct a dialogue with the students. The first demand was more important to us, because it made us remember a Chinese saying, *"Qiuhousuanzhang,"* "One settles scores after autumn." We were afraid that if the government did not say that our movement was patriotic, we would be persecuted after it was over.

So many people were gathering to debate the hunger strike that the news center lowered the broadcast equipment from the second floor down to the Triangle. Our loudspeakers could be heard from very far away and brought more people, about four thousand in all, to the Triangle. They were passing the microphone around, giving speeches, some of which were rather bizarre. One person talked about *qigong,* a martial arts technique for regulating your breathing. "I have been practicing *qigong* since I was a child," he said. "I have gone on many hunger strikes against my father. You must master it if you want to survive hunger. It is the secret to victory. I want to be a hunger striker," he added, to a round of applause. "I want you to join me in the hunger strike." The applause grew louder. "I want all of us to practice *qigong!*" Everyone burst out laughing.

I wasn't sure the hunger strike was such a good idea. A lot of the speakers supported it, but none of them seemed to have any convincing reasons for doing so. This was on my mind as I went to an appointment with one of the advisers the government official had arranged for me to see. He was a young social science professor, and I immediately asked him what he thought of the idea.

"Many students are determined to begin a hunger strike, so it looks like that's what will happen," he said. "Therefore, you should do everything you can to help them make it effective. Your role should be to draft a petition supporting their cause and have it signed by as many people as possible, not just intellectuals. This petition may not seem important now, but if the strike lasts for a long time, the strikers will have the backing of many people and the government will not be able to say that it is merely a few hundred students who refuse to eat."

That night the professor and I drafted a very short open letter of support, at the bottom of which we drew lines for eighty signatures. I took the letter back to the publishing center, where we ran off 2,000 copies overnight, enough for 160,000 signatures.

On my way back from seeing the professor, I stopped by the Preparatory Committee office and learned that Wuer Kaixi, Wang Dan, and four other students had announced that the hunger strike would begin the next day, May 13, in Tiananmen Square. The students in the office told me that although the federation was opposed to the hunger strike, Wuer Kaixi, Wang Dan, and some other students were going ahead with it. At Beida, only forty students had signed up to be hunger strikers — a disappointingly small number compared with the number of students who had gone to Tiananmen Square for protests during the past month.

When I went downstairs around ten o'clock, my dorm room was dark and empty. Almost everyone was out in the Triangle. I could hear the speeches about the hunger strike still going on, so I just lay on my bed listening, without turning on the lights. Through the window I saw that the streetlamps were already on; they gave the tree branches and leaves outside a yellow hue. I felt sad all of a sudden, and very tired.

Just after I closed my eyes, Chai Ling's thin voice came over the loudspeakers. "I am here to tell everyone that I want to go on a hunger strike," she said. "Why am I doing it? It is because I want to see the true face of the government. We are fortunate to have parents who raised us to become college students. But it is time for us to stop eating. The government has time and again lied to us, ignored us. We only want the government to talk with us and to say that we are not traitors. We, the children, are ready to die. We, the children, are ready to use our lives to pursue the truth. We, the children, are willing to sacrifice ourselves."

I got up from my bed and walked toward the window. Below the trees was a sea of black heads, thousands of students standing quietly, listening to Chai Ling. They were all staring intently at the fragile speaker before them. I made no sounds or motions at all; I was incredibly moved by her words. Chai Ling's speech was so personal and direct, yet it touched me as no other speech had. I had been trying all day to come to terms with the idea of the hunger strike, and no one had said anything that satisfied me. Chai Ling made me understand why students would want to make such a sacrifice. We were asking the government for dialogue and recognition. Were these two things worth dying for? I didn't think so. But Chai Ling's speech made me and many others realize that the hunger strike was about much more than those two demands. Some of the students were willing to die in order to see the true face of the government. This made me realize how important the Dialogue Delegation's work was. I felt a heavy responsibility. The lives of the hunger strikers depended on our success.

When all the speechmaking was over, I ran downstairs to see Chai Ling, to tell her how much her speech had affected me. I looked for her all night, but I couldn't find her.

May 13, Saturday

At dawn I recruited the Olympic Institute members to fan out across the Beijing campuses and collect signatures for the open letter in support of the hunger strikers. The broadcast station announced that morning that the number of Beida students who had signed up for the strike had risen to three hundred, and many more had volunteered to serve as support staff. The idea had caught many students' imaginations. Chai Ling, who had now become the leading spokesperson for the hunger strikers, had inspired people and made them emotionally committed to the strike, which they saw as the ultimate sacrifice and a heroic way to make a stand against the government.

As soon as word got out that students would be starting a hunger strike in Tiananmen Square that day, workers, teachers, and elderly women came to the Triangle to give us advice. They talked about bringing blankets and keeping containers of hot water nearby during the fast.

I was working in the broadcast station that morning when Xiong Yan came up to me. "Shen Tong," he said, "I'm going to join the hunger strike."

"I don't think you should," I replied. "You're part of the dialogue team."

But Xiong Yan insisted. He too felt that the hunger strike was extremely important. "I must go. I want to go," he said.

At noon everyone crowded around the May Fourth Monument to hear the declaration of the hunger strikers. I squeezed my way toward the monument and saw Ti Bo, who had been head of the Beida student marshals, reading from a piece of paper.

"On a bright and sunny day in May, we are going on a hunger strike. We are young, but we are ready to give our lives. We don't want to die so in our youth, but our country suffers from so many wrongs."

I looked around the crowd. Everyone was still. All eyes were on Ti Bo as he read the declaration.

"We want to tell our parents: don't pity us when we are

hungry. We want to tell our aunts and uncles: don't feel sad when we are gone. We have only one wish: that those whom we leave behind will have a better life. We have only one request: that you remember us as young men and women who pursued life, not death."

Although Ti Bo's reading was moving, no one was crying. The faces of the hunger strikers told me that they were determined in their action.

After Ti Bo finished reading the long declaration, the strikers headed over to a restaurant on campus where a number of Beida professors were giving a last meal as a sendoff. I went from table to table, shaking each person's hand and asking them all to sign the open letter. I knew many of them because they had volunteered at the news center. They seemed at peace with what they were about to do. After the meal ended, around three o'clock, they left for Tiananmen Square, where they settled in front of the Monument to the People's Heroes to begin their fast.

I went straight from the restaurant to a meeting of the Dialogue Delegation. We wanted to start preparing, because there was a good possibility that the government would finally contact us now that some students had begun a hunger strike. Everyone at the meeting was talking about the strike, which some people were still against. Two other delegates besides Xiong Yan had also left our group to join it.

As we prepared for our discussions with the government, more delegates arrived to take part. We were surprised to find out that the authorities had scheduled another meeting with students for May 15; it would be similar to the one I had heard on the radio on April 29, but this time fifty students would attend, thirty of whom represented official student associations. We knew that the presence of these students would prevent a real dialogue from taking place, so we decided not to participate. In the end, this meeting had no more effect or significance than the April 29 "dialogue" had had.

While we were still discussing this, someone from the United Front Department came and told us that Yan Mingfu would meet with us, but only if we went right then. This was very sudden, but we knew that we had to agree, because we might not have another chance. We decided that Xiang Xiaoji, myself, and four others would go.

A van was waiting to take us to the United Front Department. I didn't recognize any of the passengers who were already aboard, but I soon learned that they included some of China's noted intellectuals, such as Wang Juntao and Chen Zimin, political activists and dissidents I had heard about many times. Wang Juntao and Chen Zimin had founded the Economic Institute, a totally independent research group, and some of the other intellectuals were unofficial advisers to members of the Central Committee. They told us that Yan Mingfu had met with them the night before to talk about the situation. "As a result of that discussion," one of them said, "he agreed today to meet with students and asked us to find a few representatives."

When we got to the conference room at the department, at around five o'clock, we weren't the only students there. Vans had also picked up representatives from the federation and from the hunger strikers, including Wang Dan, Wuer Kaixi, Wang Chaohua, Chai Ling, and a number of others. There were forty or fifty people in the meeting room. I wasn't nervous, but I had a strange feeling. The officials treated us like VIPs, pouring water for us and giving us pads to take notes on. They had also prepared supper for us and invited us to eat while we waited for Yan Mingfu, but none of us felt comfortable eating in front of the fasting representatives. We were there to settle very important matters; it wasn't the time for food. Everyone began talking to one another, and the atmosphere seemed curiously relaxed. Finally Yan Mingfu walked in with a number of his aides, one of whom was the government official who had been helping me at Beida.

As soon as we sat down around the table, Wuer Kaixi handed me a note that said we should concentrate on our two most important demands: that the government recognize the student movement as patriotic, and that it conduct a dialogue with us that would be broadcast live to the country. I was impressed by how quickly he had reacted; I was still looking around the room trying to get my thoughts in order and remember what the nine professors had taught me. I felt that we were working as a team, I as the negotiator and Wuer Kaixi, the representative of the hunger strikers, as my weapon against the government.

The intellectuals were serving as arbiters between the government and the students, but as they spoke, it became clear that they were not neutral. "The student movement this time has already reached an advanced stage," one of them said. "The hunger strike has just begun. The government must find a way out of this situation, and that must be through a dialogue with the students."

This support prompted me to write Xiang Xiaoji a note saying that we should express our eagerness for them to become part of the dialogue.

While the intellectuals were speaking, I began thinking about my perception of the Dialogue Delegation's role. I had been so busy emphasizing our independence and our function as a bridge between the students and the government that I had forgotten whose side we were on. After all, the delegation was definitely speaking on behalf of the students. Therefore it seemed important to establish our position while acknowledging the support of the intellectuals. "The Dialogue Delegation agrees with the suggestions that have just been made," I said. "The government and the students should move ahead as quickly as we can, as the intellectuals have recommended."

At this point Chai Ling left the room. Her face was dirty and sweaty, and she was exhausted from leading the hunger strikers to the square and speaking to them for most of the afternoon. It was unfortunate that she was not able to participate in the rest of this meeting, because all of us there got one of our clearest views of the factional infighting that was taking place in the Party hierarchy.

As the meeting moved into high gear, we were all reminded that May 15 — two days away — was a crucial date. The Soviet leader, Mikhail Gorbachev, was making a state visit to Beijing on that day. If the students did not leave Tiananmen Square before his visit, the Party conservatives would seize the chance to say that students and reformers had sabotaged a reconciliation in Sino-Soviet relations, which had been severed for thirty years. The consequences would be like those in 1987, when reformers had been blamed for social unrest and Hu Yaobang had been made the scapegoat and ousted. No one wanted to see that happen again.

"We should all admit that Gorbachev's visit is important not only for international relations but for all reformers in China," one of the intellectuals said. "This visit is the result of the open-door policy of the past ten years. It proves that reform has been successful. We must not disrupt the state visit, because doing so would disrupt the progress of reform."

"We students know how important Gorbachev's visit is for China," I said. "But this is our time to ask the government to sit and talk with us. Why don't we have a dialogue before May fifteenth? That would be a way of responding to the students' demands as well as a way to get the hunger strikers to leave the square."

"Many of you believe that there is a distinction between reformers and conservatives in the government," Yan Mingfu said. "You are in fact wrong about this, but if you believe it, then you are hurting the reformers by being stubborn. There are some things that I do not wish to say here. Everyone knows full well what the situation is. I hope all of us proceed in earnest to resolve this problem. We all know the problem." He seemed to be saying that the student movement was potentially harmful to reformers like himself and Zhao Ziyang, because the hardliners were ready to use our actions to accuse them of promoting social unrest.

Zheng Min, a dialogue delegate from People's University, said in an emphatic tone, "The ball has been kicked to the government's court. We are waiting to see how the government will kick the ball back."

Suddenly the battle lines were drawn between the students and the government. Before Zheng Min's comment, we were speaking in conciliatory language, as if we were trying to resolve the issue together. His words made it plain that it was us against them.

Yan Mingfu then said, "If the students do not leave the square by May fifteenth, the consequences will be hard to predict. None of us wants to see anything bad happen."

This signaled the end of the meeting. I was relieved; the situation was still tense and nothing had been resolved, but all my fears about the difficulty of conducting talks with the government had been put to rest, because the meeting had shown me that it could be done. As we were walking out, I heard Yan Mingfu say to Wuer Kaixi, "We have very few ethnic minorities working for us at the United Front. I hope you study hard, and perhaps when you graduate you will join us as a cadre here."

Afterward some intellectuals and I asked Wang Dan and Wuer Kaixi whether they thought it was possible to get the hunger strikers to leave the square by Monday. They said it was, unless Chai Ling opposed the idea.

May 14, Sunday

In the morning Xiang Xiaoji and I, still hoping to get an official meeting with someone higher up than Yan Mingfu, went to the Central Committee public liaison office. There we hoped to set up a dialogue between government officials and our delegation only, to take place before the false dialogue, which was scheduled for the next day. We met with Zheng Youmei, the liaison officer, who told us again that he didn't have anything definite to report.

"We must meet with someone today," I snapped at him. "Tomorrow will be too late. Unless we have a dialogue, there's no way the hunger strikers will leave the square."

"Students should not be so demanding," he said, frustrated. "I've been a revolutionary for many years; you don't have the right to talk to me this way."

Xiang Xiaoji and I stressed again how urgent the situation was.

"I'll do my best to get you a response today," Zheng Youmei finally said.

Xiang Xiaoji and I went back to the University of Political Science and Law, where the other dialogue delegates were gathered. After the meeting with Yan Mingfu the day before, we all expected that a formal dialogue would take place sometime before Gorbachev arrived, so we needed to be ready, in case we were called at a moment's notice.

Around midday Zheng Youmei sent word that there would be another meeting with Yan Mingfu, beginning at 6 p.m. According to him, it was at such short notice that it couldn't be broadcast live by China Central Television, but cameras would record the proceedings. The Dialogue Delegation agreed to meet under these conditions, even though we continued pushing for a live broadcast. We contacted the federation and the students in the square to alert them, and I called Andrea and asked her to get the word out to the foreign press. I also asked her to lend me her tape recorder for the meeting. When I got to the United Front building at four o'clock to prepare the room for the dialogue, foreign journalists and reporters from various Beijing newspapers and magazines were already waiting there, milling around the entrance. It was chaotic.

We were meeting in the same second-floor conference room where we had met the day before. I spent a lot of time negotiating with United Front personnel to set up the room in a way that showed equality between the government representatives and our delegates. Eventually someone told us that the officials would sit on one side of a long oval table in the center and the students would sit on the other side. Xiang Xiaoji and I noticed that thirteen chairs were designated for the officials, so we decided that if we were to conduct talks as equals, we should have the same number of representatives. By this time more than forty of us were there, so we got together and selected thirteen to speak on behalf of all the others, although everyone would attend.

While Xiang Xiaoji arranged the seating and helped the crew from CCTV set up, I went outside and tried to organize the students who were arriving for the meeting; delegates were coming on buses from the University of Political Science and Law, and people were wandering around and clamoring to get in. Andrea found me as I was ushering students in and out. She quickly handed me the tape recorder I had asked for.

I heard some shouting at the door and saw that Zhou Yong-jun, the former head of the federation, was trying to get in. He wasn't one of his school's dialogue delegates, nor was he a federation leader. I rushed back to the meeting room to ask the delegates from his school if they wanted him to attend, but they were adamantly against letting him in, so I had to go back downstairs and tell the doorkeepers to keep him out. Blocked by the men at the door, he looked at me, his face red. I felt sorry for him. He had been the top leader of the movement at the beginning, and now he was an outcast. After he had tried to end the class boycott on May 4, some students from his school had posted *dazibao* calling him a traitor to the movement. I didn't say anything to him now, but went back upstairs to the meeting room, where Wuer Kaixi and Wang Dan had just arrived to represent the hunger strikers. Although they had not been chosen as delegates, I told them they could stay as observers if they limited their party to five people.

Just before six o'clock, we asked again whether the meeting could be broadcast live on CCTV. Zheng Youmei explained that it could not, because a soccer game was being shown. I suggested that if the meeting was videotaped, the footage could be sent back to the studio every half-hour, to be broadcast right after the game was over. I also proposed that an audiotape could be broadcast over the loudspeakers in Tiananmen Square for the hunger strikers. The liaison officer agreed to both these ideas.

At six the meeting began. Xiang Xiaoji and I looked at each

other and let out a big sigh of relief; the dialogue we had been working for was finally under way. I sat directly across from Yan Mingfu, who still looked weak from his fever. Xiang Xiaoji faced Li Teiying, the head of the state education commission. Ten deputy commissioners of other government departments were also seated, as was Zheng Youmei. I turned on my tape recorder and kept my eye on the TV cameras to make sure they were running.

I immediately reintroduced the issue of the live broadcast. Some of the newspaper reporters had told me it was possible to broadcast live when the game ended, so I suggested that we do that. "We've already told you that the television station said it's not possible," Zheng Youmei answered. I thought for a moment, then decided not to hold up the meeting on this issue.

The dialogue delegates presented the students' views to the officials, taking up in order the three areas of discussion we had been preparing since our first meeting on May 5. While we were speaking, the student observers behind us sent endless notes and proposed more questions for us to raise, so we began deviating from what we had prepared. The meeting started to get out of hand; there were so many questions that Yan Mingfu couldn't answer them all. Many of them didn't seem critical to me — almost all demanded an explanation for why the government had labeled the student movement unpatriotic and the independent student organizations counterrevolutionary.

Yan Mingfu and Li Teiying did most of the talking for the government, while the other ten ministers said nothing. I looked over at Xiang Xiaoji. Neither of us knew how to regain control. My mind was a mess; my thoughts were everywhere. The representatives of the hunger strikers raised their hands to speak, but before anyone could recognize them, and while others were still speaking, they turned on a tape recorder and played the text of their declaration. I was shocked, and didn't know what to do. Suddenly the atmosphere became very emotional. Xiang Xiaoji and I held hands tightly to give each other support.

It took us a while to regain our composure. When I looked up at Yan Mingfu, it was clear that he too had been affected by hearing the declaration, and the other officials had their heads bowed. As soon as the tape stopped, one of the student delegates said, "The only thing we ask for is that the government stop calling us instigators of turmoil." Everything the Dialogue Delegation had prepared to say was by now unimportant. Our only goal was to get the officials to recognize our actions as patriotic.

Xiang Xiaoji suddenly whispered to me, "Shen Tong, you take care of things here." He got up and hurriedly left the room. I panicked. All I could do was to make sure that people with raised hands got a chance to speak.

I could tell that something was going on outside, because assistants were giving messages to the government officials, who looked pressured. The atmosphere was very tense. Xiang Xiaoji came back in with a stern face and walked over to whisper to me. "The students outside are ready to charge the building," he said. "I'm going back outside to talk them out of it. We've got to continue the dialogue without interruption."

"Go on," I replied. "I'll do what I can here. Tell them they're hurting the discussions."

Before he left again, Xiang Xiaoji said, "Shen Tong, the government hasn't been broadcasting the meeting."

I knew then why the students had surrounded the building. The meeting had been going on for over an hour, but the audiotape was not being played in the square.

A few minutes later, around 7:15 p.m., a group of students, including Wang Chaohua, stormed into the conference room, shouting, "Stop the meeting!" as the United Front security guards struggled to push them back outside. "The Dialogue Delegation should stop the meeting now!" Wang Chaohua cried. "The government hasn't been broadcasting any of this!"

I looked at Yan Mingfu and asked him pointedly, "Why aren't you broadcasting as you agreed?"

One of the officials tried to tell us that the van with the videotape had been blocked by the students, so that it was not able to reach the television station.

"That's not true!" a student shouted. "The van with the first tape made it out, because we saw a few scenes on television. It was on for thirty seconds, but that's all. It didn't even say it was a student-government dialogue!"

I looked for Zheng Youmei, but he must have slipped out of the room earlier. When I turned to Yan Mingfu, I saw beads of sweat on his forehead. He looked as exasperated as I felt. He turned around to ask the aides what had happened, but he didn't get an answer.

"Why aren't you broadcasting this?" I asked again.

The students who had forced their way in started shouting over and over, "The Dialogue Delegation cannot go on if this is not broadcast!"

I turned back to Yan Mingfu again, desperate for an explanation that would let us continue. "Why aren't you broadcasting this?" I asked for a third time. "We can't go on if it isn't broadcast."

I could tell by the way the aides were acting that someone higher up was opposed to the broadcast and there was nothing Yan Mingfu could do. "If we can't go on, then we can't," he said. He stood up from the table, and the other ministers did the same. The student delegates stood up too, then the government officials filed out of the room.

For some reason I thought that this was just a temporary break, that somehow we would resume when things were ironed out. As I walked down the stairs, I could see through the open door that the street was packed with students, all waiting to hear what had happened inside. At the bottom of the stairs I turned into a small meeting room where the other dialogue delegates were gathered. Everyone was worried about the consequences of not finishing the meeting. We didn't know what the government would do if the hunger strikers were still in the square when Gorbachev arrived the next day.

Xiang Xiaoji was especially upset. "I said we should limit the number of student observers, but no one listened to me," he complained. "There were too many people talking, and there was no order to what we were saying." Everyone started arguing about what we had done wrong and why.

Some of the intellectuals found us and said that they were going to the square to persuade the hunger strikers to evacuate. Just then Wuer Kaixi walked in. "We've got to go to the square now," he said. "The students are very agitated because they weren't able to hear the dialogue."

I walked with him to the courtyard in front of the United Front building. The group of intellectuals was leaving. The students crowded outside fixed their eyes on Wuer Kaixi and me, looking to us for some direction.

"Shen Tong," Wuer Kaixi said, "what should we do?"

"I don't know. Kaixi, why don't you go ahead to the square? I'll stay here and take care of things in case the meeting starts again."

"All right," he said, turning to go. As I watched him walk away, his eyes full of fire and his movements self-assured, I regained some of my own courage.

I went back inside and found Xiang Xiaoji. "Is there any way we can resume the talks?" I asked him.

Before he could answer, Yang Tao walked up and told us what was happening in Tiananmen Square. "The students do not want you to continue if the dialogue cannot be broadcast."

We walked around the building and talked to some people who worked for the United Front. "You should settle for whatever you can get today, or you'll lose everything," one of them advised us. They knew that we were being pressured not to continue by the students we represented. But we knew that Yan Mingfu was powerless to do more for us if some higher-ranking officials did not agree with him. We were in a mutual bind.

"No one is at fault here," I said. "Our grievances are not with Yan Mingfu. Our grievances are with others, who are not here at the meeting. The people who were sitting across the table from us are the people in the government who are the most sympathetic to us."

Some journalists told us that they had heard that Hu Qili, the Central Committee member in charge of the press, had ordered CCTV to broadcast the meeting live, but someone higher up, maybe from the Central Political Bureau, had instructed the TV station to say it was impossible. We determined from this that there was disagreement within the Central Committee. Yan Mingfu and Zhao Ziyang's faction were eager to comply with our requests before Gorbachev's visit, but the conservatives were not willing to give in on anything, because the hunger strikers' refusal to leave gave them a powerful weapon to use against the reformers.

We were still waiting at the United Front building, hoping that the dialogue could resume when the intellectuals came back from Tiananmen Square. They began to arrive just before nine o'clock, looking depressed. They had not been successful in persuading the students to leave. I found Dai Qin, a very respected journalist, in a conference room with her head on the table. Several other intellectuals, people we admired and trusted, were also there, and their sullen faces told me that the situation was grave. One of them said that Yan Mingfu was still running a high fever.

"What's going to happen?" I asked him.

"It's been two hours now," he said. "The chances of resuming the dialogue get slimmer as time passes."

The dialogue delegates were sleeping in chairs in the hallway. Suddenly the crews in charge of the sound system began setting up again in the small meeting room. They claimed that they had been instructed to put their equipment in place. A few minutes later Yan Mingfu entered the meeting room, looking very weak. I sat in a corner this time, not at the table; I had nothing to say. Xiang Xiaoji sat in the front, and suddenly all the delegates seemed to regain their energy.

"It's a shame that we can't go on because of technical reasons," Yan Mingfu said. "I hope you will understand."

One of the students stood up and accused the government of bad faith. As some of the delegates tried to stop him, others joined in criticizing the officials. Yan Mingfu got up and quickly left the room.

It was around nine-thirty when we dejectedly filed out of the meeting room.

"You realize that if the hunger strikers don't leave Tiananmen Square, at midnight the troops are coming in to clear them out," one of the intellectuals said when we got downstairs.

"But what can we do?" I asked.

"You've got to find some way," he said to me.

Exasperated, I ran back upstairs to get away from the pressure. The reporters were still in the hallway trying to find out what had happened.

"Well?" someone from the *People's Daily* asked.

"It's all over," I said very simply. "At midnight the troops will move into the square."

The reporters gathered around me. They seemed shocked. "What?"

"Tonight at midnight, if the students don't leave the square, the troops will force them to leave," I said.

I ran away from them then and found a small conference room where I could sit down. A few minutes later the other dialogue delegates found me. Zheng Min, who had commented the day before that the ball was in the government's court, said, "We've wasted a historic opportunity. I don't know what terrible consequences will come because of our inability to succeed today."

"There are so many students in the square," I said. "What can we do? The movement has already come this far — it's been almost a month. I don't know where it's going anymore." I felt that we had started a car that was now driving off in a dangerous direction.

We all felt powerless to do anything, so we just sat there for a while, until the United Front people told us that we had to leave. Xiang Xiaoji was seething with anger and started walking back to his school. The others asked me where I was going.

"I'm going to the square," I said.

"Let's all go to the square," suggested a delegate named Li Peng, whom we called the Good Li Peng.

As we walked, many people dropped away and went back to their universities. By the time we reached Tiananmen Square, there were only five of us: Jun, the undergraduate law student who had been helping me on the Dialogue Delegation, and three delegates from the Institute of Social Sciences. I didn't know what we were going to do, but we kept moving as if we had a mission in mind. We walked toward the broadcast station that Feng Congde and the news center people had set up, using the two small speakers that we had first used at Beida. As I passed the fasting students, I saw that their faces were dirty with sweat, and they were wrapped in blankets. There were over six hundred now, half of them from Beida. The whole square was a mess, with people camping out all over. There were no footpaths for us to walk on, so we had to step over the sleeping bodies and on people's blankets to get to the station.

Along the way we heard some of the students say, "The dialogue delegates are here." Many woke up and waved to us, and people who recognized me called out my name. A runner, part of the support staff, went to the broadcast station and reported that another hunger striker had fainted; after just a day and a half, twenty-seven had already fainted.

Feng Congde, who had been in the square the whole time running the broadcast station, looked like a wounded animal. He was dirty and tired, and was trying in vain to maintain some kind of order. He didn't seem to recognize me.

"I want to say something," I said.

"No, you can't," he said, not even looking at me.

"Feng Congde, it's Shen Tong," someone explained. Only then did he realize that I had been standing there.

People came up and patted me on the back, asking how the dialogue had gone. I must have looked like a wreck myself, because someone started to massage my shoulders. I saw Chai Ling's small body at my feet; her eyes were closed, and she didn't seemed to have an ounce of strength left. She didn't budge as people stepped right over her. "Feng Congde, you'd better take care of her," I said.

He handed me the microphone, and I tried to gather my strength. I wanted to tell everyone exactly what had happened inside the meeting room, but most important, I wanted to persuade them to leave the square. I took a deep breath and raised the microphone to my mouth.

"My fellow students, my name is Shen Tong. I am here to apologize and ask for your forgiveness," I said.

As soon as the words came out, hands reached out to clutch my arm and hold me steady. "Don't," those around me said. "There's no need to apologize."

I tried to continue. "The Dialogue Delegation did not complete our mission. I am so sorry . . ." I didn't finish my sentence, but broke down entirely.

Jun quickly grabbed the microphone from me. "Shen Tong is too upset to continue. Let me tell you all what happened at the dialogue meeting." As soon as he began, I let go. Several people behind me held me, and I sensed the darkness all around and felt very cold and tired and helpless. I saw some Hong Kong reporters watching us with great emotion on their faces. Jun's voice, broadcast over the two small speakers, was too weak to pierce through the darkness. Only a few of the hunger strikers sitting close by could make out what he was saying. Jun didn't care. Like a man trying to keep a friend alive by speaking to him nonstop, no matter if the friend is already dead, he kept talking.

"Despite what happened tonight, we sense that there are some in the government who are earnestly trying to help us," he said. "We've already gained a great deal in this movement. We wanted to see the true face of the government, and we have seen it. It is divided. Internal struggle is clearly going on. Gorbachev is coming. We have to remain reasonable and leave the square."

When he finished, the three delegates who had walked to the square with us took turns addressing the crowd. Someone draped a blanket over me because I was shivering. I saw some of the hunger strikers who had fainted being carried away, but as dawn broke, I fell asleep.

· 10 ·

Gorbachev
Is Coming

May 15, Monday

A gust of cold wind woke me up. I was leaning against a flagpole in the square, and people were walking around me with blankets draped over their backs. Everything was very quiet, because it was still early. Suddenly I thought, *Today is May fifteenth! In a few hours, the welcoming ceremony for Gorbachev will take place right where we're sitting!* I jumped up, grabbed the microphone at the broadcast station, and started shouting. "Fellow students, today is May fifteenth, and in a short while Gorbachev will be here. We should leave the square." I woke up the people near me, but the loudspeakers were weak and many kept on sleeping. As I continued, some students came up to stop me, and arguments broke out over whether we should leave or stay.

Even though the troops hadn't come, as people had said they would, I felt strongly that we should get out before something bad happened. "I'm not saying we have to stop the hunger strike. But we should evacuate the square temporarily." I yelled into the microphone so that more people would hear me. "We can't let our emotions make us forget all reason. Gorbachev is leading the Soviet Union to political reform one step at a time. His visit to China could be beneficial and useful to us. By staying here, we are giving the conservatives an excuse to crack down on the reformers."

An older man, one of the workers who had come to the square

to support the students, had walked up and was staring at me. "You are a student leader. You must see this through to the end," he told me emotionally. "You have all of our support."

I tried to convince him that the hunger strikers had to leave before Gorbachev came, and to explain why our presence would be harmful in the long run to what we wanted.

"Are you worthy of being a student leader?" he asked. "You're letting all of the people of Beijing down; you're letting the workers down. To say you want us to leave makes you a traitor to the movement."

By now a lot of students were coming up to take the microphone away from me. They didn't want to hear what I was saying. Suddenly Wuer Kaixi appeared.

"I'm moving the hunger strikers to the east side of the square," he said.

"Isn't there a way of getting them out of here?" I asked, with urgency in my voice. "I'm worried that the troops will come if they stay."

"It'll be impossible to get them to leave completely," he replied.

"All right, at least we can evacuate half the square and show the government that we're still acting in good faith," I said.

Wuer Kaixi said that he would talk with the hunger strikers from each school, to convince them to move to the east side of the square, and I agreed to see what I could do to convince the other students to stay put. Once Kaixi set up an orderly camp on the east side, it would be easier to move the others.

As Kaixi walked off, I grabbed the microphone again. "Please sit and don't move," I shouted. "Student leaders of each school, please keep your contingent together and seated."

An hour or so later we heard from several students that Wuer Kaixi had moved the majority of the hunger strikers. But there was still general chaos, with people standing around and roaming from place to place. I stood up on the monument steps to get a better look at the whole square, and from there I could see that over on the north side the hunger strikers from Beijing Normal

— Wuer Kaixi's own school — had not moved. A ring of students surrounded them as if to protect them. I thought they might follow the others if we moved the broadcast station, along with the school flags and other banners, closer to the new camp. When this didn't work, I ran to them to ask them to cooperate. They began asking all sorts of questions — "Why the east side? Where are we supposed to set up over there?" — which told me that they weren't budging.

I was running back and forth between the broadcast station and the strikers when I saw a huge group of students entering the northwest corner of the square from Changan Avenue, carrying banners and flags. Just as we were about to vacate that half of the square, more people were coming. I went back to the Beijing Normal camp, but its leaders insisted on staying where they were. I had done all I could to move them, but thousands of students were spread out everywhere. It was nearly an impossible task, but I went from school to school, asking each group's leaders to take everyone over to the east side of the square and leave the other half clear for the Gorbachev ceremony. It was really frustrating, because the leaders always said, "If the others move, we'll move too." And when some of them did shift, columns of students poured into the square to take their place.

I looked at my watch and saw that it was almost ten o'clock. Gorbachev was due to arrive at any moment, and there was nothing more anyone could do. I went back to the broadcast station and waited with everyone else to see the limousines carrying the Soviet leader down Changan Avenue. Some of the students held up a large banner that said, "Welcome Mr. Gorbachev, the great reformer."

I knew my worst fears had come true when, at 11:30, there was still no sign of him. We had disrupted the first Sino-Soviet summit in thirty years. I was worried that the government was now infuriated and would never grant us a dialogue. Since there was nothing more I could do in the square, I decided to go back to the news center at Beida to find out what had happened, and on the way I stopped at home to watch the noon news broadcast. The welcoming ceremony had taken place at the airport instead of in Tiananmen Square. When Gorbachev and his wife stepped off the plane, they were greeted by Party officials and given flowers by grade-school children. The news footage showed the limousines coming into the city via Third Ring Road — not the usual route for diplomatic VIPs — to avoid the congested downtown area.

On my way back to school, I tried to imagine how embarrassing it had been for the government officials not to have been able to hold the formal welcoming ceremony they had planned. I still thought the students should have left the square; it would have shown that our movement was not intended to create havoc. Our leaving would have been a gesture of good faith to our countrymen, and the world media, which were in Beijing for the summit, would have reported our ideals and goals. It was a shame things didn't happen this way.

When I got back to Beida, the news center was broadcasting constant updates on what was happening in the square. The faculty and staff had formed a support team to assist the hunger strikers, and buses were shuttling students back and forth. Toward the end of the day we heard that some students in the square had written their wills and gone to buy gasoline to set themselves on fire. This news set off a panic on campus. No one felt that such drastic acts were called for, but we were afraid that some of the students might actually go through with it. People streamed into the broadcast center to try to stop them.

"We must save our children," one woman pleaded over the loudspeakers. "We cannot let them set fire to themselves. We can't let them die this way."

An economics professor who I had never thought was interested in politics was racing around in a frenzy. He was wearing an armband that said he was part of the Beida faculty support group for the hunger strikers. "We have to help the students," he said over and over again as he ran around in circles in the Triangle.

Qing Nian, the Giant, and I took one of our big white bedsheets and wrote in large characters, "We cannot die today," then rode a shuttle bus to the square to hang the banner. It was around nine o'clock when we got to the monument's east side, where we pointed our banner toward the hunger strikers, hoping they would see it.

Some of the dialogue delegates were also at the monument, so we exchanged information. "More than ten hunger strikers from the Institute of Social Sciences have already been sent to the hospital," one of them said.

I was angry that even when students' lives were on the line, the government and the Dialogue Delegation were still at an impasse. An idea suddenly came to me. "Let's go charge Zhongnanhai," I said.

Four of the delegates and I walked to the northwest gate of the Zhongnanhai compound. A lot of people were already gathered there, but they were keeping a distance from the actual gate. A white line was painted in front of it to keep out anyone who didn't have an official reason to be in the compound. I walked right up to this line and was about to cross it when two guards, armed with loaded rifles with bayonets, stepped in front of me.

"I want to go in," I said.

"What for?" one of the soldiers asked.

"Two hundred and sixty hunger strikers have been sent to the hospital. I want to see Li Peng."

An officer came out of the gate and said, "Let's talk over here." He walked me to the side away from the others, but a crowd gathered around us. "It's almost midnight," he said with a phony smile on his face. "All the Central Committee members are sleeping. You can't go in." Obviously, he was not taking me seriously. I became enraged.

"If your child was on a hunger strike and had already fainted, would you still be laughing?" I said.

"We're very sympathetic to the students," he replied sarcastically, the smirk still on his face.

"Why are you smiling?" I asked him. I was very aggressive.

"You should take off your insignia, because you're not worthy of being in the People's Liberation Army. You're nothing more than security here. I want you to get someone who is really in charge. I want to talk with him, and I want to see Li Peng. You have fifteen minutes."

He turned and went inside. By this time at least four hundred people were standing behind me. More soldiers came out and lined up behind the two guards at the gate. After about ten minutes, a student standing near us had to lie down on the ground; he was exhausted from fasting. The crowd started crying that the soldiers should get him a drink of water, and when there was no response, several people began screaming that we should charge the gate.

"Can't anyone inside get him a drink of water?" I asked the guards. They didn't move. "Someone is dying in front of you and you can't move?"

They thought for a few seconds, then called for someone to come out of the compound. There was no response. Suddenly all the soldiers went inside, including the two watching the gate. We were still waiting behind the white line. We knew that if we crossed it, the soldiers had the authority to arrest or shoot us.

"Fifteen minutes have passed," I said. "I'm going in." I walked across the line and was about to enter the gate when an officer ran toward me.

"We're contacting the people in charge," he said.

"We want to wait inside," I told him.

"That's not appropriate," he answered.

"This compound is paid for by the people of this country. There is nothing inappropriate about our waiting inside."

He started to get worried. "You can't all come in."

"Only five of us here represent the students," I said, waving for the other four delegates to join me. We went into the reception area, where a guard sat behind a desk with a telephone.

"Just wait here. We're trying to contact the people," he said, seeing that I was staring at him.

"I don't see you making any phone calls," I said. "I think you should call."

He snickered but picked up the phone and dialed. "Can you come out for a minute?" he said into the receiver.

During the next fifteen minutes no one else appeared, and the crowd outside began yelling, "Let the students go!" They must have thought the soldiers had arrested us. We didn't want them to charge the compound, so one of us went outside to say we were all right.

Soon after that a black car pulled up and two men got out — the deputy liaison officers for the Central Committee and the State Council. "What is the problem here?" one of them asked.

"There are two things you can do," I said, thinking fast. "First, you can have Li Peng go to the square and talk directly to the students. Second, the government should talk with the Dialogue Delegation tomorrow afternoon at two o'clock." I was becoming very emotional. "This is not negotiable. Both of you are old enough to have children our age. If your children were in the square eating nothing and sleeping in the sun and rain just to have an open dialogue with their own government, would you be so relaxed and nonchalant about this? We're not discussing anything with you. We want Li Peng to come to the square for a dialogue. Your job now is to get the message to Li Peng."

"There's no need to talk that way," one of them said. "Don't get so excited."

I pounded the guard's desk. "I won't hear any more of your nonsense!"

The other deputy immediately asked, "What are your names?" He was trying to frighten us.

"I'm Shen Tong — Beida biology department. I'm co-organizer of the Dialogue Delegation." I gave them all the information they wanted about me, in order to show them that their scare tactics wouldn't work. The other delegates also identified themselves.

"I know the two of you are just bureaucrats sent to appease us. You don't have to pretend you're really talking with us," I said. "Just get our message to the people at the top. The hunger strikers don't have time for us to exchange niceties." I couldn't stop scolding them; my anger had run away with me. "Has your conscience been eaten by dogs? You've become mindless machines for the government."

"If you talk like this, we can't go on," one of them replied. Evidently my tirade had made them furious, because they turned around and left.

"I never wanted to talk with the two of you. You're not worth talking to!" I yelled after them. "I just want to give you the message that people are going to die in the square!" I chased them and put my face right up next to theirs, but the other delegates grabbed my arms and pulled me away.

The two officials took a step back, then left in the black car. One of the dialogue delegates pounded the guard's desk and yelled out after them, *"Goguan!"* which means dog official, a name that Chinese people in feudal times called the authorities when they were heartless and corrupt.

When we got outside, even more people were waiting for us.

"They're still stalling," I said, loud enough for everyone to hear. "They don't care about the students who are dying in the square. These people have no conscience." I turned to the two soldiers still guarding the gate. "The two of you should take off your PLA uniforms and go home. This place is not worth your protection," I continued. "By being here, you are helping the government and letting the students fall. You should just go home."

The four other delegates had been surprised by my actions, and my outburst had shaken all of us. We couldn't stay at Zhongnanhai any longer, so we headed back to Tiananmen Square. Several of the people who had been crowded around gave us a ride on the back of their bicycles. I found Qing Nian and the Giant at the broadcast station, and they told me that no one had killed himself that night.

May 16, Tuesday

At eight the next morning, I left my house and went out onto Changan Avenue. People were everywhere, moving toward the square. I walked with the crowd until I passed the Zhongnanhai gate, where Wang Wen, one of the first hunger strike organizers, was talking with a soldier and a female hunger striker. (Wang Wen designed the federation flag, which looked very much like the American flag.)

"What's going on?" I asked him.

"Mind your own business," the soldier said to me.

"Twelve people started a water fast today," Wang Wen said, ignoring the soldier. "They're from the Central Academy of Fine Arts, and they're lying on Changan Avenue in front of the Great Hall of the People under a big banner." Wang Wen and the girl had tears in their eyes as they described these people. "We tried to pour water down their mouths, but they refused. We tried to force their mouths open but couldn't," Wang Wen said almost frantically. "They'll die this way."

"Let's go inside here," I said. "We've got to do something about this."

They followed me to the gate, and again I tried to enter. When the soldiers stopped us, I demanded that someone in charge come out to talk to us in fifteen minutes. The crowd from Changan Avenue had followed us, but it was much bigger this time. The street was full of Beijing residents, many of them yelling, "Let's charge in!"

I turned back to the crowd. "Our movement is peaceful!" I shouted above the noise. "We started as a peaceful movement. The hunger strikers are using their bodies and their lives to convince the government that our intentions are peaceful. This morning twelve people started a water fast. If this government continues to ignore us, these students will die." It may have been because of fatigue and frustration, but I had been emotionally on edge since the dialogue had ended on May 14. Now my voice started to break. "We are here to give the government one last chance to answer our peaceful petition."

The crowd calmed down, but after fifteen minutes no one had come out. I thought for a few minutes, took a deep breath, and began walking through the gate toward the large letters on a back wall that said TO SERVE THE PEOPLE. Just as I went through the second of two gates, a group of soldiers suddenly came out of nowhere and lined up in front of me. I was taken into a room beside the gate where the sentries slept between shifts. Wang Wen and the girl ran in after me, and two more groups of soldiers immediately went outside to cordon off the front of the entrance and stop others from crossing the white line.

Inside, the soldiers seemed really nervous, as if they didn't know what to do with us. The people beyond the gates saw the troops that ran out after we disappeared and were afraid that the soldiers had captured us. I heard them shouting, "Let him go, let the student out!" so I stepped out of the room to let them see that I was all right. Wang Wen and the girl were very quiet. Their whole purpose in coming here had been to have a confrontation, to negotiate with the soldiers, but suddenly they were afraid to say a word.

After a few minutes Zheng Youmei, the Central Committee liaison officer who seemed to be dispatched every time something involving students occurred, came into the room. As soon as I saw him, I knew we weren't going to get anywhere. Still, I repeated the demands I'd made the day before: Li Peng must go to see the hunger strikers, and the government must talk with the students that afternoon.

"We will transfer your requests to the central leadership of the Party," Zheng Youmei responded. "The government understands what you are doing."

I had had enough encounters with Zheng Youmei to know when he was stalling, and I didn't see any reason to wait around for an answer.

"Let's go back to the square," I said to my companions. "It would be better for you to take care of the hunger strikers than to wait here for an answer that probably will not come."

We went out of the gate, through the crowd in front, and into the square, arriving around noon. A lot of people who supported the students had managed to enter the square and were crowded around the monument, and some members of the federation asked me to help restore order. Later I met up with Xiang Xiaoji and some of the other delegates, who had made a huge banner for the delegation and were wearing red ribbons that said "Dialogue Delegate" on their jackets. Together we walked to the broadcast station at the monument, where we were told that the United Front office had sent for student representatives. Wang Dan and Wuer Kaixi had already gone, so I rushed to the office, where I found everyone waiting in the lobby.

Some of the dialogue delegates were sitting around sipping tea with the United Front officials, which I thought was odd. After all, it might be a good idea to be friendly toward the people we were negotiating with, but we hadn't gotten very far with the United Front. I suppose these delegates somehow hoped we might get a dialogue with the government through Yan Mingfu, but I no longer believed that Yan Mingfu could help us. I now saw myself as an opponent of the government. Before the May 14 meeting, I had thought of myself as a negotiator, someone bringing two sides together, but my thinking had changed over the past couple of days. Why did we need to be recognized by the government? We didn't need our opponent's blessing to know that we were a legitimate force. It was useless to wait at the United Front office, because the government obviously didn't want a dialogue.

I was just about to lose my patience when Yan Mingfu came out to talk to us. "I am willing to be your hostage in the square if you agree to stop the hunger strike and the water fast," he said. "I will stay there as your hostage until the government agrees to have a dialogue with the students."

We were all impressed by his commitment to help us, but no one believed that this was a solution. It would be almost impossible to keep a hostage, and holding a government official captive was not compatible with our tactics. Nonetheless, the group decided that Yan Mingfu would go to the square and present his proposal to the students there, so at about 5 p.m., Wuer Kaixi and Wang Dan took him to Tiananmen Square, where all three gave very inspiring speeches. But in the end, not very much came of this. The hunger strikers would not accept Yan Mingfu's offer.

Meanwhile, those of us still at the United Front office were furious that we had been called there yet again, only to have the government present us with a weak gesture. The Good Li Peng suggested that we go to the Zhongnanhai compound and stage a sit-in hunger strike until a high-ranking official agreed to talk to us. About ten of us headed over there and formed a group between the white line and the gate. We held hands, raised them, and declared, "We will sit here and die until we reach our goal."

More and more people gathered behind us. I spotted Andrea in the crowd, but she was too far away for me to say anything to her. Instead I took out the small notebook that Qing Nian had given to each member of the Olympic Institute and managed to pass a page from it back to her. "I don't know if I'll ever leave this place. Take care. I love you," I had written on the little piece of paper. We were all aware of how dangerous the sit-in was; at any moment the army troops could rush up and clear us away.

Andrea passed back a note, on one side of which she had written in Chinese, "Dialogue Delegation President Shen Tong," and on the other side in Portuguese, "I love you." When I read this, my eyes filled with tears. I looked at her, but her sister and a friend were leading her away, trembling.

As word got out about our sit-in, many people came to show us their support, including a group of workers who made a mock coffin to symbolize the death of the government and a Buddhist monk wearing saffron robes who came up and said that he was in favor of the student movement. The crowd eventually sat down on the sidewalk, spreading the sit-in way up Changan Avenue, alongside a line of soldiers. Every now and then someone in the crowd stood up and spoke on behalf of the students. After a while the street was so crowded with onlookers that people climbed up in the trees to get a better view.

At one point one of the nurses who was there in case the strikers needed medical help gave me a note. "Yuan Yuan," it said, "Nainai, Dad, Mom, and I all love you. Your sister, Qing."

I grabbed the nurse's arm. "Where is the person who gave you this note?" I asked. "She's my sister."

"She left," the nurse told me sympathetically. "She look worried, almost as though she were about to break into tears."

I looked around some more, but Qing had vanished.

Sitting there, I could see that Changan Avenue was very different from normal. The traffic had halted; the public buses were not running; no policemen were in sight. The government had quietly ordered all public transportation stopped so it could blame the students for disrupting life in the city. In response, to preserve order and to keep the traffic moving, student marshals began to line the avenue, standing ten meters apart. This line of marshals became a great way to send messages quickly up and down the thoroughfare and in and out of the square. Also, some students served as patrols, running around delivering messages.

When the leaders in the square heard about our sit-in, they sent these student patrols to find out what we needed and to form a barrier to keep the crowd from surging forward through the line of soldiers and trampling us. As a reminder to the officials that there was a sit-in just outside the gate, I wrote down slogans and passed them back to the patrols, who were leading the crowd in chanting. Their voices rolled over my head like tidal waves. One of our favorite chants was *"Zongli zongli, renmin jiaoni, weihe buli, haipa zhenli, biedang zongli,"* "Premier premier, the people are calling you, why do you ignore us, If you're afraid of the truth, don't be the premier." I will never forget this sight. Sitting there, I could see in front of me the words TO SERVE THE PEOPLE, and behind me was an ocean of Beijing residents.

At around eight o'clock I heard people shouting my name. I looked back and saw a group of dialogue delegates calling me, trying to get me to go with them to the United Front office.

"I can't leave here," I shouted back. "I vowed to stay."

For more than an hour the delegates kept calling to me. "You've got to go, it's urgent," one of them cried out. "Xiang Xiaoji is waiting for you. You must go now."

"I declared that I would not leave until we get a satisfactory response from the government. I can't leave," I told them.

They didn't say why I had to go to the United Front, but there was only one thing I could think of: a meeting with government officials might soon take place. We had started the sit-in to pressure Party leaders to come to the table. If a dialogue was about to happen, I should be there. I was still unsure about what to do when the delegates called for me for the eighth time, so I told the other sit-in students that I would go and see what the emergency was.

When I got to the United Front office, shortly after 10 p.m., I found the other delegates waiting in the lobby. Their faces were tense.

"You've set off a bomb in front of the Zhongnanhai compound," one of them said to me. They had called me there to tell me that they thought I had so antagonized the government with the sit-in that the officials would never meet with us.

"What did you people drag me over here for? It looks like nothing is happening," I said angrily. I waited for a few minutes, and no one said anything. "I'm going back."

I was heading out the door when one of the United Front officials stopped me and said quietly, "I think you may want to stay a while. There's a very important meeting going on. If anything good comes out of it, you'll need to be here." He went on to explain that the five members of the Standing Committee of the CCP Politburo — Zhao Ziyang, Li Peng, Hu Qili, Yao Yilin, and Qiao Shi — were meeting secretly with Deng Xiaoping. The meeting was expected to last two hours, and there was a slim chance that a real dialogue might result from it.

The other dialogue delegates filled me in on what had happened during the day. When Zhao Ziyang had met with Gorbachev, he had disclosed a political secret that effectively ended his relationship with Deng Xiaoping: he had told the Soviet leader, and therefore the world, that Deng was still the supreme leader even though in name he no longer held a position of power. There was a delicate balance between the reformers and the conservatives in the Politburo, and Deng Xiaoping always cast the deciding vote. Although it wasn't much of a revelation that Deng was still in control, Zhao's comment signaled that he and Deng were at odds, and as a consequence we were afraid that Deng would cast his vote in favor of Li Peng's faction.

While we were waiting, I tried to speculate on what might be going on in the meeting. I knew that Yao Yilin sat on the fence and could vote either way. Qiao Shi and Li Peng were the most conservative members. The problem was Hu Qili. In 1987 both Hu Qili and Zhao Ziyang had agreed to make Hu Yaobang the scapegoat for the student movement, a betrayal that had also been a show of allegiance to Deng Xiaoping. If Hu Qili decided to ally himself with Deng once again, Zhao would cast the only vote for the students.

It was almost two in the morning when the United Front people told us not to wait any longer and ushered us out. From the way they acted, we guessed that they knew what had happened in the meeting and had already given up any hope that we would have a dialogue.

I ran to Tiananmen Square to spread the word about the secret meeting of the Standing Committee. It took me a long time to find all the other members of the Dialogue Delegation, and while I was looking, at dawn, I heard that Zhao Ziyang had made a speech shortly after 2 a.m. I was eager to find out what he had said, so I watched the replay of his speech on the morning newscast at home. Nothing in his speech told me what had happened in the meeting. Zhao Ziyang asked for calm and restraint and begged the hunger strikers to stop their fast. He also promised that when the movement came to an end, the government would not punish the students who had participated. But seeing his face on the television screen, I could tell how tired, frustrated, and hopeless he felt.

May 17, Wednesday

Two million people — what seemed like all of Beijing — lined the streets for the biggest rally China had ever seen. The hunger strike was now in its fifth day; more than 2000 of the 3600 strikers had been sent to the hospital, and six were critically ill. Every half-hour or so ambulances rushed into the square and then out again, their sirens blaring through the streets, to take fallen strikers to the hospital. The people of Beijing could no longer stay on the sidelines, and everyone was calling for a dialogue.

The *laobaixing*, the ordinary people, were now actively involved in the movement. I heard that even the city's thieves had agreed to go on a two-day strike to show their support for the students. In fact, the crime rate went down in May. People on the crowded buses were friendly to each other instead of fighting, as often happened. Everyone was concentrating on the student movement, and there was a great spirit of comradeship.

Yan Jiaqi and some other intellectuals responded to Zhao Ziyang's disclosure about Deng Xiaoping with a May 17 declaration. "The problem of China is exposed fully to the country and the whole world," it said. "The dictator has unlimited power. The government has failed; it is no longer human. China is still ruled by an old and aging emperor, even though he does not wear the crown. . . . The Chinese people should not wait any longer for the dictators to criticize themselves. . . . Down with dictatorship! End government by old men! The dictator must resign!" I thought this declaration was too drastic and radical. Yan Jiaqi was talking about overthrowing the dictatorship, and though I knew that Deng Xiaoping was the supreme leader, this was the first time I had ever heard anyone publicly call him a dictator.

Before I left the house in the morning, my father told me that my passport was ready and suggested that I pick it up as soon as possible. I agreed, then left for the square. I was carrying a big megaphone and had a pair of binoculars around my neck, and my dialogue delegate badge and my pass were on my denim jacket. Anyone who wanted to enter the square had to have a pass, because security had become tighter and tighter to make conditions more comfortable for the hunger strikers. I also wore a red scarf given to me by the federation, signifying that I was a special delegate.

On Changan Avenue I hitched a ride with a pickup truck from a factory that had closed for the day; all the workers were going toward the square, and the truck in front of us was carrying cases of soda that were being donated to the students. Four other young men, two of them students, were also hitching a ride in the pickup truck. When the two students saw the credentials on my jacket, one of them asked, "What do you do at the square?"

"I'm with the Dialogue Delegation," I said.

One of the other two young men asked me to sign my name on his vest as a remembrance. His companion, who was wearing a red headband, said, "I've been supporting the students all along. I closed my small restaurant, but whenever students come to eat, I open it, no matter what time of the day or night it is. The students have been very nice to me too. They gave me 4000 yuan so I could give free food to other students who come by." I nodded and expressed my appreciation. "I want you to sign my arm," he said, moving over to sit next to me. "When I get back to the restaurant, I'll peel off the skin and hang it on the wall next to my restaurant permit." These permits are hung in the most visible place because they are a store owner's most important document, so I thought he was joking. But he held out a ball-point pen and his forearm. I put the pen to his arm, and my hand trembled as I wrote my name.

The truck started going more slowly than the pedestrians because the streets were so full of people. When we finally reached the square, I jumped off, thanking the driver for the ride. It was clear as soon as I entered that Tiananmen Square was now completely controlled by the students. Each school had its own marshals to check passes and keep order, and the marshals cooperated with one another to form a special security service. Four paths, called lifelines, had been cleared on May 15 to move hunger strikers to the hospitals, and these were still in place.

Most students did not leave the square. Everything was available — bread, sodas, blankets, tents, portable toilets. Much of this material had been donated by Beijing residents, and the students in charge of supplies had one of the most difficult jobs in the square, since they had to maintain an orderly storage space and deal with all the requests. They did their best, but a lot was wasted. Distribution was also a problem, because many students were far from the tents where the food and drinks were kept and had trouble getting to the supplies.

When I got to the monument, I found about thirty of the dialogue delegates standing around waiting for a meeting with the federation and hunger strike leaders. We had all been saying among ourselves that the three groups should form a joint conference, but the delegates told me that nothing had happened. Instead, the hunger strikers and the federation leaders were fighting over control of the square. The hunger strikers felt that they should be calling the shots because now the whole movement revolved around them, but the federation people felt that they were still the overall leaders and that the hunger strikers were no longer physically capable of making decisions. It didn't look as if these groups would ever be able to agree, and the Dialogue Delegation did not want to get in the middle of the power struggle, so we decided to leave the square and meet somewhere else.

One of the delegates, a student at an arts institute, suggested that we go to his school. We left at the height of the day's rally, when the streets around the square were mobbed with demonstrators. Groups were carrying banners that stretched across Changan Avenue, some of them so long you had to move your head to read the entire message. There were workers, teachers, high school and grammar school students, intellectuals, peasants, journalists, medical workers, and even customs officials and employees of the State Council and the Foreign Ministry. We tried to avoid the crowds by walking through some of the smaller alleys, but there were always more groups of demonstrators trying to find their way onto the avenue.

People noticed our dialogue delegate badges and cheered us. When we passed the Zhongnanhai compound, we shouted, "What does this place need? A conscience! What do we want? Dialogue!" The banners in front of the gate directly attacked the leadership, calling for Li Peng and Deng Xiaoping to resign.

So many things were going on in my head as I walked through the crowds. I thought about what this movement could mean for Zhao Ziyang, and about the student leaders — we were arguing too much, and there was too much dissension among us. I also thought about the young man who had asked me to sign his forearm. As I moved among all the people and saw the workers cheering, I remembered something Yang Tao had said early on: that this might become another movement for national salvation. His point was that in recent mass movements in China, very few people had been aware of the ideology behind the demonstrations, and their involvement had been based solely on emotion. I was overwhelmed by what I was seeing on the streets, but I was worried that what Yang Tao had said was true. The people were looking to the students to lead them out of discontent.

It would usually have taken us an hour to get to the arts institute, but this day, with all the crowds, it took six hours. Once we got there, we decided to regroup and start again by electing a new five-member standing committee to head the Dialogue Delegation. Xiang Xiaoji and I were both elected. I always felt that the Dialogue Delegation was very democratic, because we paid a lot of attention to procedure, an important element of democracy.

After our meeting we gathered around a television set to watch the news. Starting on May 17, the press in China operated without censorship from the government for a few days. In this atmosphere, we soaked up every detail of the broadcast. The cameras showed all the people in the capital supporting the students. Spontaneous rallies had also broken out in twenty cities across the country, with hundreds of thousands demonstrating to support the Beijing students.

The television reporter read a moving letter that had been issued by the All-China Women's Federation, appealing to the hunger strikers to stop their fast: "Children, you have already given much to the nation. We the citizens understand, sympathize with, and support you. You are patriots. But you have done enough." The rest of the letter tried to reason with the strikers, almost directly telling them that the government was not worth dying for. The reporter also said that numerous other national organizations, including the China Democratic League and the China Federation of Literary and Art Circles, as well as the presidents of eight universities, had asked the government to hold a dialogue with the students. All of these organizations operated as if they were independent groups for and by the people, but actually they were all controlled by the Communist Party and answered to the government. For the first time they were acting independently and openly disagreeing with the Party. The All-China Workers Union, China's only labor union, which was also under the Party's control, publicly gave the students in the square 100,000 yuan to help the hunger strikers, an amazing and exciting act, since the government had already labeled the strikers counterrevolutionaries.

One of the delegates had been given the telephone number of the Political Bureau, the policy-making organ of the Party, by a contact in the government. Very few people, even in the Party hierarchy, knew this number. It was top secret.

"Let's call the Political Bureau," I said. "We'll make our demand for a dialogue again and wait for a reply at the northwest gate of the Zhongnanhai compound."

We ran to a public phone in the building. I dialed the number and got through immediately.

"Who is this?" the man who answered said.

"I am a dialogue delegate from Beida, Shen Tong. Third-year biology student," I said quickly. "I'm sure you've been watching the news and know that the whole country is asking the government to talk with us."

"You have the wrong number," the man replied.

"I don't have the wrong number. I know I'm not supposed to have this number, but it's becoming a life-and-death situation now, and I had to call." I was speaking quickly, afraid that he would hang up. "I know you have a hotline to the top leaders. You must call Li Peng and Deng Xiaoping and tell them that in a half-hour we will be waiting in front of Zhongnanhai for their answer."

"I think you should be contacting the liaison officer of the Central Committee," he said, referring to Zheng Youmei.

"We've done that several times already, and nothing ever happens," I explained. "We'll be waiting at the northwest gate."

"Wait, wait, wait!" he said. "You shouldn't be so hasty."

"I'm not being hasty, " I replied. "The hunger strikers are going to die."

I hung up the phone. Then about twenty of us hitched a ride to Zhongnanhai with a man driving a large van filled with his family, so we had to pack ourselves in. When we got to the northwest gate, it was mobbed. I ran up to the same officer I had encountered earlier and told him we wanted an answer in fifteen minutes. While we waited, a group of little kids, about five or six years old, gave us Popsicles and drinks. Fifteen minutes went by, but we didn't hear anything. We gave the officer another deadline, and then another; we waited for two hours, and still no one came out. I don't know why we continued to think the government would pay any attention to us. The hunger strikers were starving themselves in the square, but the nation's leaders didn't seem to care. Why wouldn't they ignore a small band of dialogue delegates sitting outside their gate?

Finally we gave up and went back to Tiananmen Square. The hunger strikers had now set up their headquarters in a bus parked on the north side. The Red Cross was bringing in more buses that night, seventy in all, to shelter the strikers from the severe thunderstorms that were expected the next day. It was becoming increasingly hard to keep up with what was going on, because various people claimed to represent the strikers. When I asked who was in charge, I was told that Chai Ling was managing the camp and that Zhang Boli and a man named Li Lu were her deputies.

Chai Ling was a very charismatic leader. She could move you to tears with her speeches, and without her the hunger strike would not have held together. Her leadership came directly from the heart. She was an idealist, but I thought her ideals were based very much on emotion and not on a real philosophy. I knew Zhang Boli from his work on the *News Herald*. We had met because he was a member of the Beida writers' seminar, not through any previous demonstrations. To my knowledge, he had never participated in any political activities before the hunger strike. I didn't know anything about Li Lu. I had heard that he was from Nanjing, which made him the only person from outside Beijing to assume a top leadership role. People were a little worried about him because no one had ever seen his student identification card. When I heard about this leadership, I became concerned. Our movement was about democratic reform, but a lot of people in the square had lost their vision of what we were after, which was going to make it more difficult to accomplish our goal.

Every few minutes someone else came up to us and said he represented the hunger strikers, and at some point a number of these people called another joint conference with the Dialogue Delegation and the federation. Chai Ling, Wuer Kaixi, Wang Dan, Wang Wen, Ma Shaofang, Chen Zhen, and several others who had been recognized as representatives were gathered in the headquarters bus, but I thought having all these meetings wasn't getting us anywhere, so I was glad when Xiang Xiaoji volunteered to represent the Dialogue Delegation. Several people came out of the bus while I was standing nearby and told me that arguments had broken out — most of them concerning the hunger strikers' lack of cooperation — and that nothing was being accomplished. It was getting late, so I walked away from the camp and headed for the broadcast center.

That night I slept in a corner on the third step of the Monument to the People's Heroes, with a blanket draped over me. It was quieter there than most places, and I was able to doze for a few hours. Half-asleep, I remembered that I hadn't done anything about my passport. *For my father's sake,* I told myself, *I must remember to go and get it.*

May 18, Thursday

The Good Li Peng woke me up in the morning to tell me that some workers were organizing at the foot of the Gate of Heavenly Peace, on the north side of the square. He had talked to me the day before about the workers, as he believed we should try to help them put together a general work strike. Now he wanted me to go with him and Xiong Yan to see their leaders. I kept the blanket wrapped around me, because I felt chills and my body was achy all over.

"Take that thing off, you look ridiculous," the Good Li Peng said. But I felt too sick to care how I looked.

At the north end of the square, as we crossed Changan Avenue, we had to wait for about four thousand workers on bicycles who were riding around Beijing yelling slogans in support of the students. Seeing them made me very happy; their energy and enthusiasm were contagious. When we got to the steps at the foot of the Gate of Heavenly Peace, we saw that the workers had taken over a large chunk of space and set up their own broadcast station. They were dirty and looked tired, and I could tell that they had spent the night setting up a headquarters for themselves. Their chief organizer came over to greet us.

"We borrowed 9000 yuan to buy the broadcast equipment," he explained. "We've established the Workers Autonomous Union and are going to invite intellectuals to come and speak to us. We want to do our part to support the students. We don't have anything to ask of you, except one thing," he said. "Could the federation lend us some money to buy blankets? The workers who stayed here last night didn't have anything to sleep on. We would ask the federation ourselves, but we can't get past the marshals to go into the square."

His sincerity and modesty were very moving. I had learned

from a friend of mine, who was one of the three students in charge of finances for the federation, that it had recently been given 170,000 yuan (about $46,000), as well as some money from Hong Kong and the United States. The federation had probably received up to 300,000 yuan altogether, so it certainly had enough money to help the workers buy blankets. "Follow us — we'll take you to see the right people," I said.

After we connected the workers with the finance people at the federation, the Good Li Peng and Xiong Yan said that they were going to some factories to meet with other workers. I just stood there listlessly, with the blanket still wrapped around my body.

Xiong Yan touched my forehead. "You're running a fever," he said. "Why don't you go home?"

I managed to get to our house, but I felt even worse as I lay down in bed. I was so tired, though, and so many things were running around in my head, that I couldn't sleep. I kept thinking about the workers and what the Good Li Peng had said about a general strike. It seemed very drastic, and the consequences could be devastating. The student movement was meant to push the country toward faster and more extensive reforms, but I had always thought of reform as a gradual process. If the workers went on strike, it could push China into economic paralysis. I was very confused about this. I still thought of myself as a reformer, but I wasn't sure that any of us were ready to be revolutionaries.

In the end, I decided that even if I was sick, I couldn't stay in my room when so much was happening. I got up and started to head for Tiananmen Square.

"Where are you going?" asked Nainai, who was the only one at home. "You're too sick to go out."

"Don't worry, there are plenty of doctors with the students," I said.

As I walked out of the courtyard, Nainai called after me, "Your father wants you to pick up your passport. Don't forget it!"

I arrived at the monument at about 1 p.m., looking for the

Good Li Peng and Xiong Yan, but before I found them I ran into Wang Chaohua.

"Shen Tong, I just got back from the Great Hall of the People," she said. "I was looking for you and Xiang Xiaoji, but I couldn't find you."

"Xiang Xiaoji is probably back at his school," I said. "The Dialogue Delegation has moved to the University of Political Science and Law. I was sick this morning, so I went home for a while."

"Early this morning we suddenly got word from the government that a meeting would take place at eleven o'clock," she said. "We were looking for student representatives. Wuer Kaixi was taken to the hospital last night, but we yanked him out to go. He fainted during the meeting."

"What else happened?" I asked. I was surprised that after all this time the government had called such a meeting.

"There's not much hope."

"What do you mean?"

"I wish the Dialogue Delegation had been there," Wang Chaohua said. "We weren't prepared. It was too disorganized. It wasn't a dialogue; the two sides were just making statements at each other. Li Peng made his position clear. He wants us to leave the square, but he's not willing to give an inch."

I was feeling too sick to think about having missed this meeting. It was a very important event in the movement, but I didn't know that until later, when I found out that it had been broadcast nationwide. At the time I saw it as one of many times that the government would talk to us, but in fact it turned out to be our last meeting.

I walked the four blocks from the square to the Public Security Bureau to get my passport. I was still wearing my red scarf from the federation, the badge that said I was a dialogue delegate, and my pass for the square, all of which clearly showed that I was active in the student movement. It didn't even occur to me that the bureau might not give me my passport when they saw that I was involved in the demonstrations, but fortunately, the man behind the desk just handed the passport to me, and I walked out of the building holding it. I was extremely lucky to get it so quickly, because the procedure for getting a passport in China is very bureaucratic, involving a number of approvals and checks with your school or workplace, which usually takes a very long time. Many people helped my application move along by pulling many different strings, but even though I was grateful to have my passport, I put it in the outside pocket of my denim jacket and forgot about it.

Walking back to the square, I had to pass through thousands of people who were again marching in the streets. Every day now the area around Tiananmen Square was mobbed with people, all of them celebrating and cheering the students on. When I saw a public phone, I called the Dialogue Delegation headquarters at the University of Political Science and Law to find out what we were doing about the meeting with Li Peng and whether another one was scheduled. A delegate there told me that the delegation had already drafted a statement denouncing that morning's meeting because it had not been a real dialogue and restating our demand to meet with the government to discuss substantial issues. This statement was given to the CCTV English-language news program anchorwoman, who read it over the air that night.

At the square I ran into one of the students who had been at the meeting with Li Peng. He said that it had been highly confrontational and that the students had been especially indignant; in fact, Wuer Kaixi had spent much of the time scolding Li Peng. From what I was hearing, I could see that Li Peng had called the meeting simply to find out whether the students would leave the square. When they told him they would stay until the government agreed to discuss our demands for reform, it all fell apart. Many other students came up to me to say what a shame it was that none of the dialogue delegates had been at such a critical meeting, but from what I could gather about Li Peng's position, it didn't matter who had been there.

Everyone was talking about the thunderstorms that were predicted. We could feel them in the air; the wind had already started blowing. We began moving the hunger strikers into the buses, but many of them didn't want to leave their makeshift tents. Their leaders were afraid that this was a trick set up by the federation to drive them off the square, so the drivers were booted off their buses and some of the hunger strikers, weak from fasting, punctured the tires.

"How are we going to explain this?" the drivers cried.

The federation people tried to calm them down, saying, "Don't worry, it's not your fault. We'll take care of it."

Eventually, after a lot of work, the federation leaders convinced the hunger strikers that the buses were there to provide shelter from the storm, and people began to board them voluntarily.

Another meeting of the joint conference was called at a trailer in front of the Museum of Chinese History, and this time I decided I had better go. Outside the meeting place I saw Wuer Kaixi sitting on the ground, leaning against a column and eating a bowl of rice. He was surrounded by bodyguards and medical personnel. He looked terrible; the hunger strike had clearly taken a toll on his health. For days I had seen him running around in the camp. Now, when he saw me, he said, "Get some food for Shen Tong."

"We've just run out of food," someone said.

"Here, take my bowl," Wuer Kaixi offered.

"No, I can't take your food," I replied. "I'll get another chance to eat."

I was shocked at first to see one of the hunger strike leaders eating, but someone standing near me quietly said, "His health is really bad now. He has to eat." After a minute's pause, he added, "Did you know that Wang Dan is not really a hunger striker?"

"That's impossible," I said. Rumors about the student leaders were flying everywhere around this time. This one about Wang Dan, like many of the others, turned out to be false; there was never any evidence that he was faking his fast. In fact, Wang Dan was one of the few hunger strike leaders who remained in the square and refused to be hospitalized. I came to admire him more than I ever had.

"Wang Dan set up a bed near the square, and he disappears for a time every day to eat," this fellow went on. "Haven't you noticed that he's never been to the hospital?"

"Where did you get this information?" I asked.

"Everybody's talking about it."

"Who is everybody?" I said, very annoyed. "Name someone I know."

"Everybody is everybody," he said defensively.

"The government may have started these rumors about student leaders to hurt the movement," I said. "Don't spread this around."

Just then the meeting started. With a very serious look on his face, Wang Dan walked in, sat down, and didn't say a word. The meeting had been called because several student representatives from outside Beijing were complaining that they were not part of the leadership in the square.

"The square no longer belongs exclusively to the students of Beijing," one of them said. "Thousands of us have come from all around the country to join the student movement. We want to be included in making the decisions."

That morning, when I had taken the workers' organizer to get money for blankets, we had walked through an underpass beneath Changan Avenue and had seen thousands of students from other cities huddled on the cold cement floor. They had no food and no blankets, and the sanitary conditions were horrible. Tiananmen Square was so tightly controlled by the Beijing student marshals that they couldn't get in for supplies. Understandably, their representatives were asking for a place in the organization so they could ensure better conditions for their fellow students. Finally a compromise was reached: the students from outside Beijing announced that they would form their own association instead of joining the Beijing federation, but agreed to cooperate with the federation leaders in organizing the square.

I walked toward the monument after the meeting, but before I got there, someone told me about another meeting of the federation. *What is it with these meetings?* I thought. *Didn't we just have one?* I went to see what it was all about, but I didn't recognize any of the people. "Who are you guys representing?" I asked.

"We're the new leadership of the federation," they answered.

Things were getting out of hand. Conditions in the square were becoming more confusing by the minute. I made my way over to the hunger strikers' headquarters, where Chai Ling and Zhang Boli were sitting with several reporters from the *People's Daily* and other Chinese newspapers. Wuer Kaixi boarded the bus and told me that the *People's Daily* was doing a special profile of him. I don't know whether it ever appeared, but I was amazed that a government-controlled newspaper would feature a student leader.

While I was on the command bus, we heard that some people in the square were calling for an end to the hunger strike, so the leaders decided to drive the bus around to encourage the students to continue it. As we slowly made our way through the square, cheers went up everywhere, and people reached into the windows to shake hands with us. I stuck my arm out and made the V for victory sign.

After about an hour I got off the bus to walk around. Soon after that the skies opened up, and the rain came down in sheets. I was given a plastic poncho by one of the people in charge of supplies, but it stuck to my skin and made me feel even colder. The students sitting out in the open were miserable, but I thought the rain was a good thing, because the square needed a thorough cleaning. We had set up portable toilets, but there weren't enough for everybody, and some hunger strikers were too tired to make it to them, so people urinated in the open. The stench had become unbearable.

That night, when the rain stopped and after I had slept for a while in the command bus, I went to the monument for yet another meeting of the joint conference. This time most of the important student leaders were present, debating what to do next. It was totally chaotic and disorganized, with everyone trying to talk at once.

"We need a unified leadership," someone said.

"But without a common vision for the movement, we can't expect other students to follow us," another replied.

"The most important thing for us to do now is to take the movement outside the square to other parts of the country," I heard a third person remark.

"The situation is so out of hand that there is nothing we can do now," I said. I was so pessimistic that some of the other students got angry with me for throwing cold water on their efforts to renew everyone's enthusiasm.

While we were meeting, one of the marshals kept interrupting to tell me that someone was asking for me. Finally I walked over to where he was arguing with a young man.

"I want to see Shen Tong," I heard the young man say.

"What is it?" I asked.

"None of your business. I want to see Shen Tong."

"I am Shen Tong."

"I've come to tell you that your sister is looking for you," he said.

I came down from the monument steps and saw Qing standing there, almost crying. "I've been here for two hours, and these people won't let me through to talk to you," she said angrily.

The area around the monument and the hunger strike buses had become a forbidden zone; it was hard to get in and equally hard to get out. Many students wanted to meet Wuer Kaixi and Wang Dan, who had become cult heroes by this point, but it was impossible to get near them.

"I'm sorry," I said. "You're lucky you even got into the square."

"Dad sent me here in the rain to take your passport away from you, so it doesn't get wet or lost."

I took the passport, which was already soaked, out of my jacket pocket.

"Mother and Dad are really scared," my sister said before

leaving. "They know there's nothing they can do, but they want you to take care and take it easy."

I returned to the meeting, but it was still as disorganized as it had been when I left. Everyone agreed that we should have a joint conference, but we couldn't decide who the real student leaders were and who would lead this new organization. There were always a few people who missed a meeting and then objected to what had been decided. Discouraged by the disorganization, I went home to sleep. It was around 4 a.m. when I left the square.

· 11 ·

Martial Law and the Goddess of Democracy

May 19, Friday

The next morning I turned on the television and saw footage of Zhao Ziyang speaking to students in the square. I rubbed my eyes in disbelief as I watched pictures of Li Peng shaking hands with the hunger strikers. Holding a megaphone, Zhao Ziyang said in his heavy Sichuan accent, "We're old, it doesn't matter. You are young, you should take care." I was still woozy with fever and half-asleep. *What's he doing in the square?* I thought. Then Zhao Ziyang said, "I've come too late. I'm sorry." At last someone in the government was apologizing to the students, although I took his words to mean that he could do nothing to help because he was finished in the Party. This was Zhao Ziyang's last card in the power game, and that was bad for the students, because if any high-ranking official was going to be sympathetic to us, it would be Zhao.

I dressed quickly and went to a public phone to call some of the reporters I had gotten to know through the news center and the Dialogue Delegation. I checked in regularly with a number of journalists, especially some of the reporters from Hong Kong and France. This time I reached one of the Hong Kong reporters first.

"They came right after you left," he said, explaining that Zhao Ziyang had tried to go to the square secretly to let the students know he was opposed to the conservative faction's handling of the situation, but Li Peng's people had found out about this plan and had rushed the premier to the square to blunt the effect of Zhao's visit. To those of us who were trying to figure out what the government would do next, it was clear that Zhao Ziyang was losing power and that the hardliners would soon begin to crack down on the student movement.

After I got off the phone, I went to the square, passing the headquarters of the Workers Autonomous Union, whose organizer I had met the day before. He came right up to me, angry about something.

"What is it with you students? What did they think they were doing, getting the autograph of the enemy?" He was referring to some students who had asked Li Peng for his autograph when he was in the square. I didn't know what to say, so I just nodded.

When I got to the monument, I was told to rush over to the United Front Department. Almost all of the key student leaders were there. The United Front people had given the others a nice meal, and they urged me to have a bowl of noodle soup as soon as I walked in. They seemed genuinely concerned about us.

I finished eating, then went to the conference room where the others were gathered. The atmosphere there was very relaxed, almost like a big party. For the first time in weeks, many of the students in the room were well fed and reclining on comfortable sofas. Wuer Kaixi, who was running around, knocked over three containers of hot water, which made everyone laugh.

"What are you all doing?" I asked.

"We're collecting each other's autographs. There's going to be martial law," said a student by the door.

"So soon?" I said. I was shocked. I then remembered that Gorbachev had just left China. Li Peng wasn't wasting any time.

Wang Dan, Xiang Xiaoji, Wang Chaohua, and the rest were signing their names for one another as remembrances, because once martial law was declared, the end of the movement would be near. Even some of the United Front employees were crowding around Wuer Kaixi, whom they recognized from his meeting with Li Peng, asking for his autograph.

I took off my red scarf and began exchanging autographs too, but at the same time I thought that if we really believed that the movement was almost at an end, we should rush back to the square to tell the students to leave.

"What are we going to do?" I asked Wuer Kaixi, who was now in the hallway.

"What do you mean?"

"I mean about martial law."

"We should establish a directorate, with me in charge," Wuer Kaixi said very matter-of-factly.

"How are we going to do that?"

"We'll go to the monument and announce that we are forming a directorate, with me in charge," he said again.

"Who's going to join the directorate?" I asked.

"Anybody can join. I'm the head of it."

I suddenly thought, *What's gotten into this guy?*

Xiang Xiaoji was leaving the building, so I followed him, because I thought he was also concerned about what martial law would mean for the hunger strikers. We both thought that in order to avoid bloodshed, we should end the fast and get the students out of the square. As we were leaving, the other student leaders began to go too.

"Where is everyone heading?" I asked.

"Back to the square, to tell everyone that martial law will be imposed," someone answered.

"Now is the time to end the hunger strike and get everyone out," I suggested.

I was getting ready to give them my reasons when someone said, "All right, we'll end the hunger strike at the same time we report the news about martial law." The others agreed immediately.

We made that very important decision on the way out of the United Front office. I was mystified. The others must have had this on their minds already, because after all the meetings in the past few days, it was hard to imagine that we would have no discussion at all.

The United Front people had ordered cars to take us back to the square. (Wuer Kaixi was still ill from his hunger strike, so he had his own vehicle equipped with medical facilities.) The man driving the car I was in asked us for our autographs. He didn't work for the United Front but had been so touched by the student movement that he was working as a volunteer. "I'm going to give your autographs to my daughter," he told us. "Working for free today will be well worth it."

I never felt comfortable when people viewed the student leaders as VIPs. None of us was that important alone. But this attention did show how much our movement had come to mean to the people of Beijing, as well as to the other students.

We entered the square via one of the lifelines and went to look for Chai Ling to discuss ending the hunger strike. But the people on the command bus would not let us on, so we began meeting outside the bus. Before long Chai Ling came out, and she and Wuer Kaixi got into a heated argument. I thought at first that she was opposed to ending the strike, but as I listened to them, I realized that they were fighting over who would make the announcement that it was ending. Wang Dan was also standing nearby, and when it became obvious that the argument was going to continue, he left. The meeting went on for some time, and they still hadn't resolved their differences when Wuer Kaixi fainted and had to be taken to the hospital.

"I don't know what the result of their discussion was," Wang Chaohua said, "but let's quickly go and announce an end to the strike."

Wang Chaohua, myself, and four others held hands and walked to the federation broadcast station at the monument. It was an adventure just to get from one place to another; at each blockade of marshals we had to show our identification badges and say who we were. After we made our announcement, I ran to the buses where the hunger strikers were stationed to be sure they knew what was happening. That's when I heard that someone who disagreed with us had gone from bus to bus telling the students that the hunger strike was continuing.

I was just about to leave one of the buses when I saw a familiar face. It was Li Jin, a friend I had met when I was on the official Beida Student Association. Li Jin was one of those students who devoted all of his energies to going abroad, and almost every time I saw him he was studying for the TOEFL exam. He had urged me not to be involved in student movements, and after I got into trouble in 1988 with the Committee of Action, he jokingly called me "the veteran troublemaker" whenever he saw me. Now here he was, quietly reading a book. I was astonished that he had joined the hunger strike.

"I didn't know you were a hero," I said to him, half in jest.

"I'm not." He smiled weakly, the effects of the fast visible on his face. "Don't tell anyone, but in the first few days I was sneaking chocolate bars."

I laughed with him, glad that he still had a sense of humor.

"So you've given up your plans and become a revolutionary?" I kidded him.

"Nope," he said, waving a book in front of my face. "I've been reading *New Concepts in English*, getting ready for the day I go abroad."

I wished him good luck and returned to the command bus to help make plans for ending the fast. It was past nine o'clock when Chai Ling called a press conference and announced that the hunger strike was ending and becoming a peaceful sit-in. Just after her announcement, the public address system in the square broadcast a speech by Yang Shangkun, the president of China, saying that the army was moving into Beijing.

In response to the broadcast, Chen Minyuan, the first professor to support the student movement publicly, grabbed a microphone and called for a new hunger strike to be made up of 200,000 participants. Thus the hunger strike ended for only a few hours before it was back on again. The students were so angered by Yang Shangkun's speech that everything quickly returned to the way it had been just hours before. Chen Minyuan had joined the students in the hunger strike early on, and as he fought for the microphone, he seemed emotionally drained. He later suffered a breakdown and was hospitalized.

I was feeling very weak from my fever, so I went to a back seat on the command bus and lay down. The hunger strikers were busy puncturing the rest of the bus tires and removing all of the steering wheels so the army could not come and drive them out of the square. As they ran around poking holes in the tires, I heard a few of them say they would rather die than give in to the government's threats.

My head was spinning, and I tried to block out the noise around me. The nurses who visited the bus wanted to give me intravenous glucose, but I wouldn't let them. They also asked me if I wanted to go to the hospital, but I said no. Rather than have them fuss over me, I went home.

May 20, Saturday

The morning news broadcast showed Li Peng making a speech in which he called for an end to the turmoil and stressed the importance of stability. Just the sight of him made me angry. He had come to represent everything many of us disliked about the government. Some students called him a eunuch because of his high-pitched voice, baby-white skin, and pudgy face. Li Peng said that starting at 10 a.m., martial law was being imposed to restore order to the city. This made it illegal to hold demonstrations, class boycotts, work stoppages, or any mass gathering. It also gave the armed police, PLA soldiers, and other security officers license to do whatever was necessary to stop any violations. For Li Peng to say that martial law was necessary at this time was maddening, because Beijing had never been as orderly as it was during the student movement.

My neighbors found out that I was recuperating at home, and they all came to see me. While they came in and talked to me in my room, Nainai was busy cooking chicken soup to make me well. Dakun also came by, as did Rong Dong, who had returned from Shanghai because the students there were also boycotting classes.

Rong Dong said he had been hearing so much about the

excitement at Tiananmen Square, the first thing he wanted to do was stand there with the thousands of students who had taken it over. Dakun added that Xiaoying, my old girlfriend, and his girlfriend had become hunger strikers.

"I'm not going to the square ever again," I said angrily. "Everyone's gone crazy there. You shouldn't go either."

"Are you serious?" Dakun asked. "You have to go back and reason with the people you say are crazy."

I wasn't really serious about not returning to the square; I was just venting what was by now an enormous amount of frustration over some of the things that had happened among the leaders recently.

"Do you really think I could stay away?" I said to Dakun. "Today is the first day of martial law. I've got to think about my ideas for the movement and write them down. I'll go to the square later and state them publicly."

When my friends left, Andrea came to tell me that ABC News and the Canadian Broadcasting Corporation wanted to interview me. Under the martial law order, students were forbidden to talk to the press about the movement, so we were very nervous when we left my house to go to the meeting place set up by ABC. Andrea went to hail a taxi, because this was usually easier for a foreigner, but this time the taxi driver said to her, "The students have risen up against the government. We don't have to be afraid of you foreigners anymore." As soon as I told him that I was one of the student leaders, his attitude changed. He wanted to help me, he said, but he and a lot of the other drivers had turned in their car keys as part of a strike, so he couldn't take us anywhere. Instead we called the ABC reporter, Todd Carroll, from a nearby hotel and asked him to meet us in the lobby café.

When he came, the first thing Andrea asked was whether ABC could protect me if I was arrested for violating the martial law order. Carroll said that there was nothing he could do. "There is danger, and we cannot guarantee your safety. Do you still want to be interviewed?" he asked me pointedly. I was thinking about it when he said, "If you do, you have to come in the ABC van to our hotel for the interview."

I said no. I did believe that the student leaders should continue giving interviews despite martial law, but if I got in the ABC van and then walked into the hotel with ABC personnel, I was almost sure to be arrested.

I noticed on my way home that fewer people were on the streets than in the past couple of weeks. I spent the rest of the afternoon drafting a speech I wanted to give that night in the square, to get everyone's attention and appeal to their reason. Just before I left the house, my father and mother came out of their bedroom, and my father handed me a sheet of paper.

"I have written something for you and your friends," he said. "I hope you will read it carefully and publicly in the square."

I took the paper, but I didn't look at it and I didn't pay any attention to how serious he looked. My mother was acting a little strange, being unusually quiet, but I didn't pay any attention to that either, because the news that martial law had been declared seemed to consume every thought I had and influence every action I took that day. Both my parents seemed especially worried and looked very sad, but I assumed it was because they thought there was a good chance I would be arrested that night. After taking the paper from my father, I ran out of the house.

I couldn't get into the square at first because I didn't have that day's pass, and it took a lot of explaining before the marshals let me in. On my way to the monument, I was stopped just before crossing one of the lifelines, which the marshals were clearing so that some of the ambulances could get out. I stood next to a man who was well dressed and didn't look as if he belonged there.

"What school are you from?" he asked me.

"Beida. What about you?"

"Oh, I'm from a school in Fujian Province."

We chatted a little bit while the ambulances were going by.

"Do you know who I am?" he asked me, very mysteriously.

I took a good look at him for the first time. I knew that many spies and plainclothes police were in the square, but I could always tell who they were. Sometimes I walked right up to them and said, "Working hard?" But this man didn't fit the description.

"Are you from the Public Security Bureau?" I asked.

"No, I'm a soldier," he said. "A group of us are in the square now."

This made me very tense. "How many are here?" I asked.

"I can't tell you."

"You must know the plan for tonight," I said.

"Of course," he replied, proud that he knew such important information.

"Can you tell me?"

"No, but I will say that you will never guess how the troops will come into the square."

I wanted to pump him for more information, but I didn't want to scare him away with too many questions. "I'm pretty worried about getting hurt," I said casually. "If the soldiers start using tear gas, I won't know what to do."

"Let me tell you," he said excitedly. "Take the tear gas canister and throw it in a bucket of sand."

"All right, thanks," I said. The ambulances had passed and we were allowed to cross. "Take care," I said to the soldier, and then I walked on.

All of us were thinking that the square would be cleared that night, but talking to this man made it seem more real to me. Many of the journalists I had been friendly with throughout the movement pulled me aside and asked me what I thought would happen. Because I thought the 38th Army, the regiment that was stationed in Beijing, would be sympathetic to the students, I was not worried that a real massacre would occur. But the journalists told me that huge numbers of troops had been transferred to Beijing from remote parts of China and that the 38th Army might not be the one carrying out the martial law order.

"We've heard that these troops from outside Beijing have not seen a newspaper in two weeks," one of the journalists said. "The only thing they've read is the April twenty-sixth *People's Daily* editorial."

Once these troops were in the city, we began hearing various rumors about them. Beijing residents who had been chatting with some of the soldiers told us that the troops had been told there was a great flood in Beijing and they were here on a rescue mission. Other soldiers said they were told that an ethnic minority uprising had taken place in Tiananmen Square.

When I reached the broadcast station near the monument, a marshal I didn't recognize stopped me from going on. All of the student marshals were now from outside Beijing. The hunger strike leaders had started using them as a way of keeping a lot of federation and Dialogue Delegation people away from the monument.

"It's okay," I said. "I'm an organizer of the Dialogue Delegation."

"I don't know anything about a Dialogue Delegation."

I didn't want to argue with this marshal. Fortunately, behind him I saw a friend from Qinghua University who worked in the broadcast station, so I asked him to help me. "I have something important to say, but I can't get through," I told him.

"Shen Tong is a student leader, and he's very good at making speeches," he said to the marshal. "On a night like this we need him to speak to the students."

The marshal finally let me pass. I took the microphone and gave the speech I had written earlier. "The three steps of the movement are proceeding, and we have already achieved the first," I said. "We have gotten the attention of the whole nation. Now we have to establish democratic institutions on our campuses. We should have left the square and returned to our schools, despite what the government has done, but now that the government has declared martial law, we must not leave. Our movement is nonviolent, and we cannot be frightened by a violent threat. The government will have to move us physically. In order to remain a nonviolent movement, we cannot panic. Each school should organize its marshals to direct the students in an emergency. All tents and flammable materials should be torn down and cleared out of the square. The lifelines should be preserved in case we have to run. We should have towels ready to combat tear gas."

I spoke for twenty minutes, but was interrupted several times by other students who wanted to grab the microphone. It was very noisy and people were moving all over the place, so I wasn't sure how many heard what I said. After giving my speech, I sat down on the monument steps and looked out at the sea of people. Some students were giving away all the food and medical supplies because they thought that this was our last night in the square. Someone handed me some ginseng and all sorts of pills. A young high school girl with a round face and a childlike voice came over with two large bags of food, including a plate of stir-fried meat, rice, and vegetables, and a steamed bun. I was told that she had been bringing homemade food to the square for the past several days. "I brought extra tonight, since it's the last trip I'll be making," she said.

I thanked her, but I had no appetite. I sat staring at the food; then I remembered the letter my father had given me to read to the students. I took it out and began to read.

"When I was young, I was a student at Beida. I understand full well your enthusiasm and patriotism," my father had written. "Children, you have won so many victories. You have won the hearts of all the people of this country. Your efforts have awakened the political consciousness of ordinary people. It is time to withdraw and regroup so that your second effort will meet with even greater success. I share your dreams. My beloved son will forever stand with you."

Maybe my mind was too exhausted and confused, or maybe I was just stupid and insensitive, but my father's words did not make me realize that something serious was happening to him. His letter should have moved me to tears, but it didn't. I should have realized that something was wrong with him, but I had no idea. I didn't even take the time to think about why he had written this letter. I asked my friend from Qinghua University to read it aloud, because I felt uncomfortable doing it myself. I'm not sure that it was ever read.

The young girl came back and saw that I hadn't touched the plate of food. "Why don't you eat? Eat, eat," she insisted.

So many people were running around giving things away that I decided to escape from the madness. Some people had heard my message and were taking down the tents, but most students weren't moving at all. As I walked through the crowd, I met a group of students who said they were part of the dare-to-die corps.

"What do you do?" I asked.

"We're going to protect the hunger strikers," one of them said. "If the troops come in, we will die rather than see them get hurt."

Stunned by their commitment, I asked them to help clear the square of all flammable materials and to make it more orderly, in case we had to evacuate quickly. They agreed immediately and began collecting things into piles.

As I walked toward the north side to get a cleanup effort going over there, I saw three large tents with about three hundred people sleeping underneath. I had never seen any of them before.

"What group is this?" I asked.

"We're hunger strikers. Some of us have been here since May thirteenth."

I was shocked. I had thought that all the hunger strikers were now on buses — especially tonight they should be on the buses, so that the marshals could push them to safety if we had to flee.

When I told them this, one of them said, "No one told us to leave. We've been waiting for the people at headquarters to tell us what to do."

"Don't worry, I'll go and tell them you're here," I replied.

I ran to the command bus, where Zhang Boli was lying across a seat. "Did you know that there are about three hundred hunger strikers still in tents?" I asked him.

"Don't ask me, ask Li Lu," he said, waving to a man at the back of the bus.

I walked over and finally met Li Lu. He wore tinted glasses. "You still have three hundred people in tents. You've got to get them on the buses," I said. "Where's Chai Ling?"

"Why are you looking for Chai Ling?" he asked.

"She should move the hunger strikers."

"I can take care of that," he said.

"All right then, if you'll take care of it," I agreed.

"All of our people are on buses. I don't know what you're talking about," he suddenly said.

I explained, "I just saw three tents full of hunger strikers. I don't know why they weren't moved on the day of the thunderstorm. I just talked to them."

"If I say there aren't any hunger strikers under tents, then there aren't any," Li Lu said.

I was dumfounded. "I came here to tell you that your people are still out there," I said, my temper rising. "Why don't the hunger strike leaders ever want to cooperate with the rest of us? We're at a point of life and death. I'm telling you that three hundred of your people are still sitting out there."

"Get this guy off the bus," Li Lu said to the other students.

Zhang Boli suddenly sat up, and the others on the bus who knew me came between Li Lu and me. Someone said to Li Lu, "That's Shen Tong." I began moving toward the front of the bus to leave, still thinking about his remark, but my anger overtook me and I rushed back.

"You bastard! What kind of student leader are you if you don't care about the lives of those hunger strikers?" I said.

I knew if I stayed another second I might hit him, so I quickly got off the bus. Li Lu followed me and put his hand on my shoulder. I shrugged him off, but he put his arm around me.

"Shen Tong, there's been a misunderstanding. I've long heard about you," he said, with his arm still on my shoulder. "Listen to me," he continued, in a friendly tone of voice. "Take off all your student badges and the scarf. I'll issue you the best bodyguard. When the army comes, run. A hero knows how to adapt to a situation. I've taken off all of my badges so no one can tell I'm a student leader."

"I don't need a bodyguard," I said angrily.

"Don't be that way," he urged. "All of the top leaders have one. You should have one too." He called over a student who was at least a head taller than I. "This is Shen Tong. You take care of him."

I left him and went to look for Wang Chaohua and the other federation leaders. The bodyguard followed me, even though I tried to lose him. When I found Wang Chaohua, I told her what had happened.

"We've never been able to take care of the problems with the hunger strikers," she replied sadly. "Why don't you just continue your efforts to get the square into some order?"

After this I ran into Lao He, the professor from the Institute of Social Sciences whom I often talked with about politics. He was working at the broadcast station in the square. We had both been too busy to have the long conversations we enjoyed so much, so we began walking around, catching up with each other and sharing our thoughts about what might happen in the next hours and days. I told him that I was trying to get the square ready for an evacuation.

"The situation tonight could be very bad. There is really no use in preparing," he said. "Even if the square is a little more orderly, it will not change the overall picture."

I realized then that he was probably right. I must have been busying myself as a way of coping with the martial law order. If the government cracked down on the movement that night, there wasn't much any of us could do.

The bodyguard was still following me, and I felt sorry for him. I asked him to leave several times, but he refused. "I'd rather walk around with you than stay on that bus," he said.

"Where are you from?" I asked.

"I'm from Hunan Province, Chairman Mao's hometown," he said with a trace of a smile.

Like many students, he had wanted to be part of the movement but hadn't quite known how. He had volunteered to be a bodyguard to the student leaders because it was a way to be useful and also to be in the thick of things.

As we started walking again, I asked Lao He what he had been doing over the past few days.

"I've been running a democracy salon right here in the square," he said. "Leading the discussions makes me feel the same way I felt during our talks."

As we reminisced about the times we had spent talking freely in my dorm room, I felt very close to him. I knew he was in his thirties, but I didn't know anything about his personal life.

"Are you married?" I asked.

"No, I missed some opportunities to get married because I was too idealistic," he said wistfully. "I knew a girl whose father was a successful businessman in Japan. I never considered marriage then because I was so busy chasing after my ideals. I wish now that I had married her. I would be in much better shape financially, and that would allow me to be involved politically over the long run."

We walked in silence for a while, the bodyguard still behind us. My mind drifted back to what might happen now that martial law was in effect.

"I'm not afraid of death," I said, breaking the silence.

Lao He stopped, grabbed my arm, and said, "Are you sure?"

I thought long and hard about it and answered, "Yes, I'm sure."

"I'm not afraid either," he said. "If we need to die today, I am ready."

We continued walking, then we brought up the name of Tan Sitong, an intellectual who led a campaign for reform during the Qing dynasty. Before he was executed for leading the dissident movement, Tan Sitong had said, "If not I, who?" Pointing out that reform movements in every country had historically taken the blood of reformers, he had said, "If it is necessary in China, then let it start with me." We were both looking to him for inspiration.

"If nothing happens to us today and we get out of this alive, let's take a trip together," Lao He said, trying to lighten the mood.

"Sure," I agreed, and then we talked about some of the places we might visit.

"Even if nothing happens tonight, I don't think we will be able to escape this fate," he said, sounding pessimistic again. Many of us knew that somehow or other, the government would find a way to punish each of us. "I've already chosen three places in Jiangsu and Yunnan provinces to hide," he told me. "If the situation is such that I can stay in Beijing, I know two hospitals that will help. I've given them your name, and they have agreed to hide you as a patient until the fury subsides. I'll take you now to introduce you to the nurse who is my contact, and she will give you the best food in the square — and in the world."

We walked to one of the medical stations set up in the square. The nurse was especially pretty, and I gave him the eye.

"Stop it," he said. "I'm not going to marry her."

He introduced us and asked the nurse to bring me something to eat. She came back with salted eggs wrapped in hot pancakes. Suddenly I felt hungry. He was right: her food was the best I'd had in the square.

Lao He had to go back to the broadcast station, so I returned to the hunger strike headquarters to get some sleep.

I was awakened an hour or so later by shouts that the army was moving into the downtown area. The news set off a panic in the square. After my conversation with Lao He, I was not scared; instead I lay back down on the seat as if waiting to die. But a short while later the broadcast stations were reporting that the people of Beijing had come out and lined up in front of the troops, building barricades with steel dividers that resembled bicycle racks and anything else they could find to prevent the army from advancing. They were very friendly to the soldiers, explaining what the students were doing and appealing to them not to disturb our peaceful demonstration. Some of the people even gave them food and drink.

The students around me were elated by this news. But I remembered what the plainclothes soldier had told me about the army coming into the square in an unusual way. We then heard that whole regiments of troops were in the subway system. That would be the end for us, because there was a train station right at the southern edge of Tiananmen Square. This news set off another panic. The federation leadership asked the dare-to-die corps to go to the subway station and block the exits, but before they set off, we were told that subway workers had cut the electricity; the troops were stranded underground.

As updates were broadcast over the loudspeakers, the mood in the square swung wildly. Very soon the sun came up, and we realized that we were still in the square and we had lived through the night. We were ecstatic. There were hugs and handshakes all around. Everyone broke out in song, singing the "Internationale" and shouting, "Long live freedom!"

May 21, Sunday

In the morning I went to see two Hong Kong journalists who were staying at the Beijing Hotel, near the square, and who always had the best information. They told me that they had seen many tanks, army trucks, and even missiles advancing toward the downtown area, and they showed me photographs they had taken. I could hardly believe the government was dispatching such heavy artillery to deal with unarmed students. They also said that Zhao Ziyang had stepped down as general secretary of the CCP. It was rumored that he had been put under house arrest.

After lunch with the reporters, I returned to the square. Now that we had stayed through the first night of martial law, I thought we should consider ourselves victorious and leave the square, ending the movement on a high note. Most of the student leaders agreed with this, so we held a meeting that afternoon, with about seventy students in attendance, to vote on the question "Should we leave?" More than fifty people were in favor of going, but all of us leaders knew that our authority was uncertain and that such an important decision would have to have the support of the other students. We decided to take a poll to determine what we would do. In the end, I thought the majority had decided, and I walked away from the meeting and headed back to Beida, thinking that we would begin pulling out that day and that the focus of the movement would shift back to the campuses, which would be the start of the second stage.

But that never happened. Chai Ling and her group were among the minority who felt that we should stay, so later Li Lu called another meeting with about three hundred different student leaders, most of whom were from other cities and didn't have an understanding of and perspective on the whole movement. A new majority decided to remain in the square.

I hadn't been to my dorm for almost a week. The news center was running out of funds and needed everything; if something wasn't done, we would soon have to stop publishing and broadcasting. I remembered that my friend who was one of the students in charge of the federation's money had told me that he thought a large part of the money should go to the *News Herald* because he believed it could last beyond the movement, so I returned to the square to tell him we needed the federation's help now. He was very receptive to our needs, but because of martial law, a lot of the money had been secretly taken elsewhere. I managed to get 5000 yuan.

When I got back to the news center, I received a call from one of the well-placed sources in the government with whom the news center and the Dialogue Delegation had maintained contact throughout the movement. He said he was sending us a transcript of a speech Yang Shangkun had given to a secret meeting of senior cadres from the Party and the army, in which he had discussed the government's view of the student movement and stated that because the students had broken the law, the army should go into the square no matter what they did now.

As soon as the three-page transcript was delivered, I took it to Ji An, the person now in charge of the publishing center. One of the Olympic Institute members who had tried to keep away from politics and controversy, Ji An had agreed to help us when the movement started by keeping an archive of all of our leaflets. He then started working in the news center and eventually took over the broadcast station and our publishing operation.

"This is a copy of the transcript of the secret meeting," I said, handing him the pages and 500 yuan to cover the expense of reproducing it.

His hands were sweaty as he took it from me. Pushing his glasses up, he didn't say a word, but headed for the mimeograph machines. Seeing his serious expression in the dimly lit hallway made me realize for the first time how far he had come as a political activist. That night he printed 20,000 copies of the speech and sent out teams of students to post them on the electricity poles in the downtown area.

Being back in the news center gave me a better sense of what people outside the square were feeling about the student movement. Martial law had scared many people, but not everyone; in fact, it showed us just how strongly the *laobaixing* supported us. Workers and city residents had formed their own dare-to-die corps and were marching around Tiananmen Square to protect the students inside.

I discovered how much the people were behind us when I stopped at home that afternoon. One of the old ladies in my alley, whom I never thought would be sympathetic to us, told me, "Yuan Yuan, I've been sleeping in the daytime so that I'm wide awake at night. If any soldiers come, I'm ready to hit them over the head with my rolling pin." Even the hooligans had gotten together. "We collected logs to stick in the wheels of the tanks so they won't be able to move," one of them explained to me.

Many of the young punks in my neighborhood had joined a group called the *feihudui*, the Flying Tiger Brigade, made up of about four hundred young men on motorcycles. They rode around Beijing, usually in groups of about forty, giving students information about troop movements. The Flying Tigers became famous overnight, and everywhere they went, traffic and pedestrians moved out of their way and cheered them on. Sometimes their girlfriends, who usually wore chic biker outfits and heavy makeup, rode on the backs of their motorcycles.

One of the Flying Tigers from my neighborhood stopped his group of thirty or so on the corner of Xidan and came over to see me. "He's a student leader," he told the others. "Yuan Yuan, if you ever need news from any part of downtown, I can get it to you in ten minutes."

"That's great," I said, impressed by the group's organization and enthusiasm. "Why did you get involved?"

"I had nothing better to do at night," he joked. Then he became very serious. "People like me have never had any status in this society. We have no money, we have no education, we are the lowest class. The people who work with me got together and donated money, but we couldn't even buy respect. We want the same things that you students are after. The officials are corrupt, but we're the ones who are looked down upon. This is the first time that the people of Beijing have recognized us," he said emotionally. "They actually respect us and like us. Everywhere I ride, the people yell, 'Long live the Flying Tigers!' It's worth dying for." I understood then that the Flying Tigers were not just joy-riding around town; for the first time in their lives, they believed they were doing something good and right for the country.

As I was standing there talking to him, another Flying Tiger rode down the street yelling, "The troops are at Fuxingmen!" which was only a few blocks west. Within two minutes the people in the neighborhood put together six blockades by pushing cars and buses and metal barriers across Changan Avenue. They were incredibly efficient. A few minutes later, when we heard that it was a false alarm, everyone slowly moved the blockade away.

I went on to the Beijing Hotel to see the two Hong Kong reporters again. It had become such a routine for me to visit them daily that I had begun giving their phone number to various people as a place where I could be reached. That afternoon I received a call from a group of intellectuals who had come to

Beijing from elsewhere in the country. They were meeting with various Beijing intellectuals and wanted me to connect them with other student leaders to devise a strategy.

To help them out, I went to see Chai Ling and Li Lu. But Chai Ling was preoccupied with the hunger strikers, some of whom were quite ill, and Li Lu was concentrating on a plan to reorganize the square. He showed me on a map how he was going to set up some brand-new tents that had been donated by people in Hong Kong, with red tents on one side and blue tents on the other. From the way he talked, I thought he planned to stay in the square forever. It seemed clear that he had no time to hear about the intellectuals' idea.

As the hunger strike leaders began exercising more control over what was happening in the square, there was yet another meeting, at which they asked the federation people to leave. The federation people went back to Beida to regroup. Tiananmen Square was now controlled by a new organization, the Safeguard Tiananmen Square Headquarters, with Chai Ling as commander and Li Lu and Zhang Boli as deputies. The hunger strike leaders had completely taken over.

May 22, Monday

Two days into martial law, Wuer Kaixi made an impassioned speech in Tiananmen Square, urging the students to retreat to the embassy area, a few blocks to the northeast, for safety. Many students denounced him as an alarmist, and he was expelled from the leadership in the square. He moved to the Jimen Hotel, about ten kilometers west of the square, which became a new center of activity because many intellectuals had moved there as well, and he and Wang Dan began spending most of their time there. The intellectuals were interested in helping set up a secret publishing apparatus to combat the government's propaganda should there be a crackdown. The government would not last more than a few days, they reasoned, if people around the country were told about its use of violence against the peaceful students.

The Canadian reporters from CBC still wanted to interview student leaders, so I went to their office to make arrangements. There I saw a well-known Chinese television journalist working as a translator, which meant that reporters, both Chinese and foreign, were continuing to work despite the martial law order. After suggesting that they interview Wang Chaohua, I went to the square to look for her, but I was told that she had left with the other federation people. While I was there, I saw six helicopters — special high-tech helicopters called yellow jackets, which I was told had been used in the massacre in Tibet — flying over Tiananmen Square, dropping leaflets warning the students to evacuate. Everyone was shocked and angered by the loud sound of the blades sputtering overhead, and after reading the government leaflets, the students pointed to the helicopters and shouted obscenities.

Wang Chaohua wasn't at the new federation office in No. 38 dormitory, but I ran into Yang Tao, who had stayed on campus as head of Beida's Preparatory Committee since early May.

"So where do we go from here?" I asked him.

"Since there is no hope of negotiating with the government," he said, "I think we should declare our independence, hold direct elections, and form a very strong grassroots student association here at Beida."

"I'm worried about the square," I pointed out. "Most of the students left there now are from outside the city. The hunger strikers who monitor the place told me that more than seventy percent are from out of town. They have no place to go, no plans at all."

"That's why those of us from Beijing have got to be especially organized and clear about our next step," Yang Tao said. "They will have to follow our lead."

He told me about the idea for an "empty school movement": all the students in Beijing would leave the universities and travel around the country, taking the movement to the rest of China. He also told me that people were talking about mobilizing the 10,000-yuan households, the families who had made a lot of money from the opening of limited free markets. These house-holds supposedly had 9 billion yuan deposited in Chinese banks. If we could persuade them to pull out their money, the economy would be crippled. This conversation with Yang Tao convinced me that the movement's future rested with the think-ers and intellectuals behind the scenes, not with the students still sitting in Tiananmen Square.

I finally reached Wang Chaohua on the telephone and asked her to join me in an interview with the CBC.

"Oh no, no interviews," she said.

"Why not?"

"I don't want any publicity."

"The movement has come to this crisis," I told her. "You are a major player. You have a responsibility to tell the world what you are thinking and why you've done what you've done. The Western media are very powerful. It's your chance to explain our motives."

Reluctantly, she agreed, and we made an appointment to meet later in the Friendship Hotel. I was standing around wait-ing for her when a middle-aged woman wearing very plain clothes and a straw hat walked up to me. When she took off her hat, I realized that it was Wang Chaohua. She was very nervous. Her face was full of lines, and her fingers were constantly wring-ing the hat in her hands.

We went up to one of the rooms, where I first heard about Wang Chaohua's colorful past. "My background is very different from that of the other students," she said when asked to describe herself. "I have been involved politically since grade school. Because my father was a professor, I attended the grade school operated by Beida, and during the Cultural Revolution Beida was a hotbed of Red Guard activity. I organized the first group of Little Red Guards to support the high school and university students."

Until I heard Wang Chaohua's story, I thought that all the students who joined the movement, except for Wang Dan and a few others, were participating for the first time. It was wonderful to know that someone I already admired so much had a background as fascinating and passionate as Chaohua's. We had become good friends, and I felt a very strong bond with her.

May 23 through 28, Tuesday through Sunday

Every day for the next six days I went to the square. During this time it seemed that there was a stand-off between the students and the government; neither side knew what the other was going to do, and each seemed to be waiting for something to happen. There was definitely an atmosphere of crisis.

I no longer held out any hope for a dialogue with the government, but I was frantically looking for a way to prevent a crackdown. One of my ideas was to contact Li Xiannian, the former president of the country, who was now retired, and ask him if we could draft him as a transition leader if Li Peng was forced to resign. Li Xiannian was part of the Old Guard, but he was well respected by the military as well as by other Party officials. I thought he could take on a caretaker role, like the one Hua Guofeng had played after Chairman Mao's death.

I called the intellectuals I knew and my contacts in the government to find out how I could reach Li Xiannian. One of the intellectuals said my idea was worth trying, but he wasn't at all enthusiastic about it. "By my estimation," he said, "since Li Xiannian has gone this long without expressing his position, I doubt he will be receptive to the idea, nor can you count on him to oppose Li Peng."

A well-placed government contact I had met in the square said that it was very possible that Li Xiannian was fully behind Li Peng. After several days of trying to contact the former president, with little success, I finally dropped the idea.

While I was trying to reach Li Xiannian, a rumor was going around that Deng Xiaoping had said he would sacrifice the 200,000 lives in the square to buy twenty years of stability. I heard on the news that a group of students had gone to see two senior army generals, Nie Rongzhen and Xu Xianggian, and asked them to state publicly that the troops would not fire on the people.

They had also asked them to denounce Li Peng, who had reportedly ordered the Beijing jails vacated to make room for mass arrests of students. Nie Rongzhen and Xu Xianggian had said that the students should not believe rumors and that the army was in Beijing only to preserve order, not to move on them.

I was partly encouraged and partly distressed by this response. I was glad that two senior army officials were assuring us that the army would not attack, but I was distressed that they had not gone one step further and publicly denounced Li Peng for ordering the troops into the city. By echoing Li Peng's position that martial law was meant to preserve order, these men showed their continuing support for the premier.

When I was in the square, I went from tent to tent and talked to the students. It was almost like the survey I had done when I was in high school, only this time I was asking about something much more important. Every time I talked to my fellow students, I was encouraged. No one knew what was going to happen, but instead of talking about death, people were talking about building a better life for themselves and for China. They wanted to move forward from what we had achieved. I was proud of my generation.

The students had set up little camps for themselves, with pillows and blankets and mattresses that had been donated by various sources. Those on the perimeter tended to have better provisions than those in the center, who were harder to reach. Many people were reading. Some of them were preparing for their TOEFL exams so they could go abroad to study; others read novels or fliers we called "fast news," which were printed by the hunger strike leadership at the monument. A lot of students listened to music on personal stereos, and others brought portable stereos so music was heard all over the square. Two of the most popular singers were Qi Qin and Cui Jian, the John Lennon of China. As I walked around, I saw couples arm in arm, and the boy was often singing one of Cui Jian's songs to the girl: "I was looking at you very closely, and this made me feel so good that I forgot I was without a home . . ."

Rumors flew all over Beijing in those days, some of them positive signs from around the country and the world, which gave us momentary flashes of hope that we might still succeed. We even heard that the Shanghai branch of the Communist Party had declared itself separate from the Central Committee and that ten southern provinces were thinking of breaking with the central government.

It was true that seven senior PLA generals had written a letter to the Military Commission urging that the troops be withdrawn from Beijing, and there was a rumor that the military was so deeply divided that a civil war might break out. The intellectuals, who had been publishing a newspaper since May 15, had become an active political force. Beijing residents presented an open letter to the government saying that they would stand forever with the students. The workers were contemplating a general strike.

Hearing all this made me think that perhaps the government would cave in, but it was impossible to know how much of what we were hearing was true. I was still a reformer, but the reformers in the Party had lost the battle: Zhao Ziyang was formally dismissed as general secretary of the CCP on May 26. But it seemed that the conservatives had lost too, because they were still unable to control the situation. I started to think that maybe, just maybe, the whole government hierarchy would have to undergo dramatic change.

May 29, Monday

I was in the broadcast station at Beida when some officials from the government came to tell us that what we were doing was illegal and we had to stop immediately. When we argued with them, saying that we did have the right to broadcast on campus, they backed off and said instead that we were disturbing the peace. To appease them, we removed a loudspeaker that was directed at the streets outside the campus. But we refused to take down our whole operation. The officials left, not knowing what else to do with us.

Everyone at the news center had been talking for days about a statue that was being built by a group of art students, who were calling it the Goddess of Democracy. With two French journalists, I went to the Central Academy of Arts, where this much-talked-about Goddess was being constructed. The art students had finished it by the time we got there. The sculpture was in four sections, and I couldn't tell what it was going to look like when it was assembled.

One of the French reporters said, "It's a great idea. The student movement has become so complicated. What it needs is a new leader. This is the perfect symbol."

When I went home that night, I found out that my father had been admitted to the hospital. "Please take time out to go and see him," my mother pleaded with me. I didn't think anything was seriously wrong with him; my mother had told me he suffered from gallstones. My sister didn't say anything to me.

Later that night Andrea called and told me that the Goddess was going to be taken to Tiananmen Square in an hour or so. My sister and I hurried to the Central Academy of Arts and watched as the art students loaded each of the four sections onto its own cart. Everyone was very excited about what they were doing, and they handled the Goddess as if she were a precious object.

As we walked to the square, Qing and I joined hands with the marshals accompanying the statue. When we arrived, thousands of students pushed forward to get their first look at the Goddess, and we had a hard time getting her past the crowds to the scaffolding. This was the first time that I felt afraid of being trampled. Everyone in the square was very emotional. Qing and I knew that it would take a few hours for the artists to assemble the sections, so we went home.

Dakun was waiting for me there. "I've been to the hospital to see your father," he said. He had become a surrogate son while I was neglecting my duties. "He is worried that you won't get your visa. I know you don't have time, so why don't I go to the American consulate and wait in line for you?"

This offer was tremendous; since martial law had been declared, the lines outside the American consulate were incredibly long, as people tried to get out of China while they were still able to. I thanked him, and at four in the morning I went back to the square while Dakun went to the consulate for me.

When I entered the square, I saw that the art students were just mounting the head of the Goddess. The students had been holding a vigil throughout the night, and now they stood up and cheered.

I got to the monument, where I found Wang Chaohua. We huddled in a corner, sharing a filthy old blanket. It was cold that night.

"I really don't know what I should do," I said. In spite of all my worries about how the movement was being run in the square, I was grasping for a way to remain active. "If there is work here for me, I would still like to contribute to the movement. Could you go talk to Chai Ling, now that she seems to be in charge, and see if I can still be of help? If not, I should go and relieve my friend, who is at the American consulate now, applying for a visa for me. I am seriously thinking about going abroad."

"I haven't been home for months," she replied. "I left my little boy at home with my husband. I haven't been taking care of them." Her eyes started to water when she thought about her family.

"Let's talk about something hopeful," I said. "What are your long-range plans?"

"I'd like to work for the *News Herald* if it continues publishing," she said. "The news center has done a terrific job with that paper."

"You know you'd be welcomed with open arms," I responded excitedly. "It would be wonderful if you worked for the paper."

"What about you?" she asked.

"My parents want me to go to America, but I'd like to stay in China. I want to continue what we have begun here."

When we began talking about the present again, Wang Chaohua's mood changed. "I'll go talk to Chai Ling," she said somberly.

I stayed at the monument, waiting for her to return. Sitting on the cold stone steps, I tried to imagine what going to America would be like. What I really wanted to do was take a train to Moscow and go to Europe on the Orient Express before I went to the United States. I wanted Andrea to go with me, but I didn't think she would.

The sun was coming up, and the scaffolding around the Goddess had just been removed. I took my first good look at the white figure framed against the sunrise, and I felt so at home. Beijing was my city, where I had lived my whole life. Tiananmen Square was now our town. We had erected a Goddess of Democracy to face the portrait of Chairman Mao that hung on the Gate of Heavenly Peace. *This is where I belong,* I thought. *How can I leave?*

My eyes were still on the beautiful Goddess when Wang Chaohua came back with a blank expression on her face.

"Shen Tong," she said, "you should go get your visa."

I didn't say anything. We looked at each other for a moment.

"Take care of yourself," I said, and walked down the monument steps.

May 30, Tuesday

I went to the American consulate to relieve Dakun, but when it was my turn to be interviewed by the official in charge of visas, I was still thinking about Wang Chaohua and the Goddess of Democracy.

"Why are you going to the United States?" the official asked.

"To go to school," I said, showing him the acceptance letter I had received from Brandeis University in March.

"Are you coming back to China?"

"Yes."

My mind must have wandered, because the next thing I heard was "Could you please answer my question?"

I froze. "I'm sorry, I didn't hear your question," I stammered. "I'm very tired." I was afraid I had ruined my chance of getting a visa.

The official looked at my red scarf, my dialogue delegate badge, and all the identification stickers taped on my jacket. "Take a break," he said, smiling at me. "Come back on June fifth."

May 31, Wednesday

The federation leaders decided that the only thing we could do to keep the army from moving into the square was to ask the people of Beijing for their help. Many student leaders, including me, set out in vans equipped with public address speakers to give pep talks to the *laobaixing*. Wherever we went, people gave us food and drink and applauded us. It was a wonderful feeling to know that they were still behind what we were doing.

As we drove around the outskirts of the city, I saw truckloads of troops that had been stopped by citizens. Sometimes the people scolded the soldiers, but most Beijing residents were friendly to them, giving them food and drink too. There was a general feeling that the soldiers did not know why they had been brought into the city and that they didn't want to harm the students.

On one of our trips, I saw a crowd of people gathered around an army vehicle full of soldiers and weapons — machine guns, rifles with bayonets, cases of bullets. "Those bastards in the government!" a man in the street shouted at the army officer on the truck. "How can you use these things against the students?"

Later that day I heard that Guo Haifeng was now the director of the reorganization effort in the square, in charge of replacing the old tents with the new ones from Hong Kong. Apparently he was now working with Li Lu, making preparations to dig in for the long haul.

June 1, Thursday

I went to pay my daily visit to the Hong Kong reporters in the morning and was told that someone had tried to kidnap Chai Ling. She had escaped somehow and had held a press conference, at which she showed the towel that the kidnappers had tried to use as a gag. Hearing about this made me very tense, since it made me think that the government had started kidnapping student leaders.

On my way to the square, I stopped at the hospital to see my father. This was the first time I had visited him. He was lying in bed, and my mother was sitting at his bedside. I didn't think at the time that he had a serious illness, and no one told me otherwise. He asked me again to leave the movement and get ready to go abroad.

"What more can you do?" he said.

"I don't know, but I just can't leave," I replied.

I stayed for only five minutes, but on my way out of the hospital I looked up and saw my father, wearing the light blue hospital-issue pajamas, staring out the window while my mother held his hand. I had never seen my parents touch each other or show any affection before. I should have known then that my father was gravely ill, but I didn't think about it. I wish now that I had known the truth; if I had, I would have spent every minute with him at the hospital.

When I got to the square, I heard that Chai Ling's kidnappers had really been rival student leaders who wanted to question her about how donations were being spent. I was very upset that relations between student leaders had deteriorated to such a point.

I spent the next two days back at my dorm. The situation in the square was now so chaotic that I thought I could use my time most effectively by working at the news center.

· 12 ·

Bloody Sunday
and Farewell

June 3, Saturday

The French journalists called me at school in the morning to tell me that troops had driven into the downtown area the night before and had left five trucks on Changan Avenue near Xinhuamen after they were stopped by citizens. This concerned me, because I knew that at this point the troops couldn't be so easily stopped, nor would they abandon their trucks unless it was part of a plan, a kind of trick. The reporters urged me to leave my dorm and come back to the area around the square. Something could happen very quickly now.

After arriving at the French journalists' hotel and checking to see whether they had any more information, I called Andrea to ask whether she had heard any news from CBC. She said that the abandoned trucks were loaded with weapons, including butcher knives, chains, and clubs. Apparently the government was trying to goad the students into taking these weapons, so it would be able to call us violent counterrevolutionaries and use this to justify a crackdown.

As we watched CNN in the hotel room, the news report showed tear gas being used near the square. I was pretty sure the footage was taken at a spot called Liubukou, on Changan Avenue near Xidan. A reporter from *Paris Match* decided to take a taxi to the square, so I rode with him. When he got out, I continued on toward the corner of Xidan. Crowds of people were running in the street. Abandoning the taxi when it could go no farther, I walked toward the place where I thought the tear gas was being used. As I got closer to Xidan, I could see the fumes rising from the street. I also saw that some of the people had blood on their faces.

My house was only a few blocks away, so I rushed home. My mother and Nainai said that they had heard loud explosions, apparently the sound of the tear gas canisters going off, and that a lot of people had run into our courtyard to wash the fumes from their eyes. All the neighbors gathered in front of our house and talked about how powerful the Chinese-made tear gas was.

Many people had also been wounded. "I was standing on Liubukou when the police charged the crowd," one person said. "A tear gas canister exploded and blew off a small boy's legs. I saw it with my own eyes. The boy's mother was holding him and crying. She just stood on the avenue not knowing what to do. She was too hysterical to take him to the hospital."

When they heard this story, the neighborhood women were so shocked that they put their hands over their mouths. Another neighbor said he had seen a man whose eye had been destroyed by a tear gas canister.

While we were talking, a few of my sister's friends who were medical interns at a nearby hospital came over. They told us that they had seen hundreds of armed police run out of the Zhongnanhai compound and use billy clubs to beat the hunger strikers, who were still holding their sit-in. The police had also started firing tear gas. When a few children were hurt by the exploding canisters, some who saw this ran to a nearby construction site and got bricks and rocks to throw at the armed police.

"I'm going to see what's going on," I said.

I was heading for the street when one of my sister's friends pulled me aside. "We need to talk to you," he said. He was standing very still, and I could tell that he had something important to tell me. "Your father has leukemia."

I just looked at him blankly. It didn't quite sink in at first. I was preoccupied with what was happening outside, so I couldn't fully comprehend what he had said. At the time I thought this meant my father had only a few years to live, not that the situation was critical then. I didn't do anything or say anything. I was trying to decide whether I should go to Beida or to the square, with no regard for my parents. I was incredibly insensitive.

My sister's friend had told me because it was so obvious that I didn't know my father was so ill. "We are doing everything we can to take care of him," he said now. "But we can't take care of his son. You should stay home and be with your mother."

My mother had already left for the hospital, so I didn't pay any attention. Instead I went out. As I walked down Changan Avenue, I kept hearing the words in my mind: "Your father has leukemia." The truth slowly began to come to me.

Soon I was overwhelmed by guilt. I hated myself for not seeing what had been happening in my own family. To do something for my father, I used the money I still had from the federation and bought two large shopping bags full of food, which I carried home. I asked my sister to take them to the hospital, and left the house again at around 7 p.m.

I walked east about a third of the way to Tiananmen Square. Truckloads of soldiers were parked on Changan Avenue, where they had been stopped by the people the night before. A warning was being broadcast over the Beijing public address system, telling everyone to stay off the streets tonight or suffer grave consequences. That same warning was being broadcast repeatedly on the radio and on television.

I wanted to call the news center at Beida to tell them what was happening in this area, so I waited in a long line that had formed at the public telephone. When I was next to use the phone, I heard the man in front of me say into the receiver, "What is going on over there?" He then turned and handed it to me. "Listen," he said nervously, "they're firing over at Muxidi."

I put the receiver to my ear and heard the sound of gunshots in the background. Muxidi was a congested downtown intersection five kilometers west of Tiananmen Square. I decided not to make my call but to start walking back home.

At this point I saw one of the student marshals racing toward the square. Blood and sweat were running down his forehead.

"What's happening?" I asked him.

"The troops are coming from the northwest corner of Second Ring Road and are already at Muxidi. They're firing real bullets, and the people are burning their trucks," he said, hardly taking a breath between sentences. "I just came from Muxidi. One of the students I was with died — I'm covered with his blood. I've got to run to the square and warn the others."

I let go of his arm and he continued running.

I ran in the opposite direction, toward my house, to tell everyone that the troops were shooting. As I entered our courtyard, I caught sight of my mother.

"I thought you were at the hospital with Dad," I said to her.

"Qing is there," she replied. "Your father sent me home to watch you. He said, knowing you, that you'd probably go to the square tonight and wait to die. He sent me back here to keep you at home."

I told my mother that I wouldn't go out, and I really meant it. The news about my father's illness was still fresh in my mind, and I wanted to do everything I could to cooperate with my parents because I felt it was important to my father.

It was just after ten o'clock. For the next hour I tried to block out what was happening nearby, but around eleven the noise became too loud for me to ignore any longer and I went into our courtyard. The neighbors were coming by to tell us that armed police were driving people off the streets, but the people were fighting back, getting into pushing and shouting matches with the police. The gunshots sounded closer and closer every minute. When the people from our neighborhood began to build a barricade on the street, I couldn't stand it any longer.

"Yuan Yuan, don't go," my mother said, grabbing my shirt as I tried to go out the door. Nainai came to help pull me back, and my uncles, who had just walked in, joined the effort.

As I gave up struggling, we heard more shots, and my uncles went out to see where they had come from. Nainai stood in the doorway while my mother, who was outside, held her arm across the frame to keep her from leaving. I was the only one still inside. The gunfire became more rapid, and tear gas canisters seemed to be exploding all over. Every few minutes someone staggered into our alley, covering his eyes with his hands, and my mother and Nainai took basins of water into the courtyard so these people could wash the tear gas out of their eyes. Puddles collected in the courtyard as people wildly splashed water on their stinging faces.

In the middle of all this chaos, I sneaked out of the house. On Changan Avenue, people were dousing the abandoned army trucks with gasoline and setting them on fire. I wanted to get a group of students together to try and persuade people to go back to their homes, because with more troops only a few blocks away, we didn't have much chance of stopping them, and I didn't want to see anyone else killed. But I looked all around and couldn't find any other students, and everything was so crazy that it would have been impossible to organize anything.

While I was standing on Changan Avenue, my uncles found me and dragged me home. On the way I saw a graduate student who had been on the first Beida Preparatory Committee with me. He was walking his bicycle calmly toward the square.

"What are you doing here?" I asked him.

"I want to be in the square," he said. "I can't stay at school any longer."

"Are many from Beida going there?"

"I don't know," he answered. "I had a hard time getting past the barriers the people put up, just to get this far."

"See if you can recruit some students to help calm this crowd down," I said.

"I'll try," he replied calmly.

As he walked on, I watched him, admiring his quiet courage. After he left the Beida Preparatory Committee, he had become a hunger striker. His commitment had never waned, even after he lost his leadership role.

My uncles urged me to get going, so we headed toward my

house. By now there were dead and wounded people all over the sidewalks and under the trees along Changan Avenue, and the alleys off the avenue could no longer hold all the wounded. When we got to our courtyard, I noticed that one of my uncles was lagging behind, dragging a man who was screaming in agonizing pain. This man had been wounded in his leg, and blood was shooting out of a main artery. There was no way we could get him to a hospital on this night. He bled to death in front of our door.

My uncles dragged some of the others who had been wounded into our courtyard to make more room in the alley. While they and my mother were busy taking care of these people, I sneaked out again. As soon as I was in the alley, I heard a low rumbling noise and felt the ground quake beneath me.

"The tanks are coming!" someone shouted.

It can't be, I thought. *How can they drive tanks into the downtown area?*

A crowd had gathered at the corner of Xidan, and when I got there a seemingly endless line of headlights stretched as far as I could see down Changan Avenue to the west. I couldn't believe my eyes. It was so bright I almost couldn't see. There were maybe twenty army tanks, but it seemed like many more, and they were headed right for us. The people around me were throwing stones at them and at the foot soldiers walking beside them, and in response the soldiers started spraying gunfire at our feet.

"Rubber bullets!" I shouted as people began to scream with fear. "Stop throwing things — there's no way to stop them!"

I fought my way through the crowd, trying to get onto the avenue, but I stopped when one of the soldiers fired rapidly at my feet. I wasn't hurt, so I tried to look for the shells, to see whether the bullets were real. Hundreds of people rushed into the avenue to put up barricades, but as soon as they reached the middle of the street, a spray of machine-gun fire scattered them. People who had been hit fell to the ground and lay still. *Those people are dead,* I thought to myself. *The bullets are real.* I couldn't believe it. It was as if this were all happening in a dream.

Everyone around me was still throwing things at the tanks, and it was odd to see people picking up anything, even a little pebble, and throwing it at the metal monsters coming toward us. It was totally useless. I grabbed a young man by the collar just as he was about to lob a small rock and screamed at him, "If you throw one more thing, I'll strangle you!"

The people near me were taken aback. I looked at the crowd and said, "When the troops come, just stand here and be still. Otherwise, go home. If you run, you're almost asking them to shoot you. If you throw things, you're asking them to shoot you. Just stand your ground."

Just then three soldiers jumped from an armored car and shot into the crowd. A flash of bright orange light went up a few meters away; two buses had been set on fire by the people. I walked toward the wreckage and stood behind a tree, watching the flames, which actually looked beautiful against the night sky. More shots were fired at my feet. When I looked in the direction of the gunfire, I found myself staring at a soldier's face. His eyes were popping, bloodshot, and dazed, as if he were on drugs.

Two tanks rolled forward and pushed aside the burning buses. Once the line of tanks began to pass, the soldiers stopped shooting and moved ahead. Some of them had large wooden clubs covered with metal on one end, and they were also armed with pistols and machine guns. Wearing leather shoes instead of canvas-and-rubber army boots, they looked ready for hand-to-hand combat with the civilians. They fired occasional shots into the air and shouted warnings through megaphones, saying that we should get off the streets.

Some people ran into the middle of the avenue to pick up the bullet casings, taking them back to the sidewalks to show the others. I don't know why we all felt so little fear. After living under martial law for so many days, and after so many nights of expecting the oncoming troops, we seemed to feel that violence could no longer defeat us. I know now that this was a triumph of our spirit.

I counted forty-six tanks and armored personnel carriers advancing steadily toward Tiananmen Square. In addition to the military vehicles there were propaganda trucks carrying public address equipment. Their loudspeakers were blaring slogans like "The People's Liberation Army loves the capital" and "We love the people of Beijing. Soldiers and people are one" as civilians were gunned down in the streets. These lies so infuriated us that people hurled anything they could find with even more hatred than before.

Two young men near me took the bloody shirt off a corpse on the ground and walked toward one of the personnel carriers to show the soldiers what their comrades had done. The military vehicles suddenly stopped. I followed the two men, and as we approached the carrier, the soldiers looked at each other, not knowing what to do. It was clear that we were unarmed and weren't throwing stones. By the time we got up to the truck, a middle-aged woman and a young girl were with us. The woman spoke up first.

"You soldiers, how can you do this?" she said.

They didn't answer. Shocked and hurt and still not quite sure that I believed what I was seeing, I wanted to reason with them. I realized that I had to control myself and speak civilly.

"What regiment are you from?" I asked.

They didn't answer.

"Do you know where you are? Do you know that you are in Beijing?"

One of the soldiers, who looked very young, shook his head.

"You don't know you're in Beijing?" I shouted in disbelief. "You are on Changan Avenue. Do you know the history of Changan Avenue? In 1949, when the People's Liberation Army liberated the city from the Guomindang, no shots were fired on Changan Avenue. When the foreign armies invaded Beijing, no one was killed on Changan Avenue. You are the People's Liberation Army and you're shooting your own people. We are students peacefully petitioning the government. We are against violence."

I was talking nonstop, desperately trying to get them to understand. The other people around me were at a loss for words. The two young men held up the bloodstained shirt and cried, but no words came out of their open mouths.

"Talk to me! You heard what I said — say something!" I pleaded. "Tell the other soldiers they cannot shoot anymore."

An officer got up, took out his pistol, and pointed it at me. I was still talking and didn't pay any attention to what he was doing, but one of my uncles came up to me, tugged at me, and said frantically, "Come on, Yuan Yuan, let's go home."

All of a sudden someone pulled me backward. Then a shot rang out, and everyone started screaming. I turned around to see the girl who had been standing next to me fall straight back to the ground. I hadn't even noticed her standing there, and now her face was completely gone; there was nothing but a bloody hole.

As the people who had gathered around ran away, my uncle and some men who recognized me as a student leader tried to get me away from the personnel carrier. "Take him home, they're going to kill him," I heard someone say. We stepped over a concrete divider separating the street from the pedestrian walkway. As they were dragging me away, I looked at the girl again, then fought their tugging and forced my way a few steps toward her. Four men had run to where her body lay. The screaming and the gunfire melded together into white noise. All I remember of this time is four men, like pallbearers, taking the girl's body away in slow motion, unaware of the chaos around them. They paused and looked back at the personnel carrier a number of times. Then they were gone.

When I looked up, I saw a group of young men running and trying to jump over a fence across the avenue. Several soldiers leaped down from another personnel carrier and went after them. One of the young men fell as he tried to get over to safety, and crouched with his back against the fence and his hands clutching the rails. I will never forget how he looked around quickly, with no fear on his face, as the soldiers surrounded him.

All at once they fired shots at his head. His skull must have shattered, because pieces of his head went flying and splattered on the white fence. As his body slowly slid to the ground, a piece of his skull landed on the gold metal ball on top of the railing.

The trucks started moving again, but I was completely numb. "Come with me, I'll take you away from here," I heard my uncle say. He took my arm and led me home. I looked down and saw that his trousers were covered with blood from the man he had dragged into our courtyard.

The moment we walked into the house, my mother came right up to us. "You can't wait any longer," she said to my uncle. "Take Yuan Yuan away quickly." Neither Nainai nor she tried to speak to me; they could see that I was in a trance. "I'm putting my son's life in your hands," my mother said.

My uncle took me into the courtyard, where he put me on the back of his bicycle. We rode down the alley, turned onto Chang-an Avenue, and headed west. As soon as I saw the scene before me, I became alert again. All the way across the six lanes, thousands of Beijing residents were jamming the avenue, following the army to the square. The soldiers on the last personnel carrier were firing at the feet of the first row of people, and their shots were hitting the legs and feet of a few of those in the front, who knelt down in pain. But the people behind them kept coming. The crowd stepped over the wounded and the dead and continued to follow the trucks.

My uncle's bicycle was now flying down Changan Avenue. "The people of Beijing are so brave," I said, uttering the first words out of my mouth since the girl next to me was killed. I looked at my watch. It was 4 a.m.

To avoid the soldiers, my uncle began taking the side streets. We passed the temple where Rong Dong and I had played. Smoldering army vehicles were everywhere, and I could smell the fumes of the burning rubber and paint.

When we entered one alley, we saw a man in an official-looking green uniform being chased by an angry mob of Beijing residents, who caught up with him at a construction site and picked up pieces of brick to hit him with. The man didn't make a sound. I jumped off the bicycle, almost knocking over my uncle, and ran toward them. Pushing the people aside, I saw him lying face down, with blood pouring out of his nostrils as he exhaled rapidly. He looked about eighteen years old.

"Stop hitting him!" I pleaded with the crowd.

"It's none of your business," a man said, shoving me away.

"Please stop it," I begged. "We have to take him to the hospital, we have to find him an ambulance."

My uncle pulled me away from the mob. "Forget it, Yuan Yuan. He's almost dead — there's no use."

He put me back on his bicycle and rode off quickly.

"The soldiers are killing the people, the people are killing the soldiers, right in the middle of the capital," I mumbled.

Eventually my uncle and I arrived at an empty apartment building that had recently been constructed. This was to be my hiding place.

"Don't use the elevator and don't let anyone see you here," my uncle warned. "Don't leave. We'll come and bring you food and clothes. You must not leave here."

He waited until I had started climbing the stairs before he left. The building had fourteen floors, and I walked to the ninth floor, to the apartment he had told me to stay in. It was almost dawn. I had seen too much to feel anything anymore. I fell asleep as the sun was coming up.

June 4 through 11, Sunday through Sunday

When I woke up late in the morning, I felt very hungry. I waited a couple of hours for someone to bring me some food, but no one came. I went downstairs and looked around to see if anyone was watching me, but it looked safe, so I walked to a food stand on the corner to get something to eat. People were gathered in clusters on the street, and I could tell that they were talking about what had happened.

"The old man next door to me went out to see what the noise was about and was shot to death," I overheard a woman say.

Another said, "My neighbor went to buy milk this morning and was killed by a stray bullet."

A young girl running down the street claimed that she had just come from Xidan, where the army had pointed all of the tank guns at the houses. I suddenly remembered what my mother had told my uncle and Nainai just before I left: "We should get ready to leave here too. So many people have died here that they'll probably raze the whole neighborhood."

I used a public phone to call one of the French journalists, who told me the *Paris Match* reporter had been shot in the waist but was going to be all right. She also said that two Hong Kong reporters had been killed and two American reporters had been wounded. Then I called home, but my mother was too frightened to talk to me on the telephone. She kept saying, "Don't leave the building." My third call was to Andrea, whom I begged to go to the United States with me. She sounded like she was in a daze too, but finally she said she would. Even though my mother had told me not to leave the building, I had to see Andrea, so we arranged to meet the next morning.

On my way back to my hideout, I suddenly remembered that my passport was at the American consulate, where I was supposed to pick up my visa the next day. The thought that I would not be able to get it back worried me.

In the morning I met Andrea, and she took me to get a haircut so that no one would recognize me. We asked the barber to cut my hair in the style that was fashionable among the hooligans: long in the front and back and short on the sides. Andrea also gave me a pair of dark glasses. I told her I was going to the American consulate to get my passport and visa, but she warned me not to go; her parents had been to the area, and they said that the army had surrounded both the embassies and the foreigners' compound. Instead she contacted a Brazilian businessman who spoke perfect English. He said that he would pick up my passport and visa and that he would get me out of China through Hong Kong by saying that I was his assistant. I didn't know what to think about this idea; I just wanted my passport and visa.

After I returned to my hideout, Dakun came to see me, bringing food. "I heard that Wang Dan and Wuer Kaixi were both killed," he said.

"What?"

"I heard that Wang Dan was shot in the back of the head and that Wuer Kaixi was bayoneted to death on the monument."

I didn't know how to react to this news, which later turned out to be completely false. Dakun and I went to one of the small food stalls nearby and ate lunch, but after he left, when I was alone in the apartment, I lay down and thought about what he had told me. I felt tremendously sad.

In the afternoon I went to Andrea's house to see whether the businessman had gotten my passport. Apparently a huge crowd of people had been waiting at the consulate, but most of them hadn't been able to get past the Chinese secretary at the door. By pretending to be an American, the businessman had forced his way in, acting very rudely to attract the attention of the military police, who had taken him inside. Once there, he told one of the American secretaries that he was picking up the passport of a leader of the student movement. She didn't react to this, but just told him to go to the front of the line. When he got to the desk, he found another Chinese. Again he started arguing loudly. The American secretary came up and said, "Why are you so impolite? Take your passport. If you are this rude next time, we won't give you your visa. Now go." He checked to make sure that she had stamped the visa in my passport, then left the consulate, the first person — and, it turned out, the only person — to get a visa that day.

On the next day, June 6, the American consulate closed. I knew my family was worried that I hadn't gotten my passport and visa, so I called home immediately to tell them. They were elated, but we still didn't know how I was going to leave the country.

My mother told me that many of my friends had come to look for me, to help hide me from the authorities. She had told them that she didn't know where I was. She also said that a group of six influential people I had met during the movement had contacted her to say that they had a way to get me out of China. We decided to put our trust in them, and soon the head of the group came to see me.

"You don't have to worry about anything," he said. "We already have someone who has gone ahead to the south and arranged everything along the way. We have paid to get you through an underground railroad to Macao. Once you are there, someone will send you to Hong Kong. If you didn't have your passport and visa, we could buy a counterfeit Hong Kong passport for you. You can leave for the south in the next two days — it's all taken care of."

"I won't go to the south," I said. "I want to leave directly from Beijing."

He was shocked that I refused to cooperate, but Macao was far away, and I knew that it could take weeks or even months to get to Hong Kong. Because I already had my passport and visa, I thought there had to be an easier way, a legal way, to leave the country. The group leader knew he couldn't force me into such a long and dangerous journey if I had any doubts about it; the whole operation could be exposed anywhere along the route.

"We'll have to see about that," he said. "In any case, you can't stay here. Every time you go out, people can see that a student is hiding here. We have three places for you to stay. We'll move you tomorrow."

Before he left, I gave him 4500 yuan of the federation's money, which I was still carrying, to pay for whatever arrangements were necessary.

On June 7 I moved to a different hiding place. The group took good care of me, and even brought me new clothes. They told me that Xiang Xiaoji had been trying to get out of Beijing on his bicycle when he had been kidnapped by the authorities — another story that later turned out to be false, but when I first heard it, it made me even more concerned for my own safety. For several days the government had been announcing on the radio and television that all students connected with the illegal student associations should turn themselves in and hand over their weapons.

When my mother came to bring me food, she told me about a twenty-five-year-old man from the other side of Changan Avenue who had been killed on the night of June 3. The top of his skull was still hanging on the white fence beside the avenue.

"I know," I said. "I saw it happen."

That afternoon I disguised myself and went to see my father at the hospital. Both inside and outside the building, small protests were being held by people who had found the bodies of relatives who had been killed.

My mother, sister, and I met my father in the garden in front of the hospital. The four of us sat on the park benches, not saying anything. All of our emotions were exhausted.

"Listen to those people and do what they tell you," my father said at last, just before I left. "Get out of this country as quickly as you can."

On June 8 the government announced publicly that Guo Haifeng was under arrest — the first announcement that a student leader had been arrested. When I heard this, I no longer believed that I would be able to leave the country legally, and I began to resign myself to going to Macao via the underground railroad. I didn't think the people helping me would be able to get me past the border examiners and customs officers at the Beijing Airport, where, I had heard, the Public Security Bureau had sent extra agents. I also learned that my name was on a list of sixty wanted student leaders.

Andrea's family was being evacuated by the Brazilian embassy, which had chartered a plane to take all Brazilian nationals out of the country. Andrea was very worried that I would be trapped in China, so before she got on the plane she called to say she had bought me a ticket for a flight leaving that afternoon. "Why don't you come to the airport?" she said. "There are so many foreigners here that you're sure to get out in all the chaos."

"I can't leave now," I told her, explaining that I had already put my trust in the group of people who were helping me, and I didn't want to jeopardize whatever plans they were making by leaving on an impulse.

She was so upset that she started crying; then she hung up. Her plane left for Brazil soon afterward.

In the evening my mother, Qing, and two of the people helping me came to see me, bringing a student from a nearby college with them. This boy said that at least twenty-seven students from his school had been killed during the massacre. A bulletin with photographs of the twenty-seven confirmed dead had been posted at the college, but the government broadcasts reported only twenty-three dead in all of Beijing. We knew this was a blatant lie.

Suddenly we heard a loud knocking on the door. We froze and looked at each other.

"Go hide on the terrace," my sister said.

I went out on the balcony, knowing that if the police were at the door, they would find me in a minute. I took a deep breath and waited. One of the helpers answered the knock, which turned out to be a neighbor who wanted to borrow something. From outside I could hear everyone in the room scolding him for knocking so violently.

Worried that I had received too many phone calls from Andrea, the group leader wanted me to move again. A military jeep had been parked on the street below for twenty-four hours. I told him that there was no need for me to move; I would wait for another two days, and if the group hadn't found a way for me to escape from Beijing, I would go south on June 10.

That night I received a call. "There is a way," the man said, and hung up.

The day before I left, my mother went to buy things for me to take to America. I insisted on going with her. I didn't really want to go, but I wanted to be with her and do the simple things we wouldn't do together again for a long time. Not many stores were open, so we went to a nearby shop and bought socks, underwear, and T-shirts. Normally this would have been an uneventful outing, but that day I felt very close to my mother.

Meanwhile my sister went to my dorm room at Beida to get some of my books and to pick up my suitcase. When she got there, she found several messages from Lao He, who said he wanted to see me about "what we talked about on May 20" — his plan to hide me in the Beijing hospitals. Qing told me that all of our broadcast equipment had been smashed to pieces and our papers had been confiscated. The authorities had broken into my room even though my friends had sealed it.

That afternoon several of my closest friends told their parents they were going to the hospital to see my father, but they really came to see me for the last time. We talked and laughed as if everything were the same as it always was, until the conversation turned to the night of June 3. One of my friends said that when the armed police had come into the square, he had been hit in the back of the head with a billy club. We all took turns feeling his bump.

"I was running out of the square when I stepped on something soft," he recalled. "It was a dead body."

Another friend said that he had gone out on the morning of June 4 to see the aftermath of the massacre. "On Changan Avenue, in front of the Telegraph Building, I saw eleven bodies all in a row that had been crushed by a tank," he told us. "It made me sick. I ran all the way home."

Dakun, Rong Dong, and Ziping came to see me too. Rong Dong and I hugged tightly for a long time. Dakun and I didn't have very many words for each other either.

"You see, I've become the jagged rock that gets swept into the great ocean of life," I said at last, referring to the letter I had sent him when we had first become friends.

Dakun thought for a moment. "I don't really want to be a rounded rock and settle at the bottom of the riverbed," he replied. Then he got on his bicycle and rode away. He never turned back.

That night my father came to the place I was staying to have dinner with me. Nainai was there too. My parents hadn't wanted her to come, thinking that it would upset her and make my leaving all the more difficult, but she had promised not to cry, so my mother had agreed to bring her. After dinner, when my father had to go back to the hospital, my mother and he walked slowly down the stairs. He didn't say a word of farewell. I ran after him and called out, "Dad!" He looked up, patted my hand on the railing, and kept going.

After my sister and mother took Nainai home, they came back to stay with me for the night. I packed a few of the books Qing had brought from my dorm, my English-Chinese dictionary, and some clothes. The only memento I had of the student movement was a red T-shirt of the Goddess of Democracy, which Andrea had given me. I stuffed it into the bottom of my suitcase.

I went to sleep thinking about how I would say goodbye to my mother and sister. I had done nothing to show my father that I loved him; I couldn't miss the chance to show them.

When I woke up, it was very early in the morning. Two of the people helping me had already arrived. I wanted to hug my mother and kiss my sister, but I didn't know how — I had never hugged anyone in my family, and I didn't do it then. I still dream about going back someday and hugging my mother.

"I'm sorry I can't be here to take care of Dad," I said to her. "You should take care of yourself too." I turned to my sister. "Stay with Dad for me. I'll be back in a couple of years."

As I walked away from them, they both waved to me, simply saying, "Goodbye." It was as if I were only going on a short holiday.

I cannot say any more about how I left China. The lives of many people depend on it. Only after I boarded a Northwest Airlines flight in Tokyo bound for the United States did I let out a sigh of relief. I was free.

Epilogue

I was free, but I longed for home almost like a sickness. For the first twenty days I sat alone, staring out a small window, and I often woke up from dreams wondering where I was. I was given hope by the good news that many others, including Wuer Kaixi, had also escaped to the West, and to keep my spirits up I continued to believe that more of my friends would escape. After a time, I was able to piece together the broken scenes of my memory into a painting.

The American people had watched us in Tiananmen Square for four or five weeks, but I felt that the story told by the Western media did not capture all that had gone on. People in the West knew about the hunger strike, the Goddess of Democracy, and the mass demonstrations, but they did not understand my generation's ideals and the driving force behind us. I felt an urgency to tell that story, and I wanted to keep alive the memory of June 3 and 4.

I started traveling around the United States speaking about the political and human rights atrocities committed by the Chinese government. I held my first press conference in Boston on June 30, and in July I went to Paris to meet with several pro-democracy movement leaders who had fled China, including Yan Jiaqi, the political scientist. There we established the Federation for a Democratic China. At the end of that month, I attended the First Congress of Independent Chinese Students and Scholars in Chicago.

Yan Jiaqi, Wuer Kaixi, and I with a number of other FDC founders were traveling around the United States when I found out that my father had died. The news came to me in a letter from Qiu, my sister's old boyfriend. I was devastated. My family had not told me, and had asked my friends to say that my father was doing well, because they didn't want to give me this news when I was alone in a new country. Qiu hoped that telling me would make me quit the prodemocracy movement and start thinking more about my family. I was about to begin my studies at Brandeis, but I wanted very badly to go back to China and be with them, no matter what danger awaited me. I could not attend my father's funeral, and I never had the chance to say goodbye to him. I thought about all the lost opportunities when he was in the hospital during the last days of the movement, when I hadn't sat at his bedside and talked to him or comforted him. For a while I was determined to go home, but in the end a number of people, including Andrea and Dakun, whom I called, persuaded me not to.

By this time my family had moved from the house where we had lived for twenty years. So many people had been killed at the intersection of Xidan and Changan Avenue, and so many more had witnessed the slaughter, that people in the neighborhood thought the army would raze the houses in Xidan. This didn't actually happen, but my mother's memories of June 3 and 4 and the death of my father were too painful for her to continue to live there.

I was still in a daze when school began in the fall, but having my studies to concentrate on calmed me down, and I slowly came to realize that my father's death had given me more strength to carry on the prodemocracy movement in exile. He would not have to worry about me anymore, and I felt even closer to him. We are no longer separated by the continents and the oceans. I feel his presence often, wherever I am.

With the help of Marshall Strauss and Juanita Scheyett, I established the Democracy for China Fund. We contacted East Germany's New Forum, Czechoslovakia's Civic Forum, and Poland's Solidarity, and met many great people, including Lech Walesa, when he was in Washington, and the Dalai Lama, in New York. In March 1990, I went to Prague with Liu Binyan, China's foremost dissident journalist, to meet with members of the Civic Forum, Charter 77, the Independent Journalists Association, and the Student Union. On March 8 we had the opportunity to talk with Czechoslovakia's new president, Vaclav Havel.

One of the great thrills I've had in the past year was serving as a grand marshal in the Martin Luther King Day parade in Atlanta, Georgia. In an effort to promote Dr. King's message of nonviolence in the prodemocracy movement, the Democracy for China Fund maintains contact with the King Center. It also organized a Democracy Tour that traveled to San Francisco, Seattle, Phoenix, Tucson, Houston, Memphis, Washington, D.C., Atlanta, and New York, to commemorate the June 3–4 massacre and to make sure that the people of this country do not forget the events of the spring of 1989.

In the past year I have learned from conversations with other student leaders and eyewitnesses a great deal more about what actually happened on the night of the massacre. I was not in Tiananmen Square, but I was at one of the two centers of the most brutal killings. Many have corroborated what I saw: most of the people who died were civilians and workers, and they were gunned down in the Xidan and Muxudi areas, on the western approach of Changan Avenue to the square.

When I began to write this book with Marianne Yen, I found out how difficult it is to tell such a story as a historian and to write about what happened with objectivity. Every time I tried to remember, I felt that I was in Tiananmen Square. The movement belonged to millions of people, and I cannot tell the whole story; my experience was only one strand of the total truth. But my personal story does explain why and how I got involved in the movement and why I was so committed to it. In telling the story in this book, I have tried to remember as accurately as possible what happened during those fifty-six days.

Unfortunately, many of the people I mention in these pages are now in jail or in some danger, so we have changed the names of those who I believe could be in jeopardy. Many of these, including most of the crucial members of the student movement, are still in China, where some are undergoing unbearable spiritual and physical torture in prison. But even such severe punishment cannot kill the seeds of hope and the determination of those who seek liberty. An underground movement has developed very rapidly and has already established contact with the overseas exiles. The dramatic changes in Eastern Europe have been immeasurably encouraging, just as our prodemocracy movement gave the people of Eastern Europe courage to rise up. I believe the end of tyranny is near.

For the people of China, the overthrow of tyranny may exact a price of blood. But thousands of years of Chinese history and the cycles of dynastic rule have shown that the fall of a tyrant is not impossible. Building a nation that fights against feudal ideas and pursues the spirit of liberty, science, equality, and fraternity is a task facing not only China but all humankind.

I feel a sense of guilt that so many people who helped me are in jail or in political trouble. Some of the Olympic Institute members have been told that they cannot apply for graduate studies, and some are still in jail. The nine Beida professors who served as my advisers have been arrested or questioned or are in hiding from the Public Security Bureau. Some of the people who helped me escape have been found out and punished. I owe so many a debt of gratitude. At first I tried to repay that debt by helping others escape, but as many of those attempts failed, I realized that there are other ways. I can pay those debts by continuing the work we began in Tiananmen Square.

When I called my sister in Beijing for the first time after I came to America, I tearfully hinted to her that I would carry on the prodemocracy movement in exile and that my mother should publicly say she had disowned me to protect the family. My sister told me that she had a chance to study in Japan, and she asked me to wait before becoming active again. But very quickly she changed her mind and said, "Don't worry. Do what you believe in." Shortly after, the government took away her passport.

In July 1990 Marianne Yen made a trip to Beijing to see my family and friends. My mother told her that throughout the student movement my father had been pressured by his superiors in the Beijing municipal government to spy on me. "He came home every night and fretted about his son," my mother reported. "He said, 'I have always done what the Party asked of me, but I will never betray my son.'" Only now do I understand fully what my father went through in order to protect me.

I know my struggle now is not to seek revenge for the violence of tyranny. Those who died sacrificed themselves so that the living could have a better future. I now persevere for the sake of a better tomorrow.

.   .   .

Update on Individuals Mentioned in the Book (1998)

CHAI LING escaped to Hong Kong in April 1990. She received her master's degree from Princeton University and is currently working in the Boston area.

CHANG JIN escaped to Hong Kong in August 1989 and is now working in Hong Kong, where he lives with his wife.

DAI QING was arrested after the massacre and was released in April 1990. She was allowed to travel outside China a couple of times and remains vocal about several sensitive issues, including concerns for China's environment.

DING XIAOPING was jailed for a period of time after the massacre. We met briefly in 1992 when I went back to China and before I was arrested and sent into exile again. He has been under constant police surveillance throughout the years since 1989.

The top eleven leaders of the FEIHUDUI, or Flying Tiger Brigade, were arrested and charged with counterrevolutionary activities just before the massacre of June 3–4. Like many labor activists, they have received much harsher punishment from the Beijing government than did intellectuals and students.

FENG CONGDE escaped to Hong Kong with Chai Ling in 1990 and has lived in Paris since their divorce.

JIAN, whose real name is Zhou Jian, was arrested in August 1989. He was kept in Qingcheng Prison till the end of 1990, without a trial. He was then expelled from Beida, and after trying to appeal to the government repeatedly and being helped by friends, he ended up working on a shrimp farm near Shanghai for many years. He managed to go to the University of Michigan with his wife in 1994 and now is working in Hong Kong.

There has been no news about LAO HE.

LI LU escaped in June 1990 to Hong Kong and then went on to Paris. He received his graduate education from Columbia University and now works as an investment banker in Los Angeles.

LIU GANG was arrested in Baoding and remained in Qincheng for over a year. He was then transferred to one of the most brutal prisons in Northeastern China, where he was repeatedly tortured physically by the prison authorities. He was released in 1995 but was constantly harassed. He fled China in 1996 and now is studying at Columbia University.

LIU XIAOBO was arrested shortly after the massacre. After his release in 1991, he continued his pro-democracy work and was arrested again in 1996. He is serving his three-year sentence in a reform-through-labor camp in Northeastern China.

MA SHAOFANG was arrested in Guangzhou and jailed for two and a half years. Like Ding Xiaoping and almost all other former political prisoners, he has been constantly harassed by the government and has remained under police surveillance since his release. We met briefly in Beijing in 1992 before my arrest.

QIGE, my neighbor's seventh son, was arrested after the massacre when soldiers came looking for me. He was accused of setting fire to the army vehicles on Changan Avenue. After being beaten severely, he was released in October 1989.

TI BO was jailed for about two years and now works in Beijing.

WANG CHAOHUA escaped in January 1990 to Hong Kong and then went on to England. She now conducts research in literature and history in Los Angeles.

WANG DAN was arrested in Beijing in August 1989. He served three and a half years of his four-year sentence. After his release in 1993, he continued his pro-democracy work by networking in China and writing extensively in Hong Kong magazines. He was sentenced again to eleven years in prison and then driven into exile in April 1998 for what the Beijing government claimed was a medical parole.

WANG JUNTAO and CHEN ZIMIN were arrested in Guangzhou in early 1990 after a failed rescue mission by Hong Kong pro-democracy movement supporters. They were both sentenced to seven years in prison. Wang was driven into exile in 1994 and is now studying political science at Columbia University. Chen was also released in 1994, but he remains under house arrest in his Beijing apartment to this day.

WUER KAIXI studied in Boston for a while and then in San Francisco. He joined the Democracy for China Fund in 1993, and we have been working together ever since. He now resides in Taiwan with his wife and son.

XIANG XIAOJI left Beijing on May 21, 1989, and escaped to Hong Kong with his wife in July 1989. After studying law at Columbia University, he became an immigration lawyer and now practices in New York.

XIONG YAN was arrested in Xian shortly after the massacre. After serving his prison sentence, he remained active in the dissident movement in China and soon had to flee. He arrived in the United States in 1992, served in the U.S.

Army for two years, and is now studying in the United States.

YAN JIAQI escaped in June 1989 to Hong Kong, then went on to Paris. He now lives in New York with his wife.

YAN MINGFU was forced to resign all of his government posts after the massacre. He was appointed deputy minister of the interior department in 1991.

YANG TAO was arrested in a forest in Lanzhou shortly after the massacre and spent two years in prison. He is now working in Hainan Province.

ZHANG BOLI was in hiding for over one year, during which time he escaped to Russia, only to be sent back to China. He eventually managed to flee to the United States and is now studying in Los Angeles.

ZHANG ZHIYONG was arrested shortly after the massacre. He has been working in Beijing ever since he finished his prison sentence. We met briefly in Beijing in 1992 before my arrest.

Acknowledgments

I would like to thank my co-author, Marianne Yen, for her heartfelt commitment to this book and to the democratic movement in China. I hope this book will be a lasting remembrance of our friendship. I would also like to thank Marshall Strauss for his encouragement from beginning to end; without his vision I would not have begun this project. I am grateful to my comrades Juanita Scheyett and Christopher Sieverts for sharing my work in the democracy movement in exile so I could have time to concentrate on the book, and for Juanita's beautiful translation of my poem in the preface. Marianne and I want to thank Cheng Mo for his help in putting together the manuscript. I also thank my book agent, Ned Leavitt; my lawyer, Jon Hecht; Liz Duvall, our manuscript editor, and Larry Platt at Houghton Mifflin; and my girlfriend, Andrea Martins. I am grateful to my mother, my sister, Nainai, and Dakun for providing precious photographs. And last, but most important, I want to thank my editor, Henry Ferris, without whose dedication and meticulous editing this book would not have been possible.

— *Shen Tong*

I am indebted to the many people who disrupted their lives so that I could take part in this worthwhile project. I want to thank the most important person in my life, my husband, John C.

Sciales, M.D., whose infinite patience and unwavering love sustained me during the five seemingly endless months I spent away from home; my parents, Jeff and Cherry Yen, for sharing their knowledge of China and for home-cooked meals; and Dr. and Mrs. William Sciales and Mrs. Jessie Petway, for taking care of Daphne and Daisy. I am deeply grateful to our editor and my teacher, Henry Ferris, who believed in this book and in us even when we doubted ourselves. Thank you, Henry, for the long hours you spent making this book worthy of history. I also thank Mark Levine, my lawyer and friend; Ned Leavitt, for holding our hands through the rough times; Bill Goldstein, for "finding" me; Larry Platt, for his good humor and encouragement; and the bottom of the alphabet, class of 1992, at Columbia Law School. Last, I thank Shen Tong for remembering and for sharing his story. The faith and resolve of his generation give me great hope that it will not be long before freedom and democracy triumph in China.

— *Marianne Yen*

Ann Arbor Paperbacks

Waddell, *The Desert Fathers*
Erasmus, *The Praise of Folly*
Donne, *Devotions*
Malthus, *Population: The First Essay*
Berdyaev, *The Origin of Russian Communism*
Einhard, *The Life of Charlemagne*
Edwards, *The Nature of True Virtue*
Gilson, *Héloïse and Abélard*
Aristotle, *Metaphysics*
Kant, *Education*
Boulding, *The Image*
Duckett, *The Gateway to the Middle Ages*
    (3 vols.): *Italy; France and Britain;*
    Monasticism
Bowditch and Ramsland, *Voices of the*
    Industrial Revolution
Luxemburg, *The Russian Revolution* and
    Leninism or Marxism?
Rexroth, *Poems from the Greek Anthology*
Zoshchenko, *Scenes from the Bathhouse*
Thrupp, *The Merchant Class of Medieval*
    London
Procopius, *Secret History*
Adcock, *Roman Political Ideas and Practice*
Swanson, *The Birth of the Gods*
Xenophon, *The March Up Country*
Buchanan and Tullock, *The Calculus of*
    Consent
Hobson, *Imperialism*
Kinietz, *The Indians of the Western Great*
    Lakes 1615–1760
Bromage, *Writing for Business*
Lurie, *Mountain Wolf Woman, Sister of*
    Crashing Thunder
Leonard, *Baroque Times in Old Mexico*
Meier, *Negro Thought in America,*
    1880–1915
Burke, *The Philosophy of Edmund Burke*
Michelet, *Joan of Arc*
Conze, *Buddhist Thought in India*
Arberry, *Aspects of Islamic Civilization*
Chesnutt, *The Wife of His Youth and*
    Other Stories
Gross, *Sound and Form in Modern Poetry*
Zola, *The Masterpiece*
Chesnutt, *The Marrow of Tradition*
Aristophanes, *Four Comedies*
Aristophanes, *Three Comedies*
Chesnutt, *The Conjure Woman*
Duckett, *Carolingian Portraits*
Rapoport and Chammah, *Prisoner's Dilemma*
Aristotle, *Poetics*

Peattie, *The View from the Barrio*
Duckett, *Death and Life in the Tenth Century*
Langford, *Galileo, Science and the Church*
McNaughton, *The Taoist Vision*
Milio, *9226 Kercheval*
Breton, *Manifestoes of Surrealism*
Scholz, *Carolingian Chronicles*
Wik, *Henry Ford and Grass-roots America*
Sahlins and Service, *Evolution and Culture*
Wickham, *Early Medieval Italy*
Waddell, *The Wandering Scholars*
Mannoni, *Prospero and Caliban*
Aron, *Democracy and Totalitarianism*
Shy, *A People Numerous and Armed*
Taylor, *Roman Voting Assemblies*
Hesiod, *The Works and Days; Theogony; The*
    Shield of Herakles
Raverat, *Period Piece*
Lamming, *In the Castle of My Skin*
Fisher, *The Conjure-Man Dies*
Strayer, *The Albigensian Crusades*
Lamming, *The Pleasures of Exile*
Lamming, *Natives of My Person*
Glaspell, *Lifted Masks and Other Works*
Grand, *The Heavenly Twins*
Allen, *Wolves of Minong*
Fisher, *The Walls of Jericho*
Lamming, *The Emigrants*
Loudon, *The Mummy!*
Kemble and Butler Leigh, *Principles and*
    Privilege
Thomas, *Out of Time*
Flanagan, *You Alone Are Dancing*
Kotre and Hall, *Seasons of Life*
Shen, *Almost a Revolution*
Meckel, *Save the Babies*
Laver and Schofield, *Multiparty Government*
Rutt, *The Bamboo Grove*
Endelman, *The Jews of Georgian England,*
    1714–1830
Lamming, *Season of Adventure*
Radin, *Crashing Thunder*
Mirel, *The Rise and Fall of an Urban School*
    System
Brainard, *When the Rainbow Goddess Wept*
Brook, *Documents on the Rape of Nanking*
Mendel, *Vision and Violence*
Hymes, *Reinventing Anthropology*
Mulroy, *Early Greek Lyric Poetry*
Siegel, *The Rope of God*
Buss, *La Partera*